T0195765

Southern Fried Life

David Luck

authorHOUSE®

AuthorHouse™
1663 Liberty Drive
Bloomington, IN 47403
www.authorhouse.com
Phone: 1-800-839-8640

Published by AuthorHouse 01/08/2015

ISBN: 978-1-4969-5671-2 (sc)
ISBN: 978-1-4969-5672-9 (hc)
ISBN: 978-1-4969-5675-0 (e)

Library of Congress Control Number: 2014921451

Dedication

This book is dedicated to all family and friends.
Thank you for all of your wonderful flaws and for accepting mine.

Contents

CHAPTER 1

The Pork Jerky beneath My Wings

It was the thirty-second class reunion for Holy Savior Menard Central High, and Norma Dubois was in her huge state-of-the-art kitchen, preparing an interesting variety of appetizers for her son Dylan and his four best friends. It was a tradition Norma started back years ago, to have a happy hour for Dylan and his companions before they attended any type of event, such as reunions, divorce settlements, births of babies out of wedlock, festivals, and funerals. Other than routine holiday celebrations, the last time Norma hosted an intimate pre-party for her middle son and company was six days after Hurricane Rita hit Alexandria back in 2005.

Norma was an extremely attractive seventy-two-year-old female, in an Ann-Margret sort of way. She had bright red hair and bronze, wrinkled skin baked just right by her latest-model tanning bed. The aged ginger had three sons. Steven and Dylan Jacobs were from her first marriage to Dr. Brent Jacobs. Kris Dubois, named after singer/songwriter Kris Kristofferson, was Norma's seventeen-year-old miracle child. She had him at the ripe age of fifty-five with her second groom, dried meat entrepreneur and one-hit wonder, Frankie Dubois. Norma felt that she could possibly be the oldest woman in central Louisiana to give birth. Norma and her entire family lived in Alexandria, Louisiana, not to be confused with Alexander, the famous Louisiana city where the brilliantly witty novel *Too Fat to Dance* originated.

The soundtrack CD from the movie *Best Little Whorehouse in Texas* was playing on the built-in stereo above the microwave as Norma struggled to get the Saran Wrap off the cheese ball. "Damn it to hell!" she shouted. Her long, manicured fingernails were covered with cream cheese.

The doorbell rang. She yelled, "Just a minute, honey … I'm coming," as she frantically looked for the remote to the stereo with her cheese-ball fingers. She gave up the search while Dolly Parton's rendition of "Hard Candy Christmas" loudly played on.

Norma quickly but cautiously, because of her five-inch high heels and tight-fitting jeans, walked through the spacious living room to open the front door. She struggled to unlock the door because she didn't want to get Philadelphia cream cheese all over the knob. She finally opened the door, and Dylan entered. He was a fifty-year-old man with a slim build, bright-blue eyes, and a full head of thick, salt-and-pepper hair. He was wearing black slacks, a white dress shirt, and a black sports jacket. He kissed his mother on her cheek.

"Why in the hell do you have the music from *The Best Little Whorehouse in Texas* blaring?" asked Dylan.

"I can't find the damn remote," Norma replied.

Dylan picked up the remote from the end table next to the sofa and gave it to his mother. The remote fell out her cheesy hands and hit the hardwood floor.

"Oh my Lord," she uttered. As she bent down to pick it up, the back of her jeans split wide open. "Damn it to hell … I just split my pants. It's those damn stuffed cheeseburgers at the Cottage!"

Dylan laughed and then said, "Such vulgar language coming from the madam of the chicken ranch."

Norma snickered at his remark and told him she needed go upstairs to change and wash her hands. On her way to the bedroom, she stuck her head into her youngest son's room and informed him that his brother was there. Kris, a seventeen-year-old young man with curly brown hair and bright-green eyes, was replying to all his Facebook messages and didn't even bother to answer his mother. He held up his right hand and gave her the okay signal while keeping his eyes glued to the computer screen.

Dylan walked into the kitchen and turned down the music with the sticky remote. He had a mild case of OCD, so immediately he washed his hands and the stereo remote.

After his washing mission was completed, Dylan looked over at all the trays of Louisiana's finest finger foods. Crawfish pizza, boudin, pecan cheese balls, and shrimp rolls covered the large, granite-topped island in the middle of the kitchen. Norma was famous for preparing or ordering too much food. Kris entered the kitchen, wearing a purple LSU T-shirt and matching boxer shorts. Although it was the beginning of September, it was not uncommon for Louisiana natives to wear shorts and flip-flops until December because of the heat.

Kris gave his older brother a hug, grabbed a handful of shrimp rolls, and with one arm lifted himself up and plopped his butt down on the kitchen counter beside the sink.

"Jesus, did you see all the food Mommy Dearest fixed? It looks like the Cajun cuisine section of Ryan's buffet. Do you believe this feast?" Dylan asked.

"Yes, I can believe it—if mom's name was Chef Lee Gwinn," Kris answered.

Dylan laughed and said, "You mean all this is from Spirits Catering?"

Kris popped another shrimp ball into his mouth and replied, "Spirits did everything except for the cheese ball and those deli spiral things that she was too ashamed to put out because y'all would know that she bought them at Sam's Club."

Dylan laughed. "You mean those little wheels stuffed with tasteless crap that you have to thaw out and everybody serves them at holiday parties?"

"Those would be the ones, my wise, old brother," answered Kris.

Dylan leaped up and took a seat right next to Kris. "Hey, ya know, Kris, the folks at my condo are having BJ's Pizza delivered. You ought to go by there."

Kris put his hand on his big brother's shoulder and said, "Are you kiddin' me? Your place is like a foster care circus of insanity. Anyway, I want to be here when Phoebe gets here. She always brings me cool Saints memorabilia."

In a joking manner, Dylan grabbed Kris's neck with both hands and said, "Have I made it clear to you lately that I really don't care for you?" They both laughed.

Norma came into the kitchen wearing a dress designed for a baby doll. She looked like a cross between an old Shirley Temple and an evangelist on the Trinity Network.

"What in God's name are you wearing?" asked Dylan.

"It's my Baby Jane Hudson dress. I was gonna change into this lovely attire after you left, but I thought, *What the hell—I'll wear it now.*"

Hoping for a reasonable explanation, Dylan gave Kris an odd look, and Kris replied, "After you old farts leave for your pathetic reunion,

Momma and I are gonna take advantage of this food that you high school rejects won't eat and have movie night for me and a few friends."

"We're watching *What Ever Happened to Baby Jane?* Kris and his buddies love the parts when Bette Davis torments the bejesus out of Joan Crawford," added Norma.

Kris chimed in, "Especially when Baby Jane tries to make her pitiful sister eat the pet parakeet."

Dylan waited for his eccentric mother and odd brother to finish laughing. When they finished, he looked over to Kris and asked, "Now, who lives in a circus of insanity?"

The doorbell rang, and Dylan was more than happy to leave the odd conversation with his unsteady kinfolk to go answer it.

Norma realized that her music was not playing and told Kris to turn up the volume. When Kris completed his mother's request, he discovered that the music was the soundtrack from *The Best Little Whorehouse in Texas*.

"What's the deal with you and this music from probably one of the worst movies Burt Reynolds ever made? I feel like I've been living in a really bad musical nightmare here lately," Kris complained.

Norma gave her candid child an anxious smile as she poured herself a large LSU Tiger wine glass of Miss Scarlett Sweet Muscadine, one of her favorite wines she had delivered monthly from the Old South Winery in Natchez, Mississippi. She took a sip, leaving most of her dark-red lipstick on the rim of the glass, and gave Kris a long-winded answer to his question.

"Besides *Cannonball Run 2*, *The Best Little Whorehouse in Texas* was your daddy's favorite movie. That Dom DeLuise would have him peeing in his pants from laughter. Ya know that beautiful actress, Adrienne Barbeau, who also played in *Swamp Thing*, was in the first *Cannon Ball Run* movie, and she's the reason we decided to have you."

Kris hopped off the counter. "I know, I know, Mom. I've heard this story a hundred times ... she had her twin boys when she was at the youthful age of fifty-one, and her pregnancy justified you having me when you were fifty-five ... I get it, I get it."

Kris smiled as his mother ran her fingers through his wavy hair and said, "I know you get it, sweetheart. I've just been thinking a lot about your daddy lately ... I really miss him, ya know."

Kris gave her a big hug and replied, "I know you do, Momma."

Frankie Dubois was Kris's father and Norma's dear second husband. He and Norma met in 1988 at a Dottie West concert in Lafayette, Louisiana. They were both waiting in line at the VIP backstage party to meet the country music icon. They both considered themselves Dottie's biggest fans. In fact, Norma made one of the bedrooms in her condo the Dottie West Room. It was a miniature museum full of the singer's albums, posters, photos, and even a mannequin wearing one of Dottie's original glitter jumpsuits designed by Bob Mackie.

Frankie was no stranger to country music. He had a momentary singing career in the seventies. "I Left You a Rose on the Satin Sheets" and "Hillbilly Love" were his two biggest hits, but unfortunately, the songs never reached the top twenty of the country music charts.

Frankie was slim and had dyed blond hair and long sideburns. It was rumored that his less than successful entertainment career was due to the fact that country music fans were unwilling to accept another Porter Wagoner into their world. Frankie played mostly rodeos and fairs. The highlights of his brief encounter with fame were performing at the Louisiana Hayride in 1973 and back in 1978, when he sang on the short-lived television show, *Hee Haw Honeys* (an unsuccessful spinoff of *Hee Haw*).

Growing up on a pig farm in Livingston, Texas, and inheriting a small fortune from his parents at the age of forty, Frankie decided to hang up his rhinestone jacket and his dream of playing at the Grand Ole Opry to become the King of Pork Jerky.

He moved to Olla, Louisiana, bought a building that was once a Piggly Wiggly supermarket, and turned it into a jerky factory. He also wanted to be near his only living relative, Aunt Dewy. In fact, Aunt Dewy was the person who Frankie named his brand of dried meats after. She had no teeth and always wore a crocheted pink cap (she lost most of hair because of hormonal changes). Frankie's aunt being toothless worked to his advantage. The first local television commercial that aired for Aunt Dewy's Jerky had her gumming the pork stick—proving that the dried meat was so tender anyone could gobble it up, even someone with no teeth.

The following three years, Frankie's business became a huge financial success. Millions of jerky sticks (packaged in a wrap with a cartoon version of Aunt Dewy's face as the logo) were sold. Aunt Dewy's Jerky was the new Slim Jim across the southern states. His little factory created over a hundred new jobs for the people in LaSalle Parish. Aunt Dewy's Jerky Factory became a main attraction in the small town of Olla because of the gigantic, bright-red plastic pig statue attached to the roof. Frankie got a good deal on the fake farm animal when he bought it from the ex-owner of the Southern Sizzlin' Pig Out Barn in Alexandria. The pig used to be in front of the restaurant that went out of business. Not only had the Pig Out Barn been suffering from lack of customers, but the counterfeit pig had been stolen every other weekend by the Jackson Street cruisers (teens who had nothing better to do than drive up and down the strip), who then placed the phony pig on people's front lawns.

The year Frankie met Norma was also the year he sold his business to a large cooperate company. He became one of the wealthiest men in central Louisiana. Shortly before Frankie made the decision to sell, he was notified by the nursing home that his Aunt Dewy had passed away in her sleep. The nurse told him that she looked so peaceful, sitting in her La-Z-Boy recliner with her eyes shut and an Aunt Dewy pork stick in her mouth; it was Cajun teriyaki, the newest flavor at the time. Frankie knew it was time to move on when the little spicy face of his jerky empire had been taken by angels to be with the Big Man Upstairs.

After the finalization of the sale, Frankie moved to Alexandria and married Norma. They bought a beautiful four-bedroom condominium and traveled a lot. Norma's oldest son, Steven, never really clicked with Frankie. Steven was twenty-seven years old and had just graduated from Tulane University's School of Medicine when Norma and Frankie tied the knot. Whenever Steven came home from New Orleans for the holidays, he always stayed with his father. Dylan, on the other the hand, really liked his stepfather. He thought it was intriguing that Frankie was a washed-up country singer and a dehydrated meat connoisseur.

Frankie was overjoyed when Norma gave him the news that she was expecting. The middle-aged couple had already experienced nine wonderful years of marriage, and the blessing of their son, Kris, made their lives even more special.

The arrival of Kris Dewy Dubois brought the entire family together. Norma's two sons, family friends, and even her first husband, Brent, were all there to welcome Kris into this crazy world.

Frankie was a hands-on father and made sure Kris had an extraordinary life. He even taught his son how to play the guitar at age six. Norma and Kris made the former pork jerky tycoon's dreams of having a beautiful family come true.

In 2003, Frankie purchased some land off of Highway 28 West and built a gigantic convenience store/gas station. He named it Norma's Cajun Rage Quick Stop after his wife and one of Dottie West's hit songs from 1981. He even had the famous pig (the landmark from the jerky factory in Olla) mounted on top of the roof of the one-stop shopping establishment.

Norma's Cajun Rage Quick Stop offered more than just gas and beer. Frankie built a deli/bakery in the middle of the store with a big neon sign above it that read Aunt Dewy's Deli. In the Louisiana souvenir section, Frankie had a cardboard figure of himself from the 1970s. The six-foot stand-up of the young Frankie was pointing to CDs and T-shirts of the first and only album he recorded. Surprisingly, the has-been singer's merchandise sold well because the CDs and shirts were autographed. Most of the buyers were tourists who weren't sure who Frankie Dubois was.

On September 24, 2005, the date Hurricane Rita hit Louisiana, Frankie had just finished making sure all his store windows were duct taped and secured. He noticed that his Marlboro cigarette stand was being blown toward the highway. Barely able to walk through the strong storm, Frankie picked up the stand and staggered back to the store. He had reached the middle of the parking lot when suddenly the notorious pig was ripped off the roof by fatal winds. With over a million places in the huge parking lot where the soaring artificial animal could have landed, it ended up plunging right into Frankie and knocking him down. When the back of his head hit the concrete, he broke his neck and died instantly.

CHAPTER 2

Seafood, Love, and Laughter

The doorbell rang several times before Dylan could open it. As he turned the handle, he heard a man and woman laughing obnoxiously outside. He opened the door and welcomed in John John and Debbie Rachel, known as the rowdy Rachels. They were two of Dylan's favorite people in the world. He had known them both since kindergarten. John John and Debbie got married one month after they graduated from high school. They owned Johnny Boy's Bistro. After Tunk's Cypress Inn, Johnny Boy's Bistro happened to be the second best seafood restaurant in town.

John John, a heavyset man with a baby face, was wearing a tux T-shirt and jeans. His LSU cap was turned around on his bald head. Staying with the theme of purple and gold, his wife, Debbie, was wearing a tight purple evening gown. Similar to her husband, Debbie hadn't missed a meal for quite some time. Her wit was just as bright as her bottle-blonde hair.

Dylan gave them both a hug, and before he led them to the kitchen, he looked at John John from top to bottom and said, "Boy, you outdid yourself for this formal affair."

John John held in his stomach as he placed his hands on his hips and replied, "Don't hate me because I'm beautiful, you jealous bastard."

All three laughed, and then Debbie said, "You two are both handsome devils, and I sure do feel bad for them poor husbands of all the lonely and horny female classmates of ours." Debbie sniffed the aroma in the air coming from the kitchen. "I smell somethin' crawfishy that wants to add more pounds to my already voluptuous curves."

Dylan positioned himself between the rowdy Rachels, placing an arm around each of the lovebird's shoulders, and ordered, "Get your asses in this kitchen! The hostess with mostest is waitin' on ya'll!"

Norma was arguing with Kris about eating all the shrimp rolls when Dylan, John John, and Debbie entered the kitchen.

"What's up, my people?" shouted John John. Norma gave the redneck clown a big hug as Debbie embraced Kris with a kiss on the cheek. Then the rowdy Rachels switched people to greet. John John acted as though he was going to hit Kris but delivered a gentle bear hug instead.

After Debbie hugged and kissed Norma, she stood back and took a good look at the sweet woman's rather peculiar choice of dress.

"Oh my, that's a rather unique outfit you have on there, Norma," Debbie politely mentioned.

"She looks like an Amish grandmother on crack," joked Dylan.

After they all shared a good cackle, Debbie and John John gathered around the kitchen island piled with catered munchies and listened to Norma's (Baby Jane Hudson) explanation. Dylan grabbed a shrimp roll out of his little brother's hand and popped it into his mouth before he started mixing cocktails for the adults. While Debbie was looking at all the mouth-watering food, she realized that she had left her contribution to the feast in her vehicle.

"Baby, go get the food out of the truck," she told her husband.

"Honey, there's enough grub here to feed an army of elephants, a tribe of hogs, and your side of the family!" John John teased.

John John took his truck keys out of his pants pocket, tossed them to Kris, and told him to go get the damn food out of his truck because he was too lazy. Kris had no problem with the big man's request and left the room.

Dylan brought Debbie and John John Crown and Cokes while Norma asked the jolly couple about their daughters. Debbie and John John grinned at each other before Debbie gave Norma the report.

"Well, ya know our youngest, Savannah, made tenth-grade cheerleader, and ah, she's also taking two honors classes. I believe they're English and social studies."

"Baby girl is like her mother here. She ain't worth a dog's turd in math," John John blurted out.

Norma smiled at the chatty parents as she waited patiently to hear about their oldest daughter, Amanda. Dylan tried to change the subject by asking Debbie if her drink was okay. Debbie gave him a wink and the thumbs-up signal while Norma continued to wait for a brief report on John John and Debbie's firstborn. After twelve seconds of silence went by, Norma finally asked, "What about your oldest? What's going on with her?"

John John guzzled his Crown and Coke while Dylan poured more wine into his mother's glass. Debbie cleared her throat before giving Norma her long-awaited explanation.

"Amanda's doin' just fine ... ah, she's still living in Opelousas and working at that veterinarian clinic ... and ah, she got married a month ago in Vermont."

"Oh my Lord, is her husband from Vermont?" Norma asked.

"Ah ... no, she's from Ville Platte ... and I'm not sure who the bride is and who the husband is in this ... ah, arrangement," answered Debbie.

John John placed his arm around Debbie's shoulder and shouted, "I'm tellin' ya, woman, it's all them damn glitter glam pageants you had her in when she was a kid!"

After Dylan and Debbie laughed at John John's remark, they all looked at Norma to see what her reaction to the gay marriage was. Norma appeared to be daydreaming. Then she smiled and said, "I'm very fond of lesbian love ... hell, I have every CD that K.D. Lang has ever made."

Debbie proceeded to tell Norma all about her new daughter-in-law and how much she and John John adored her. Five seconds after Debbie said the last positive statement about her daughter's life partner, Norma burst out into song, singing "Constant Craving" (K.D. Lang's biggest hit). Norma's voice was getting higher and higher as she belted out the lyrics of the love song. Not sure how to react to the songstress in a baby-doll dress, everyone smiled as they listened to Norma ruin a beautiful ballad. When she finished her performance, her confused audience was not sure whether to applaud or go onto another subject. John John broke the silence by saying, "Norma, you are one crazy old lady."

They were all laughing when Kris entered the kitchen with the box of appetizers (the ones Debbie forgot in the truck). He placed the box on the island and said, "Look, Momma, Debbie brought those little gourmet pinwheel things you love so much."

"Oh, Debbie, thank you so much. You shouldn't have," said Norma.

Debbie bragged, "Honey, they're the best things ever. All you have to do is thaw them out, and there you have it—the perfect little knickknack snack for office parties, holiday affairs, baby showers—"

"Lesbian weddings," interrupted John John.

Once again, everyone laughed except for Kris. He didn't know what was so hysterical, and he couldn't imagine why a lesbian wedding would be a particularly funny punch line. Suddenly, the doorbell rang. Hoping it was Phoebe with his New Orleans Saints goodies, Kris gladly volunteered to answer the door.

CHAPTER 3

Opposites Really Don't Attract

Kris slid on the hardwood floor in his socks all the way to the front door and shouted, "I predict a fantastic gift coming my way!" He opened the door and saw Stuart Dauzart, his wife, Mary Beth, and his stepson, Paul.

"I don't know how much of a present it is, but we're letting Paul spend the night with you," responded Stuart.

Kris showed the new arrivals in and closed the door behind them. "Dylan! More of your friends and my surprise guest are here!" Norma had conveniently forgotten to inform Kris that she had called the Dauzarts earlier in the day and invited Paul for a movie night and sleepover.

Stuart was another one of Dylan's life-long buddies. The fifty-year-old was in very good physical condition. He had a full head of gray hair, hazel eyes, and olive skin. In the close circle of friends, Stuart was the one with photographic memory. He could recall what he, John John, and Dylan had for breakfast on the day the three juvenile delinquents decided to skip school and play Pac Man all day at the video arcade next to Godfather's Pizza. The date was Tuesday, March 9, 1982. Stuart lived for the past (eighties), and he proudly held the title of the group's unofficial social director. His accurate recollection had made him an extremely successful accountant.

Running out of time to find the scheduled love of his life, he married Mary Beth when he turned forty. They met on the Internet through eHarmony.com. Mary Beth, somewhat of a plain-Jane brunette, who could pass for a fairly attractive librarian, was looking for security and settled for Stuart. She was freshly divorced and had an eight-year-old son when she decided to hunt and trap Stuart—by use of a keyboard.

There was little to no probability that true love was actually involved in this relationship. It was more regrettable comfort. Stuart followed a detailed guide to much-wanted validation, and Mary Beth was becoming an unwilling endorsement.

Dylan walked in from the kitchen and greeted the counterfeit couple and silent child. "Ya'll look nice. Come on into hell's kitchen. We've all been waitin' on ya." Stuart, dressed in an expensive black suit, gave his old pal a hug as Mary Beth, who was wearing a standard black cocktail dress, stood still in hopes that she wouldn't receive an embrace from Dylan.

Her son, Paul, a rather pudgy young man with thick glasses and a bad case of acne, was too busy playing a game on his iPhone 6 to acknowledge anyone in the room. Kris observed Paul's overnight bag and dreadfully requested that the future manager of the Geek Squad follow him upstairs to the TV room.

Dylan, Stuart, and Mary Beth entered Captain Norma's galley of eccentrics, and the dismal twosome was welcomed by all. Mary Beth gazed at Norma and tried to figure out whether she was attempting to be Naomi Judd (the elder of the famous duet) or a sexed-up pilgrim. In return, when Norma saw Mary Beth with her hair up and no makeup, she considered the possibility of Mary Beth being the newest church member of the Pentecostals of Alexandria. After all the kind exchanges, Stuart asked, "Where in the hell were ya'll for the pep rally this afternoon?"

"It's called a lunch crowd at Johnny Boy's Bistro," replied John John.

"Ya'll are such losers," joked Stuart.

"By the way, I'm surprised that you or one of them class committee turds didn't hit me up to cater one of them borin' reunion activities like you always do," protested John John.

Stuart replied, "The food and beverage committee chose Robbie G's for the Sunday reception because everyone felt your catfish was too greasy and your hushpuppies too dry."

John John looked over to Debbie and stated, "Somebody's fixin' to get an ass whippin'."

Debbie told her husband to shut up and then joined everyone (except for Mary Beth) in laughter. After the final cackle, Dylan took Stuart and Mary Beth's drink orders. Stuart requested a vodka and tonic, and Mary Beth asked for water. Debbie nudged her obnoxious husband and commented on Mary Beth's wish for water. "Hot damn! We got ourselves a designated driver!"

With his back turned from his guests as he sliced a lime to put in Stuart's cocktail, Dylan yelled back, "Good deal. Usually that's my role." Mary Beth forced herself to grin.

The Rachels and Dylan were not on Mary Beth's list of favorite people. She didn't care for the fact that Dylan's son, Hunter, was in drug rehab and his girlfriend and daughter lived with Dylan, the carefree dad.

Mary Beth had never been fond of John John and Debbie. The final straw that broke the camel's back for Mary Beth occurred two years ago when she was rejected by the seafood scoundrels.

Stacy Dinnat, Mary Beth's hairstylist for seven years, was fundraising for her neighbor (who was paralyzed from a four-wheeler accident). The generous beautician decided to bake chocolate-chip cookies and sell them to provide a little safety net for the victim of the mud ride disaster. Mary Beth and Stacy each took a large basket of cookies, individually wrapped in cellophane and tied with a camouflage ribbon, to Johnny Boy's Bistro. Mary Beth was sure that her husband's dearest friends would be happy to place the cookies in front of the cash register where their unhealthy customers would see and buy them. Debbie, as always, was working the register when the two crusaders approached her with charity details. The first warning sign for Debbie was the salon's title was written on each of the ribbons. "Cuttin' Up and Fancy Free," she read out loud. Debbie told the ladies that she would have to sample the goods before she could sell them. She unwrapped a cookie, chewed, concentrated, and said, "This is horrible. It's made from generic cake mix and cheap chocolate chips."

There were many things Debbie had no knowledge about, such as world history and the warning signs of homosexual tendencies in youth, but one area of expertise this woman had mastered was desserts.

John John walked up to Debbie and took the half-eaten cookie out of her hand and gorged it down. After his last swallow, he stated, "This tastes like a Dollar Store markdown." Debbie chuckled at her straightforward husband's opinion, looked at the ladies, and told them that she would not sell their tasteless treats, but she would write a check for the four-wheel driver with special needs. Both Mary Beth and her haircutting sidekick were mortified and stormed out of the restaurant.

While Dylan brought Stuart and Mary Beth their beverages, Norma observed the attractive accountant and said, "Stuart, you have turned into such a handsome man. I remember you as a short and skinny teenager who would come to the house and was so shy and insecure."

"You got the insecure part right," muttered Mary Beth.

Mary Beth's criticism made everyone uncomfortable. Suddenly, the doorbell rang. Just as in a climax scene on a soap opera, the ringing of the doorbell was a perfect segue for Dylan to remove himself from a potentially gruesome battle between husband and wife. He excused himself and ran to the front door. When Dylan made it to the door, he collided with Kris, who was jumping down from the stairs. Almost knocking each other down, the brothers laughed at each other while fighting to turn the handle. Knowing that there was a prize behind door number one, Kris shouted out, "I'm coming for you, Phoebe!"

CHAPTER 4

Black Magic Woman

After a playful struggle, Dylan managed to push Kris to the side and open the door for his number-one female comrade of all time to enter. Phoebe Werner-Sury, dressed in a gray Valentino pantsuit, walked in. She immediately tossed a Drew Brees Jersey to Kris and then gave Dylan a kiss and a hug.

Phoebe was a strikingly beautiful African American woman who could easily pass for a supermodel. The fifty-year-old had an undeniable aura. Dylan felt Phoebe was just as dazzling as the magnificent jewelry she designed. If there was one person on this problematic planet he trusted, it was her.

Although she gave him the same article of clothing for his birthday last year, Kris thanked Phoebe and then darted back upstairs. Dylan put his arm around his pretty partner in crime, and they walked slowly to the kitchen.

"What have I missed so far?" asked Phoebe.

"Let's see ... Stuart's wife is planning on making his evening a miserable disaster," replied Dylan.

"Mary Beth? Didn't we decide to destroy her months ago?" inquired Phoebe.

Dylan chuckled and then said, "We did, but Stuart was too busy planning this reunion, so the murdering of Mary Beth had to be put on the backburner."

Phoebe and Dylan entered the kitchen and saw John John and Stuart arguing about LSU Coach Les Miles while Norma was searching for a platter for Debbie to place her thawed-out Sam's Club delights on. Mary Beth was sitting at the corner of the island and appeared bored as she nibbled on a cheese ball.

Debbie was the first one to notice Phoebe and screamed, "Hey, girl!" She dropped her box of store-bought appetizers on the counter and ran over to her friend. They shared kisses and hugs. Norma, Stuart, and John John eagerly waited in line behind Debbie to greet Phoebe.

While receiving hugs from each person, Phoebe said, "Jesus, I feel like I just won the Miss Black America Pageant. Y'all are too kind."

Mary Beth remained seated and continued munching on a cracker topped with a decent portion of Norma's cheese ball. She felt out of place as she observed the group of old friends instantly bond. Suddenly, Mary Beth started gagging. Her face turned red as she coughed up a large hunk of cream cheese into a napkin. Everyone's attention was now focused on the choking outsider. "Honey, are you okay?" asked Stuart.

Mary Beth nodded her head "yes" and then took big swallow of water. "I bit into something sharp," she declared. The shaken woman looked down at the napkin and discovered a red-painted fingernail in the middle of the chewed-up cheese. "It's someone's fingernail!" shouted Mary Beth.

"That someone would be me. I'm so sorry," Norma ashamedly admitted while holding up her right hand with the pinky nail missing.

John John and Debbie were the only ones laughing while Norma continued to apologize to the humiliated housewife. Dylan dodged the tense moment by fixing Phoebe a cocktail. Stuart, also escaping the embarrassment, turned to the refrigerator and studied the many photos of Norma's children, grandkids, and deceased husband. Phoebe remained standing in place as she observed Norma attempting to use her sweet southern charm to comfort Mary Beth.

A smile came across her face while watching the two women interact. Phoebe's grin was caused by the combination of the fingenail incident and Norma's choice of fashion. She couldn't figure out the reasoning for the Ellie May Clampett look.

Dylan and Stuart kept up the good work in mastering the art of avoiding anxiety, and Debbie's never-ending compassion for John John was still intact. He roared in laughter from a tacky comment she whispered in his ear. Pleased with her accurate observation, Phoebe's smile extended. She knew she was home.

The doorbell rang, and before Dylan could attempt to bail out of redirecting the conversation to bypass the uneasiness of Mary Beth, Phoebe gladly volunteered to answer the door.

The music from *The Best Little Whorehouse in Texas* continued to play throughout the condo as Phoebe danced her way across the living room to get to the front door. She giggled because she had never danced to a song titled, "A Lil Ole Bitty Pissant Country Place." The baffled hoedown queen from New Orleans opened the door, and in walked four teenagers (one female and three males).

Sky Bordelon, a lovely blonde girl wearing a nose ring, led the three young men (who all looked like coffeehouse performers) into the living room.

Phoebe welcomed the flower children in and then shouted, "Kris! Your friends are here!" Kris ran downstairs and gave his girlfriend, Sky, a hug. Paul slowly walked down the stairs to join the party that he wasn't invited to. Phoebe saw Mary Beth's introverted son strolling toward the kitchen to avoid interacting with Dylan and his modern-day hippie support system.

"I know you're not walking into the kitchen without giving me a hug," Phoebe called out to Paul. He turned around and apprehensively walked over to her, and of course, she initiated the embrace. Phoebe hated to see anyone being socially rejected. Her arm remained around Paul's shoulder as they both followed Kris, Sky, and others to the kitchen.

When Phoebe and the teens entered the kitchen, Debbie had the floor. She was explaining to Norma, Dylan, John John, and Stuart about certain groups of customers who did not tip at Johnny Boy's Bistro. According to Debbie, the women of the Central Louisiana's Quilting Club and the members of the Rainbow Church of Christ were all lacking in gratuity etiquette. Mary Beth continued to isolate herself by pretending to be checking text messages on her cell phone.

Kris's girlfriend and buddies burst into laughter when they saw Norma. "It's Baby Jane Hudson!" yelled out one of the adolescents. Norma immediately began introducing Kris's friends to everyone as Paul went over to his mother and shoved large pieces of boudin into his mouth. He looked like a starving chipmunk storing nuts.

John John noticed Paul's aggressive eating method and said, "Settle down, junior! What the hell are you doin'? Practicing for the Nathan's Hot Dog Eating Contest?"

Once again, a member of Stuart's family was now the butt of the joke, and John John's rude comment infuriated Mary Beth.

Amidst the laughter and small talk coming from the party of all ages, Paul looked at his mother and whispered, "I'm not staying here tonight." Mary Beth, ignoring the chewed-up bit of boudin hanging from the right side of Paul's mouth, nodded her head yes in agreement.

Stuart looked at Sky and asked, "Is your mother coming to the reunion tonight?"

"No, sir. She heard that my dad was going to be there," answered Sky.

"Oh, I love your mother. If I'm not mistaken, I think we were both cheerleaders for the football team," Phoebe added.

"No, no, Melissa Walker was an alternate, never an actual cheerleader," corrected Stuart.

"I know what it's like to be just an alternate," Mary Beth said, just loud enough for everyone to hear.

There was an awkward silence throughout the room until Phoebe looked at her Rolex and asked, "Are you all about ready to go?"

"Yeah, we better go; we're already behind schedule," replied Stuart.

The middle-aged classmates took the last sips of their cocktails as Kris and his friends replaced the older crowd and were now the second shift at Norma's all-you-can-eat buffet and movie night. Mary Beth thanked Norma for her hospitality and also informed her that Paul would not be spending the night due to having suddenly developed a migraine headache. Stuart frowned as he watched his cold wife and socially inept step-son complete their mission. He knew that he would have to drop Paul off, which meant it would be just him and Mary Beth driving to reunion. Stuart realized that it would be too good to be true for his wife to want to be part of the only group of people who made him happy. He explained to Dylan, John John, and Debbie that he would meet them all there because of the unexpected side trip of dropping Paul off at home.

Phoebe grabbed her cell phone out of her purse and called her cousin LaToya (who owned a medical transportation company) to come pick up her and her pals and take them to the reunion. It was extremely important to her that there was no drinking and driving, especially for Dylan. In the past, Phoebe was the only person who could make Dylan give her his car keys when he was inebriated.

As they all headed out the door to go to the reunion, Dylan's cell phone rang. It was his son, Hunter, who was attending a substance abuse recovery program in Florida. Immediately, the father and son's conversation turned into an argument. Dylan had mailed Hunter the wrong type of underarm deodorant.

CHAPTER 5

Rebel with a Cause

Out of the party of five very different friends, Dylan was the wild child. He was the trailblazer of the incredibly unique pack and known all through high school as the Jackson Street Cruiser. There wasn't a pill he wouldn't try or a young woman he couldn't charm. The drug-seeking Don Juan didn't get by on just his good looks; according to his close friends, he was extremely intelligent and had a beautiful heart.

Dylan had compassion for people with special needs. His sympathy for the handicap developed when he received his first DUI at age seventeen. For his community service, he was ordered by the court to work at the Louisiana Special Education Center. He literally fell in love with these extraordinary individuals. In fact, he continued volunteering as a teacher's aide long after he had earned his hours to get his driver's license back. Every day after school, he would spend at least an hour with the delayed teenagers. Although his newfound passion to help people played a huge part in his decision to become a registered nurse, Dylan's womanizing and partying remained intact.

Dylan somewhat followed in his father's and brother's footsteps. Both his dad and older brother were well-respected and gifted gynecologists. The rebellious Romeo did not want to invest the time to go to med school; besides, he became a father at age eighteen. Dylan slept with his biology professor during his first semester at LSU of Alexandria. The brief affair wasn't a devastating moment for him because his instructor was a single woman in her late thirties, whose biological clock was ticking. His pregnant professor ended up moving to Shreveport to be closer to her family. Basically, Dylan was just a sperm donor to her. She was very grateful to him and had no regrets. No one, not even Phoebe, ever found out about Dylan's encounter with the fertile educator.

Until this day, Dylan has never heard from the mother of his firstborn, and he is unaware of whether he has a daughter or son. Even with providing a baby for the lonely biologist, Dylan ended up with a C in the class and eventually hooked up with an economics major who was closer to his age. Because of his endless carousing and bad habits, it took Dylan five years to earn a two-year degree.

After receiving his associate degree in nursing, his father, Dr. Brent Jacobs, gave Dylan a beautiful, three-bedroom condominium. Dr. Jacobs owned several rental properties throughout Rapides Parish. During this time period, Brent was the Tiger Woods of the late eighties. The sex-craved doctor slept with any woman with a pulse and a zipper. Therefore, the condo was not only a graduation present; it was a donation to distract his guilt from having cheated on his son's mother.

All through the last two years of high school, and the five years he attended LSU-A, Dylan continued to volunteer at the special education school and work full-time at Pearson's Drugstore. Just about everybody who attended Holy Savior Menard Central High had worked at Pearson's at one time or another. Dylan's hard work and knowledge of Pearson's sales items in the coupon section of *Alexandria Daily Town Talk* paid off. He was promoted to manager of the liquor department and received a pay increase from $3.25 to five dollars an hour. Dylan wasn't popular with his coworkers (peers) at that time in his hectic life. He ended up firing several of his friends for robbing the local drugstore blind. He even gave the boot to Stuart and Phoebe. He caught Phoebe placing a small bottle of Forever Krystal Perfume, which was by Linda Evans, (the star of the TV show *Dynasty*) in her purse. He was forced to let go of Stuart when he discovered that he was only charging his friends fifty cents for a fifth of Crown Royal. While Phoebe brushed off the minor crime, Stuart still had nightmares of having to take a lie detector test while the store's jingle, "We care for you at Pearson's Drugs," was piped into the interrogation room. Of course, Dylan never told Mr. Pearson that he fired these inexperienced criminals for stealing. Laziness and pouring too much syrup in customer's Slush Puppies (an ICEE but much sweeter) were the reasons given for termination.

While flying by the seat of his pants in nursing school, helping special people with disabilities, and playing with the big boys in retail management, Dylan made the time to travel back and forth from the Cotton Gin Bar to the Bayview Yacht Club. The two bars were located across from each other with a small piece of land that separated them. Local bar goers felt it was rather unique that there was no water near the Bayview Yacht Club. The Field View Meat Market would have been a more appropriate name. Regardless of the bars' names, Dylan was a regular customer at each cocktail lounge every night, except on Sundays. He spent Sunday nights at a country and western bar named Fool's Gold. Dylan had an unexplained desire to escape at that time in his life. Norma, never a stranger to a stout bourbon and water, believed that she evidently gave birth to the *Six Million Dollar Man*, and not because Dylan was in good physical shape. She was baffled by how any human being could stay out drinking until two every morning and function the next day. Both Norma and Brent overlooked Dylan's damaging decisions. They thought that maybe it would take him longer to get the college partying years out of his system than his older brother, Steven.

Steven Jacobs was four years older than Dylan and was the perfect child. With light blond hair and sparkling baby-blue eyes, Steven was a lot better looking than Dylan. The brilliant individual finished high school at the age of sixteen and went directly to Tulane University and majored in premed.

Steven was out of med school and finished his residency by the age of twenty-five. He wanted to keep the family legacy alive and became a partner with his father. The young gynecologist was also a phenomenal golfer.

Dylan and Steven loved each other, but they were definitely not friends. Steven felt that his younger sibling was a waste with good intentions.

As soon as Dylan received his nursing degree, it did not take him long to find a job. During the time he was in clinical rotation, he became fascinated with the mentally ill and landed a position at Briarwood Psychiatric Hospital. For seventeen years, Dylan was the head nurse/program supervisor of the ICU Unit. He treated bipolar patients suffering from the most severe cases of schizophrenia.

During his eighth year of working as a psych nurse, he met a beautiful brunette named Jaclyn Hernandez. Jaclyn was the unit secretary on the adolescent ward. She was freshly divorced from an airman who was stationed at England Air Force Base. Jaclyn was looking for a free-spirited Prince Charming and found a Duke of Dysfunction.

Dylan knew he had hit the jackpot when the stunning secretary asked him to go to happy hour the first day they met. From that day forward, the kindred spirits spent happy hour together every day after work. Red Beard's Bar was the two lovebirds' home away from home.

It only took two weeks of dating for Jaclyn to move in with the partying nurse. During the fourth month of the couple's chemical dependency courtship, Jaclyn found out she was pregnant. Dylan was thirty-one years old when his twenty-two-year-old bar mate told him about her bun in the oven. He somewhat expected she might be pregnant because she started having only two glasses of white wine every night instead of the two bottles of Chablis and the four shots of Jagermeister that she normally consumed. Jaclyn told him the news over beef po-boys at Lou & Laura's, which was located next door to Red Beard's. The two often walked over to the restaurant and ate there after their extended happy hour. They felt the grease from the curly fries would prevent a hangover. Dylan took the news well and decided they should get married. He appreciated that Jaclyn could go with the flow of his unhealthy routine, and she loved that Dylan wasn't a challenge and came from old money.

Dylan's family and best friends didn't know Jaclyn well enough to form an opinion. They all thought she was nice and very attractive, and that was about it.

Out of everyone, Stuart knew her the best because he met the lovely lushes often for after-work cocktails. Stuart could not keep up with the couple in the alcohol marathon, but he made sure to be at Red Beard's as much as possible because of his fear of missing out on reliving historical milestones from the good ole days. The follower made sure that he, Dylan, and Jaclyn would always have the table next to the jukebox and with a clear view of Jackson Street, the street that Dylan ruled in the early eighties. Stuart had at least twenty-five dollars invested in the jukebox, which made him feel he had a sense of control.

When Jaclyn and Dylan chatted about their work at the hospital, Stuart would gaze out the window and focus on the street full of memories while listening to the soundtrack from his never forgotten past, thereby reassuring his acceptance and status of being a part of Dylan's intimate army of admired soldiers.

It was on a Saturday afternoon at Red Beard's in October 1995 that Dylan and Jaclyn were married. Dylan was nursing his fifth beer while Jaclyn was showing the bar owner's wife, Sue (a.k.a. Mrs. Red Beard), her engagement ring. Dylan bought the ring from Schnack's Fine Jewelry. It was a Jacob Family tradition to purchase all gifts from Schnack's; the store also carried Phoebe's line of jewelry. The numb groom had Phoebe handle everything. All he had to do was give her Jaclyn's finger size.

Dylan was pretending to be listening to Stuart's story of how he couldn't wait for his favorite movie of all time, *Fandango,* to come out on a new digital device called a DVD when all of a sudden Dylan blurted out, "I want to get this over with!" After Dylan shared the unexpected news of becoming a husband and father to Stuart, Stuart was ecstatic that Dylan asked him to be his best man in the wedding scheduled to happen in an hour.

Along with Dylan's sentimental request came a long list of verbal orders for the honored admirer. Stuart immediately called John John and Debbie. John John couldn't make the ceremony because he was tailgating at Tiger Stadium. Debbie screamed with excitement when she received her call at the restaurant. It was all-you-can-eat fried fish and ribs night, but because of the LSU game, business was slow, so she told her sister, Darlene, to take over. Then she grabbed an aluminum tray of ribs and fish and ran out the door.

Stuart had to call Phoebe's cousin, LaToya, to pick up Judge Tom Young. Tom agreed to marry Dylan and Jaclyn at the bar, but he was at a friend's house getting tanked before the LSU game and needed someone to drive him. The soused man of justice would have had his wife take him to the refined ceremony at Red Beard's, but unfortunately she was banned from the bar for throwing darts at a woman who was flirting heavily with her hubby.

All of Dylan's family was in Baton Rouge to see the LSU Tigers play, and Jaclyn's folks lived in San Antonio, Texas. Therefore, only Debbie, Stuart, the bar regulars, a few coworkers from the psychiatric hospital, Mrs. Red Beard, and LaToya the medical transporter (chauffer for the intoxicated) attended the rushed wedding. During the less than ostentatious ceremony, Stuart held the bar phone receiver up so that Phoebe (who was in Dallas at a jewelry show) could witness her best friend make one of the worst mistakes of his life. She sat in the lobby of the Ritz-Carlton and listened to Judge Young perform the ceremony. All that Phoebe heard was a male's voice that sounded like slurring from a stroke victim and a cheering crowd. She thought to herself that Dylan should have had a tradition wedding with beautiful flowers and a three-tiered cake. Instead, he settled for a Stepford barfly under a Miller Lite neon sign. After the couple said their I dos, Dylan took the phone from Stuart and said, "Hey, Phoebe! I did it."

"You sure did," she replied.

Dylan knew that Phoebe was apprehensive about his sudden decision and gave the phone back to Stuart. Phoebe then instructed Stuart to have her cousin, LaToya, call her back from the payphone located outside the front of the bar.

LaToya, a heavyset, black female with a Marge Simpson type of hairdo, called her cousin shortly after Stuart told her to. But first she had to grab a paper plate of fish and ribs.

LaToya walked out of the bar toward the payphone while carefully holding her plate of wedding food like she was a surgeon holding a heart during a major transplant. She leaned against the wall as she multitasked dialing the payphone and chewing on a rib. The out-of-place wedding guest called her apprehensive cousin collect, of course. The only word Phoebe could get in was, "Hello." LaToya dominated the one-sided conversation that went like this:

"Gurrrl, you are friends with some crazy white people. First, they had me going to that high-class Landmark neighborhood to pick up that crazy drunk bastard, Judge Young … no tellin' what could of happened to me—a big, black woman drivin' a medical transportation van through that fancy neighborhood. I finally found that crazy-ass man in front of a mansion.

That bastard was in the front yard dancin' with a huge blown-up LSU tiger; it looked like that damn judge was trying to have sexual relations with that overgrown tiger balloon. When I got that liquored-up bastard in the van, the first thing out of his drunken mouth was, 'I know you.'

"I said, 'Oh, no, sir, you don't know me.' That crazy white man has sent just about everybody in my neighborhood behind bars. Then he asked me if I had any laughing gas in the back of the van. He then told me that he couldn't bring his wife to the club - cuz that crazy bitch tried to cut up some skinny, white tramp that was trying to talk to her man. Gurrrl, that ride to Redneck's or Red Beard's or whatever the name of this club is was one long, messy drive."

"When we finally got here, I walked into this smoky, white club like I was walking into a damn Klan meeting, and your boo, Dylan, looked like he had been hypnotized by a witch doctor. Now, you know that man has no business marrying that Selena look-a-like gold-digger. You know Miss Norma is gonna be crying every night when she finds out her baby boy got married in this rebel flag juke joint. And gurrrl, there's no wedding cake to be found. I'm gettin' the hell out of here. That crazy-ass judge can call a cab or have that crazy-ass Jack-the-Ripper wife of his pick his drunk ass up. I'm goin' back in there, and I'm gonna get more fried fish. It's not too bad, but it sure ain't no fried catfish from Tunk's Cypress Inn. Did you hear what say, gurrrl?"

"Yeah, yeah, let me get off this phone and get my fish and money from Stuart, that other crazy-ass friend of yours."

LaToya hung up the phone before Phoebe could say good-bye. Phoebe sat back in her chair and stared at all the people walking back in forth of the hotel lobby. She went into a five-minute depression, then got up and made it right on time to a cocktail party given by a fellow jewelry designer from Plano, Texas.

Not much changed during Jaclyn's pregnancy. She and Dylan still got together every evening at Red Beard's. Slowly but surely, Dylan became aggravated with his new bride. He felt smothered by her because they worked at the same hospital, and the excitement of the alcohol-induced romance had sobered up into a toxic relationship.

On June 10, 1996, Hunter John Jacobs was born. He was a beautiful, healthy baby. He was named after his father's middle name and his mother's dad, John.

Shortly after the miserable couple's son was born, Dylan and Jaclyn separated. She couldn't take his obsessive compulsive disorder. Dylan worked hard at making his home clean and crisp; he had always despised clutter. Even as a youngster, he would keep his room spotless. His strange interior decorating style came from his appreciation of chain motel rooms. No matter how hard he worked or played, it was a must that Dylan come home to his tidy palace that could pass for a suite at the Courtyard Marriott. Keeping immaculate living quarters signified new beginnings and hope for Dylan. He inherited the need to clean from his mother, Norma, and older brother, Steven.

Jaclyn couldn't take living with Mr. Clean. The first red flag for her should have been when she opened the kitchen pantry and there were eighty boxes of Glade PlugIns arranged in alphabetical order by scent. The imaginary love affair came to end when Jaclyn's expectations were shattered. She felt that since Dylan came from a prominent family, she would be set for life. Deep down, Jaclyn knew that Dylan was not in love with her, but she was willing to ride on the boat through rough waters to the island of security.

Unfortunately, Hunter's arrival didn't save the marriage. Jaclyn moved into a two-bedroom apartment and immediately started dating Keith White. Keith owned several payday loan businesses throughout the state. He was a regular at Red Beard's and had his eye on Jaclyn for quite some time. Keith wasn't the most handsome man in Alexandria. In fact, he was downright ugly. He looked like a potbelly pig in need of tan and a weight-loss program. Unlike Dylan, Jaclyn knew that she could make this pig love her, and she would be financially taken care of.

Dylan and Jaclyn decided to share joint custody of Hunter. Dylan instantly fell in love with his son the second he saw him at the hospital. Hunter looked just like his father but had his mother's dark complexion. He was an easygoing toddler who always appeared to be happy. The young man had the best of both worlds. One week, he would stay at Dylan's condo, which was like staying at a Holiday Inn Express, and the next week, he would be with his mother and stepfather in a mansion located in Alexandria's subdivision for the new rich.

It seemed as if everyone was involved with raising Hunter. Dylan hired a nanny and had help from his parents. Even his brother Steven included Hunter in family outings. With all the support from his family, Dylan was able to continue his routine of work and then spirits afterwards.

Hunter was five years old when his mother became pregnant with the first of the four children she had with his step-father, Keith. Eventually, Hunter felt that his mother rejected him because of her new family.

When Hunter reached the age of nine, he went to live full-time with his father. Jaclyn couldn't handle his bad behavior caused by his resentment for his siblings. Dylan couldn't have been happier to raise his son. He even gave up his habitual happy hours at Red Beard's and cut down on smoking. He substituted his poor lifestyle by chewing Copenhagen and drinking Bud Light at home instead of Budweiser at the bars.

Hunter did extremely well in elementary school. He was the type of child that did not require a lot of friends. The young man inherited the art of compulsive cleaning and organization from his father and his grandmother, Norma.

Hunter spent a great deal of time with grownups. He loved going over to Norma and his step-grandfather Frankie's condo. The adult in the nine-year-old body was fascinated with the Dottie West room and being one year older than his uncle. Hunter and his uncle, Kris, were as close as brothers, and many people thought they were. Unlike Hunter, Kris was messy and had several friends. He dreamed of being a folk rock musician not the spokesperson for Clorox cleaning products like his young nephew.

When Hunter started junior high, every aspect of his life remained clean, such as his hygiene and room—everything except his drug test. The preteen loner began experimenting with his father's and grandparent's prescription drugs. He also invaded their liquor cabinets when he was left home alone. Because of his good looks and mysterious ways, Hunter was popular in school; however, the juvenile addict still did not feel the need to have friends. Eventually, he detached himself from his family.

Earning money, being with sexually active girls, and getting high were Hunter's aspirations. To distract his father from his immoral intentions, Hunter would go with Dylan every other weekend to the special education center and volunteer. To feed his drug habit, Hunter cleaned his Grandfather Brent's and Uncle Steven's doctors' offices after hours. He also did janitorial work during the weekends at Norma's Cajun Rage Quick Stop. Dylan was ambivalent to his son's corrupt customs, which was rather ironic since he was a psychiatric nurse for several years (Dylan lost his nursing license in 2004 when he got his second DUI after leaving John John and Debbie's house. It was the night that LSU beat Old Miss in the Magnolia Bowl).

It was only Hunter's second week as a freshman at Holy Savior Menard High when he was expelled for smoking marijuana in the boys' restroom. Dylan knew there was a problem with his son, but it wasn't the end of the world. Basically, he thought Hunter was just a younger version of himself.

Dylan's level of concern was no way near the embarrassment felt by his father and brother, Steven. The two doctors were disgusted and in fear for the family's refined reputation, especially Steven.

Instead of sending Hunter to another high school or treatment, Dylan allowed him to be home schooled. After losing his job at the psych hospital, Dylan took his stepfather Frankie's offer to manage the convenience store, of which he eventually became owner because of the unexpected death of Frankie caused by the flying fake pig. The career change made it easier for Dylan to keep a better eye on his at-risk son. Hunter was intelligent and had no problems zipping through the computer courses. The expulsion from school was just the beginning of Hunter's journey of reckless decisions.

It was only two months after Hunter was kicked out of high school when he met Sylvia Carrillo. The two met in the parking lot of Norma's Cajun Rage Quick Stop.

Sylvia was three years older than Hunter. She was a petite, pretty Hispanic girl with dark brown eyes. The eighteen-year-old was from Forest Hill, Louisiana, and moved to Alexandria to work. Her parents were from Mexico and moved to Forest Hill to work on a plant nursery. To be able to afford her studio apartment, Sylvia worked two jobs. She worked as a waitress at the Pitt Grill in the mornings, and in the evenings, she worked in housekeeping at the Best Western. She had Hunter's heart when she mentioned housekeeping. Being a fifteen-year-old male with raging hormones and the desire to be needed, Hunter soon became joined at the hip with Sylvia. First came love; second came in-depth discussions on the latest cleaning products; third came little Maria in a baby carriage. Dylan wasn't exactly overjoyed about being a grandfather at the age of forty-seven. He felt that the situation was possibly a sign from God for him to provide a beautiful life for his granddaughter, Maria, especially since he had become a father in his teens. The birth of Maria was his chance to make up for not having anything to do with his first child.

Dylan allowed Sylvia and the baby to move into his condo. This arrangement worked out well because Sylvia had exceptional housekeeping skills. Once again, Dylan's father and brother, Steven, were embarrassed by his and Hunter's circumstances.

Norma was beyond thrilled to have Sylvia as an official member of the family. She treated Sylvia as the daughter-in-law she never had. Steven's wife, Lauren, didn't have much to do with her. Lauren was a lot closer to Brent's second wife, Ally. Norma loved spending time with Sylvia. They went out to lunch and shopped all the time. Norma even took the new mother to get her hair done. She had her beautician dye Sylvia's hair red like hers. The pair looked like an odd version of the mother and daughter singing duet, the Judds.

Instant responsibility of having a child did not slow down Hunter's love affair with alcohol and Adderall. He did take it upon himself to work full-time at the convenience store as well as Saturday and Sunday nights at John John and Debbie's seafood restaurant.

The young man truly loved his girlfriend and daughter. He was just more partial to self-medicating. For some reason, Hunter's resentment for his father increased day by day. It was as if his dad had become father of the year. Dylan had his own front baby carrier for Maria. The middle-aged grandfather took his little grand-angel everywhere with him. Hunter wished he had one eighth of the love and enthusiasm Dylan had for Maria.

Whether it was the shock of having an infant at such a young age, the death of his step-grandfather caused by the freak accident, or the built-up bitterness for his dad, Hunter's addiction was now in full force. He secretly stole from Norma's Cajun Rage Quick Stop and Johnny Boy's Bistro to support his addiction to Demerol. He turned into a gifted thief when he visited his family members; their medicine cabinets had enough prescriptions to accommodate Woodstock. Sylvia chose to disregard her boyfriend's infrequent behavior. Hunter was extremely kind to her when he was high, especially when he smoked pot or had taken Adderall.

The incident that led to a family intervention and a stay at Brentwood Psychiatric Hospital came when Hunter had a mental breakdown, Spanish style. It was a Friday afternoon when he had purchased a tablet (only God knows what it was) from Brandon Walker. Brandon's father was a pain management physician in Pineville, Louisiana. The drug turned the usually shy and reserved young man into a wild superhero. He ended up crashing Norma's Telemundo get-together. Two of the characters from Sylvia and Norma's favorite Spanish soap opera were getting married, and Norma felt it would be fun to have a celebration at her condo. She invited Sylvia's mother and six aunts to take part in the televised fiesta. All the ladies brought a covered dish. From steak fajitas to enchilada casserole, Norma's kitchen smelled and looked like the failing chain restaurant Pancho's Mexican Buffet. Debbie was invited because she had recently become a fan of the Telemundo Network. John John had gotten her satellite TV for her birthday. Debbie, Sylvia, and her non-English-speaking relatives were in the living room watching the wedding when Hunter came in and ran upstairs. Norma was in the kitchen hiding Taco Bell bags. She wanted to make sure no one knew that she didn't make the tacos herself. The ladies (all attired in vintage Mexican sundresses) were too busy sipping sangria and viewing the ceremony to realize that Hunter was upstairs in Norma's bathroom, searching for any type of antidepressant that could perhaps bring him down from his hyper mood.

The ladies were laughing and throwing rice at the flat-screen television when all of a sudden they heard a scream coming from the staircase. It was Hunter; other than wearing Norma's Mardi Gras boa, he was naked as a jaybird. *"Buena's tardes,* my beautiful *muchachas!"* he shouted.

The staged wedding guests were in shock. Well, everyone except for Debbie. She let out a huge laugh as she focused on Hunter's rather large burrito. She then nudged Sylvia and said, "Oh, honey, with that red hot chili pepper, I bet he's like a straight—very straight—Ricky Martin in bed!"

Norma ran upstairs to Hunter, grabbed him by the arm, and took him to her room. She then made him put on a robe. Hunter took a seat on the bed, hooted for about ten seconds, and then passed out. Meanwhile downstairs, Sylvia burst into tears as her mother and aunts comforted her in Spanish.

Norma called Dylan, Steven, and her ex-husband to come over immediately and help her with Hunter. When the men got to Norma's condo, Dylan called for an ambulance right away. Hunter was taken to the emergency room to have his stomach pumped. After he was medically cleared, his uncle, Steven, had him PEC'd (Physicians Emergency Certificate) to Brentwood Psychiatric Hospital in Shreveport. Dylan felt it was a better facility than the local psych hospital where he used to work.

Hunter stayed at Brentwood for eight days, and after he and his family met with his therapist, he agreed to go to a long-term substance abuse treatment facility located in Destin, Florida. Even though there was Bayou Peace Recovery Center in Cheneyville, Louisiana, which was a notable program for individuals with addiction issues, Dylan felt it would be best for Hunter to be out of state. Hunter apprehensively agreed to seek help. He told his father that the only reason he was going through with treatment was because Sylvia and Norma begged him, and they were the only two people that he had ever trusted. Dylan couldn't have cared less at this time; he just wanted his son to get better.

CHAPTER 6

Fired from Reality

Before Dylan, John John, Debbie, and Phoebe were to make their debut at the reunion, Phoebe had LaToya take them to Sweet Daddy's, a hole-in-the-wall bar where the intimate group often met for spirits during Stuart and Phoebe's holiday breaks from college. Sweet Daddy's was formerly the Howard Johnson's cocktail lounge in the 1970s.

The old meeting place had not changed at all. The same old bartender, sofas, chairs, customers, and songs on the jukebox were intact. The unenthused reunion goers and LaToya took a seat at their old regular table where many dreams had been discussed. LaToya instantly noticed the pizza Bagel Bites on a hot tray in the corner. The snacks were leftovers from the unsuccessful happy hour earlier that evening. Feeling robbed from not being able to partake in Norma's southern-style smorgasbord, LaToya darted over to the mildly warm, miniature pizzas and gathered every single one of them as if she was participating in the old game show, *Supermarket Sweeps*.

When the famished chauffeur got back to the table, John John was taking everybody's beverage order. They all ordered Miller Lites, which was the gang's drink of choice back in the day at the legendary meeting place. Dylan and LaToya were the only two who didn't order alcohol. Because of Dylan's past slipups and having a child in rehab, he now had a two-cocktail limit, and he had already had them at his mother's condo. LaToya would have killed for a Hennessy and juice but knew it was not possible because she was a professional, safe driver. Dylan ordered a club soda while John John stood and waited impatiently for LaToya to make up her mind. LaToya, with a mouth full of Bagel Bites, said, "I want somethin' sweet with no alcohol in it."

"How about a Shirley Temple?" Debbie suggested.

"Yeah, that sounds good. Tell the bartender to put plenty of oranges, pineapples, and cherries in it. Instead of a Shirley Temple, I'll call it a Beyoncé with a twist," LaToya ordered.

"Why don't you just order a fruit salad?" snarled John John.

"Speakin' of salad, you need to do somethin' with that potato salad you serve at your restaurant. It tastes like instant mashed potatoes with a shot of expired mustard in it," replied LaToya.

Everyone laughed at the driver turned food critic's comment, except for John. He shook his head, rolled his eyes, and then walked up to the bar.

Debbie patted LaToya on the back and said, "You're a hoot! You need to come to one of my pokeno parties!"

"No, not me, gurrrl. If you only knew how much church money I've spent playing cards," said LaToya.

Debbie was not quite sure she knew what LaToya was talking about. She looked over to Phoebe for an explanation.

"She's a compulsive bingo addict," answered Phoebe.

"Oh honey, my grandmother was the same way. We buried her with her lucky rabbit's foot and bingo markers," added Debbie

Phoebe noticed that Dylan was quiet. She reached over, took his hand, and then asked, "How are you?"

"Confused with a touch of fury," he replied.

Phoebe was aware of Dylan's complications with his son and knew not to push the issue, and he appreciated that she didn't. The two old friends smiled at each other as John John made it back to the table. He was carrying the drinks on a tray. "Your hot-ass waitress is here and ready to serve with love!" announced John John.

The overweight, male barmaid called out everyone's drinks before he passed them. He gave Phoebe and Debbie their beers, handed Dylan his club soda, and last but certainly not least, he delivered a large highball full of oranges and cherries to LaToya.

"No pineapple?" she inquired.

"Damn, woman! There's enough fruit in there to fill Carmen Amanda's hat!" replied John John.

"You mean Carmen Miranda," corrected Phoebe.

"What?" asked John John.

"You meant to say Carmen Miranda, the famous samba singer," Phoebe said.

"Yeah, that Brazilian chick who had about ten pounds of fruit on her head!" hollered John John.

LaToya rapidly ripped several of the maraschino cherries off their stem with her tongue as if she were a big bass tackling a hook attached to a fishing line, before she responded to John John's foolish reference by saying, "I don't know anything about this fruit-headed woman you're talkin' about but I can tell you one thang, you can kiss my big Fruit of the Loom ass!"

"Oooh-eee! I like this crazy woman!" John John shouted.

"This intellectual conversation from you people is just mind-boggling," uttered Phoebe.

Debbie noticed John John swaying back and forth. He had bright-red liquid running down his chin. "Did your drunk butt just do a shot of Hot Damn when you were up at the bar?" she asked her husband.

"No, I did not do a shot. I did five! But I don't even have a buzz, my baby!" defended John John.

"Bullshit! You're as tight as these damn Spanx I have on!" yelled Debbie.

Amidst all the cackling from the ladies, John John realized that Dylan was somewhat distant. He placed his beer on the table next to Debbie, and then he signaled for Dylan to get up.

"Excuse us, ladies. Me and the legendary Jackson Street Cruiser here have to powder our noses," joked John John.

As Dylan got up from his chair, LaToya spat out an orange peel into a cocktail napkin and yelled out to John John, "Speakin' of powder, you need to quit puttin' so much Zatarain's filé in your gumbo!"

"Jesus H Christ, woman! Did Stuart hire you to attack my seafood bistro?" John John replied back to the culinary connoisseur.

"Ain't nobody hire me to say anythang. I'm just tellin' you—you need to shape up your gumbo or you will not see me or my sisters from Eastern Star Missionary Baptist Church at your restaurant! Now! Now! What cha got to say? You better go on to that bathroom and get that red devil juice off your face!" LaToya barked back.

"Isn't there another transportation company we could use like the Tipsy Taxi service or somethin'?" John John asked Phoebe.

LaToya instructed John John to carry his ass on, and he and Dylan walked to the men's restroom.

Right as the two men entered the restroom, John John went straight to the urinal and peed while Dylan looked in the mirror to see if he was still the most handsome of all. As John John was urinating, he spotted the initials D S JJ carved on the wall under the condom machine above the urinal.

"Oh, my Lord, our initials are still craved on the wall!" shouted John John.

"That was back when you, Stuart, and I came here for a few drinks before the very first Krewe of Boogaloo Ball. What year was that—1988 or '89?" asked Dylan.

"Hell, I don't know. All I can tell ya is if Stuart finds out about this, he's gonna want this carving famed and placed on his wall of precious pubescent memories," answered John John.

Both men chuckled as John John walked over to the sink. After he washed his hands, he wiped off the leftover Hot Damn shot from his face. He then looked over to Dylan and asked him what was wrong.

"It's a complicated time for me right now, and I'm really not in the mood to go down memory lane, which consists of endless partying and selfishness. Damn it, John John, I have a kid in rehab who hates me, and this emotional wound of mine is far from healing because of all this remorse that's eating at my soul," explained Dylan.

"That boy doesn't hate you, Dylan. He's going through some tough shit right now. My God, he's only kid and has a two-year-old baby girl, and yes, he's made some rotten choices—but he's getting help, and good help at that. Isn't it like eight hundred dollars a day at that treatment center?" asked John John.

Dylan reached into his back pants pocket, pulled out his wallet, and took two one-hundred-dollar bills out of it. He held the money up and said, "While we're on the subject of finances, here's the two hundred dollars that Hunter stole from your restaurant."

John John was dumbfounded as Dylan placed the bills into his hand.

"What the hell? What do you mean he took from my restaurant?" John John asked.

"Oh, you got off lucky. According to his therapist, Hunter robbed my entire family for much more," reported Dylan.

John placed his arm around Dylan and then said, "I'm so sorry, brother. We're gonna get through this raisin' hellions crap together."

Dylan let out a brief grin and replied, "I don't know, John John. I just don't know."

John John hugged his depressed buddy and then said, "We got this, my brother. If you need any advice from one of the best fathers, if not the best in Rapides Parish, I'm here. I mean, look at my track record; I've developed a spectacular system where I can even run off sex-craved villains from getting near my baby girls."

"Like we used to be? I know I'm gonna hate myself for asking, but how do you prevent this from happening?" Dylan apprehensively asked.

"Four simple words ... let them be lesbians," answered John John.

"Okay, okay, I can see that the cinnamon shots have altered your astonishing wisdom," said Dylan.

"And I'm just gettin' started," added John John.

John John's country-fried advice had lifted his buddy's spirits. Dylan smiled at the redneck version of Dr. Phil, and the two men left the restroom.

John John snuck over to the bar to consume another Hot Damn. He had already surpassed his limit of shots. Dylan returned to the table where the hen party was in full force. LaToya had just finished complaining that there were no more Bagel Bites left while Debbie was in the middle of telling the starving van driver where to buy the deli spiral treats (the ones she left over at Norma's). Ignoring Debbie's easy and delightful munchies suggestion, LaToya looked over to Dylan, who had just taken a seat by Phoebe, and asked, "When are you all gonna be ready to be driven to this damn reunion?"

"Actually, LaToya, I'm gonna call my little brother, Kris, to drop off my truck here, and I'll drive everyone to the reunion," Dylan replied.

"Thank you, Jesus! I can go home now and watch *The Real Housewives of Atlanta*. They're having an all-night marathon on Bravo TV tonight," LaToya stated.

"Dear Lord, please don't mention reality television to me," said Debbie.

Phoebe and Dylan burst out in laughter as LaToya waited for Debbie to elaborate on her anti-reality-TV comment. Before Debbie could speak, John John came back to the table with four shot glasses and a fifth of Hot Damn.

"What's goin' on, my peoples?" John John slurred loudly.

Dylan and Phoebe noticed the bottle, shot glasses, and the condition John John was in. They glared at one another, and then Phoebe whispered, "God, help us."

John John plopped down into his chair between LaToya and Dylan as Debbie cleared her throat, preparing to tell the long, drawn-out story. Before John John could say a word, LaToya hushed him and gave Debbie the floor. Everyone was silent, and all eyes were on Debbie. She took a big sip of her beer and then shared her experience in a reality hell. "A little over a year ago, my youngest signed me up for *Momma Swap*. Ya'll know what that is? It's that show on the Country Pride Network …"

"Yeah, yeah, channel thirty-four. It's where they have the two mommas from two different worlds and switch families for two weeks. Now go on," interrupted LaToya.

Debbie made sure everyone was still listening and then continued, "Well, I hadn't heard of it. Hell, I thought my daughter was video tapping us for being the ideal family. Ya know, like for her religion class or somethin' …"

"I find that hard to believe, but go on," interjected Phoebe.

"Oh, shut up, Phoebe," Debbie told her rude friend and then proceeded. "Well, that sneaky snake of mine mailed the video to the producers, and they picked me to swap places with a family that lives in Dallas, Texas. And I said to myself, 'Debbie you can do this. Hell, you get paid $75,000 if you can be a mother to another family for fourteen freakin' days!'"

"And I was thinkin' about all the renovations that could be done at the restaurant with that kind of dough," added John John.

"Yes, I know, dear. We really needed the money, but it's my time to speak. Why don't you concentrate on drinkin' that bottle of cinnamon crap and let me talk," lectured Debbie.

John John poured himself a shot then looked over to Phoebe and gave her a hand signal, asking if she would like to partake. "What the hell" she said to herself and agreed. The tipsy giant poured his beautiful friend a shot, and Debbie finally got to share her *Momma Swap* story.

"Well, the family I traded places with was the Gorbachovas. The daddy owned a Russian restaurant, and the momma taught ballet lessons, but, honey, let me tell you, their son was the most disrespectful son of a bitch I've ever met. That little bastard didn't respect women at all. He wouldn't get up for school, he wouldn't help clean, and I'd be surprised if the spoiled buffoon even wiped his own ass," Debbie explained.

"I heard that!" LaToya chimed in.

Debbie continued, "I had to do what their momma does, and she had to do what I would normally do. And the day I had to teach ballet was the day all hell broke loose for the Gorbachovas."

"Yeah, that Russian momma felt it was beneath her to fry hushpuppies and reload the toothpick dispenser at my place!" added John John.

"I must say, when I see someone with a toothpick in their mouth after dinner, it's a true sign of negligent upbringing," remarked Phoebe.

"Are you writing an article on etiquette for *Southern Living*, or may I finish my story?" Debbie asked Phoebe. Phoebe and Dylan giggled at Debbie's question, and then they invited her to please finish her report on her reality show from hell. Debbie took another sip of her beer and resumed.

"As I was saying, I had to teach a ballet lesson, which is a story in itself, and when I got home, Boris, the teenage demon from the deep hole of Satan's backyard, was in my room, tearing up all my things! He was a devoted vegetarian and found my family pack of Aunt Dewy's Jerky in my suitcase. Honey, when I opened that door and saw that crazy Russian wearing my eyeliner and my *LSU* robe, I was loaded for bear. He tore up everything I'd brought to this weird experiment. Honey, I went berserk! He had taken one of my crochet needles and torn up my pillows that I had just gotten on sale from Target! There were chunks of pork jerky and feathers all over the damn floor! He then got right up into my face and screamed, 'You animal killer! Get out of my house!' It looked like this psycho was gettin' ready to stab me with my own crochet needle, so I punched him in the face, and that bastard hit the floor!"

LaToya interrupted Debbie by saying, "Oooh, child! This fight sounds like the time Dr. Death and Ted DiBiase beat the Russian Destroyers and won the Mid-South Tag Team Title!"

"Oh my God!" shouted Dylan as he pointed to John John. "I remember watching that wrestling match at your house! You actually cried when Dr. Death and Ted held up their championship belts!"

"I was a kid, and it was emotional for me to see two Americans win their championship belts back from the scandalous Russians. Hell, they even had Bruce Springsteen's song, 'Born in the USA,' playing in the background to celebrate this history-makin' victory!" defended John John.

Phoebe, feeling the buzz from her second shot, said, "For God's sake, Debbie, please finish this never-ending story."

Debbie told John John and Dylan to shut up and then she continued with her story. "Before Boris could get up, the producers jumped in and stopped us from fighting, and then I was removed from the Gorbachova household and taken to a motel. I made a police report, and they immediately stopped production. I flew back here, and Anechka, the Russian momma, was flown back to Dallas. The minute I got home, I told John John to call a lawyer."

"And I called Monty K. Earl," added John John.

Dylan and Phoebe snickered when they heard the name of the attorney. Dylan asked John John, "Is this the lawyer that has the television ad where he says fair only happens once a year and it's held each October at the Rapides Parish Coliseum?"

"No, No, Monty K. Earl is that law man who parks his van every other Saturday at Church's Chicken and gives out free two-piece fried chicken dinners to anyone who may be able to use his services," corrected John John.

"I know who you're talkin' about," added LaToya.

"I figured you would," replied John John.

LaToya told John John to hush, and she pled for Debbie to wrap up the horror swap tale.

Debbie cleared her throat again and said, "What the show producers didn't know or didn't tell me was this sixteen-year-old boy had a long history of mental illness. Hell, he's been in and out of psychiatric hospitals more times than I've shopped at Walmart. I didn't think the Gorbachova family was gonna take any type of legal action against me, and to be honest with y'all, I'm done with this."

"You know you could have sued that TV show for not tellin' you that you were gonna be livin' with a crazy kid," suggested LaToya.

"Hey, be careful of the word *crazy*," corrected Dylan.

Debbie responded to LaToya's advice by saying, "Look, John John and I aren't sue-happy people, especially after all the crap his sister went through when she sued Shoney's years ago for slipping on a grape jelly packet and breaking her ankle in front of the breakfast bar."

LaToya, looking at her watch, told the offbeat crew that she needed to go because the ladies from Atlanta were waiting on her. She made sure that Dylan was going to make arrangements with his brother, Kris, to drop off his vehicle and said good-bye. When she got up, John John (who had downed a Red River of Hot Damn shots) stood up and gave her a big hug and a kiss on the lips. "Now, what cha think of that?" he asked La Toya.

"Your lips are as salty as those sorry-ass onion rings you serve at your place," answered La Toya.

John John shouted, "I'm gonna kill her!"

Roxanne Moore walked in front of the fireplace to make an announcement. Roxanne was a sixty-five-year-old, overweight woman with platinum blonde hair. She had poor posture, bad teeth, and a prosthetic left hand, caused by an accident when she worked in the circus as an ax thrower's assistant in 1965. Roxanne had been the bartender at Sweet Daddy's for over forty years. Hell, she opened the doors back when the quaint tavern was the Howard Johnson's motel bar.

The sentimental bartender loved when Dylan and his comrades made their annual visit to her cozy establishment for the elderly. Roxanne had fond memories of Phoebe and John John's classic Christmas shows. The two entertained the bar veterans by singing songs from the interesting selection of music on the jukebox.

Back in the day, and after several cocktails, John John and Phoebe started off their fictitious holiday special by sitting in front of the fireplace and welcoming everyone (regular customers over the age of sixty) to their version of a variety show. The untalented duo began by singing "My Favorite Things" from the musical, *The Sound of Music*. After the opening act, Phoebe and John John, each with a Ronco Mr. Microphone in hand, walked out into the audience of VFW members and Lawrence Welk fans and asked them what their favorite things were. Then they lip-synced a few more songs from Broadway and the Big Band era.

John John and Phoebe's special guest stars were always Stuart and Debbie. Occasionally, they let an audience member perform. Dylan never took the stage. His job was to play the songs requested on the jukebox. Phoebe and John John's Christmas concert was a combination of an USO Show gone wrong and an awful adaptation of *The Sonny & Cher Comedy Hour*.

Roxanne demanded everyone's attention in the barroom and made an announcement. "May I have ya'll's attention. We have some special guests in Sweet Daddy's tonight! These talented folks have been comin' to my bar since they were in their early twenties. Sweet Daddy's has been their holiday meeting spot for a long time, and we've been blessed to have them put on a little show for us old farts throughout the years. I've always thought of them as *The Little Rascals* featuring the sassy Buckweat-nette." Roxanne looked over at Phoebe, winked at her, and asked, "Ain't that right, Phyllis?"

Phoebe nodded and then gave the seasoned barmaid a forced smile. She got over the unintentional racial remark, but Phoebe always despised that Roxanne had never gotten her name right.

Roxanne continued with her announcement, "Let's all give them a big hand, and maybe, just maybe, they'll give us the pleasure of a long overdue performance!"

Debbie, Phoebe, John John, and Dylan all stood up as the small crowd clapped for them. Phoebe poured herself another shot, and then John John took the bottle from her and downed the rest of it. Dylan walked over to the jukebox and reprised his role as the musical conductor.

Debbie strolled to a small table located in front of the fireplace (stage) and took a seat with two older gentlemen. Phoebe and John John joined hands and made their way to the tiny platform. The odd couple welcomed everyone to their holiday special by using empty beer bottles as microphones. Comparable to a sleazy Vegas act, the two started the show by talking about their favorite things, such as sunny days, kittens playing with yarn, Green Peace, LSU becoming the BCS Champs in 2004, and Grandmother's snicker doodles. Phoebe then signaled Dylan to play Julie Andrew's version of "My Favorite Things," and it was show time!

The enchanting duet performed several other crowd-pleasing songs that brought back the good old days. For the finale, John John and Phoebe brought Debbie onto the stage to sing along with Kate Smith's rendition of "God Bless America," which brought the house down. As the self-indulgent entertainers had their egos fed by the overwhelming applause from the old-timers, Dylan looked at his watch and saw that it was almost midnight and they were extremely late for the reunion. "Oh my God, Stuart is gonna kill us," he said to himself.

CHAPTER 7

Too Old to Gator

The tardy classmates pulled into the parking garage of the Riverfront Center at 12:45 a.m. Right when Dylan parked his truck, John John let out a massive belch.

"Oh my God, that smells like a cinnamon-flavored Bagel Bite," declared Phoebe, who was sitting on John John's lap.

The four late birds got out of the truck, and immediately Debbie and Phoebe took their compact mirrors out of their purses and started touching up their hair and makeup as John John sang a revised version of his opening act song, "My Favorite Things." "A sold-out night at Johnny Boy's Bistro and Sunday Night Football ... Pamela Anderson Lee and Debbie losing her voice and not yelling at me ... These are a few of my favorite things ..." sang John John as they walked to the garage elevator.

The elevator door opened, and Debbie, Dylan, and Phoebe still appeared attractive and refreshed. John John, on the other hand, looked a mess. He was drenched in sweat and resembled a frat boy clown with dime store, floozy-red lips, caused from his overindulgence of Hot Damns.

They entered the reunion, and all stood in place at the entrance, as if they were the Fantastic Four comic book heroes observing the enemy before battle. The song "Cars" by Gary Numen was playing while about sixty members of the class of '83 were revisiting their youth by way of dance. Apart from the excessive amount of receding hairlines and Botox, the scene looked like an episode of *American Bandstand* from the early eighties.

Debbie noticed a group of eight thin, lovely, former classmates chatting and giggling with one another. The ladies could have easily met the criteria to become contestants in the Mrs. Louisiana Pageant. Debbie leaned over to Phoebe and said, "I feel like a mason jar in a china cabinet full of Waterford crystal."

Phoebe laughed.

Right away, John John's former football teammates huddled up to him, and each gave him a high five along with a hug as they shouted, "Eagles! Eagles!" John John, who could barely stand up, welcomed the rowdy attention.

Phoebe was greeted by her former varsity cheerleading squad. She politely grinned as she gave each of the hyper women an impersonal cuddle. The middle-aged cheerleaders failed miserably at trying to get on Phoebe's level. With her being the only black girl on the squad in 1982–83, the spirited team felt that they had to use words from the urban dictionary to impress the accomplished person and award-winning jewelry designer. Their misused grammar didn't surprise Phoebe; in fact, she wouldn't have had expected anything less from the superficial females.

As John John and Phoebe collected acknowledgments from their categorized equals, Debbie walked over to Dylan and said, "John John and Phoebe are taken care of. I guess we're now waiting on the cool, popular people for you and the future homemakers and 4-H Club members for me."

Dylan put his arm around Debbie and replied, "I've already had enough. This Carnival Cruise of high school recollection hasn't even sailed yet, and we know what a wonderful reputation Carnival has." Debbie grinned at Dylan and then gave him a pat on the ass.

Stuart stormed up to them and yelled, "Where in the hell have y'all been?"

"We stopped by Sweet Daddy's for a beer. Where's Mary Beth?" asked Debbie.

"Just like the four of you, she bailed out on the only important occasion that I've looked forward to for quite some time," answered Stuart.

"Well, that says a lot about your life," uttered Dylan.

Stuart looked directly into Dylan's eyes and replied, "Thank you, Dylan. I wish I could stay here and be insulted by you all night, but I have to get ready to present the awards. It's a shame there's not one for being a self-centered prick. You would win that one hands down."

As Stuart angrily marched off, Dylan looked at Debbie and sarcastically said, "I guess being named prom king is out of the question."

After clarifying to the persistent pep rally posse that there wasn't a snowball's chance in hell that she would do an old cheerleading routine with them, Phoebe escaped from her pretentious past and made her way over to Debbie and Dylan.

While the three discussed the actuality that they would rather be caned in Singapore than to be at the reunion, the DJ played "Johnny B. Goode" by Chuck Berry.

Immediately, John John's teammates drug him to the dance floor, and the gatoring began. The gator was a dance when a group of intoxicated men or plastered high school boys dropped down to the ground on their backs and flopped around, waving their hands and kicking up their legs. This dance was usually performed by fraternity brothers. Actually, this type of strange ritual bared a resemblance to a group of males having convulsions from an epileptic seizure.

John John and the entire football team rolled around the dance floor as if they were psychotic children making angels in the snow. Phoebe, Dylan, Debbie, and the rest of their classmates formed a huge circle and watched the aging athletes wiggling for mercy. During the climax of this all-male tumbling catastrophe, John John cleared the dance floor by puking profusely all over himself and his fellow performers.

Debbie and Phoebe made their way through the panicky crowd to get to John John, who was stretched out on the floor, vomiting out chunks of cheese ball, boudin, and Bagel Bites, all smothered in red alcohol gravy. Debbie and Phoebe knelt down on each side of the giant as the rest of their classmates were running off the dance floor as if they were extras in the cult classic movie *The Blob*. Debbie placed her hand on her miserable husband's face and said, "Oh, honey, the time capsule back to your wild youth has demolished into little bits of undigested party food. It's time to go home."

John John attempted to smile at his wife, but the sick feeling came up again. He turned to the other side where Phoebe was and projected out a big mass of barf on her shoulder. "Oh God, I'm sorry, Phoebe," he pleaded.

"That's quite all right, John John. I've always wanted a broach made out of tomato aspic," she replied.

Debbie then stood up and looked around the room for Dylan. She saw him talking with two striking female alumni and shouted, "Hey, slick dick! We need a nurse here!"

Dylan said his good-byes and ran over to the two generals and the wounded soldier. He had not realized that it was his buddy who didn't survive the curse of the gator dance. Right away, Dylan took off his sports jacket and helped John John get up. When several of the ladies from the Class of '83 saw that the legendary rebel and Jackson Street Cruiser had taken off his jacket, they started to chant, "Take it off! Take it all off! Take it all off!" Dylan placed John John's arm around his shoulder, and the two slowly walked off the dance floor.

Hearing the chanting from the obviously sexually frustrated women, and not knowing the yelling was directed toward Dylan, John John thought he was in a nightmare where he was the disappointing eye candy for aggressive Chippendale fans.

Coming back to life and understanding that he wasn't in a dream, John John took Dylan's coat from Debbie and covered his head with it. As he took the walk of shame, John John quoted a lyric from a Pink Floyd song, mumbling, "The lunatic is my head." Dylan grinned at his pathetic pal as they all slowly and carefully walked toward the exit.

When Dylan, Debbie, and Phoebe finally got John John to the lobby of the event center, Phoebe insisted that Debbie take John John to her room at the Hotel Bentley, which was located across from the Riverfront Center. Because of the class reunion and the Woodmen of the World convention, the Hotel Bentley had no vacancies. Debbie didn't fight her generous friend's offer. Dylan invited Phoebe to stay in his guestroom. Although, the Hotel Bentley was one of Louisiana's most magnificent historical landmarks, Phoebe didn't mind letting her best girlfriend and her lifeless husband have her room. She knew that staying at Dylan's condo was the next best place when it came to top-rated chain hotels. After they discussed the overnight accommodations, the four deadbeat classmates strolled over to the elevator.

Stuart entered the lobby and saw his best friends waiting for the elevator door to open. He shook his head in frustration. Once again, his friends had abandoned him. He watched the elevator door close, turned around, and walked back into the reunion, heading directly to the open bar.

Phoebe, Dylan, Debbie, and John John, who looked as if he had risen from the dead, entered the lobby of the Hotel Bentley. Debbie was amazed how beautiful the hotel was. The Bentley had recently reopened after being closed for several years. She was in awe of the gorgeous marble columns and stairway. The astonished woman quickly understood why the Hotel Bentley was known as the Ritz of the Bayou. John John and Debbie had been to the landmark only twice. The first time was back in the mid-eighties when John John was awarded a one-night stay and a twenty-five-dollar bar tab for the Mirror Room (the hotel bar) for being the employee of the month at Winn Dixie. The second time was in the late nineties when Phoebe had a show promoting her jewelry line.

The four entered Phoebe's suite, and right away, John John collapsed on the king-size bed. The five-star suite was grand, with a lovely view of the Red River. As Phoebe packed her overnight bag, Debbie continued to thank her. Dylan took John John's shoes off and then asked Debbie if he needed to pick them up in the morning. Before Debbie could respond, Phoebe suggested that LaToya take the couple home. "Hell no!" shouted John John.

Debbie told Dylan and Phoebe that she would call her sister, Darlene, or her daughter, Savannah, the next morning to come pick them up. Phoebe and Dylan gave Debbie a hug and said their good-byes.

Right before Dylan walked out the door, he turned around to Debbie and said, "Instead of the dinner for two at Sonic and the night of passion at Motel 6, this very well could be ya'll's second honeymoon."

Debbie looked at Dylan and then looked over to John John, who was spread out on the bed, snoring and scratching his crouch. She then looked back over to Dylan and replied, "Fat chance."

When Phoebe and Dylan arrived at the elevator, Dylan was puzzled that Phoebe pushed the up button instead of the down one.

"Phoebe, what are you doing? We're going down," said Dylan.

"I want to show you something," answered Phoebe.

The door opened, and the two entered the elevator. Phoebe pressed the number nine button and the two went to the ninth floor. The door opened, and the entire floor was under construction.

"What is this?" asked Dylan.

"It's my new home," replied Phoebe.

"No way! You've decided to move back?" Dylan asked.

"I'm afraid so," answered Phoebe.

"You mean you're gonna be right in the center of a severely dysfunctional situation that involves passive aggression, detoxification, obsessive compulsive disorder, and poorly fried seafood?" inquired Dylan.

"Hey, we go together," chanted Phoebe.

"We do go together—like rama lama lama ke ding a de dinga a donk!" Dylan sang.

Phoebe enjoyed Dylan's attempt to sing a song from the Broadway musical *Grease*. Then the elevator doors closed. When the two arrived at the hotel lobby, they walked over to the front desk, and Phoebe asked the concierge to set up a massage therapy session for the charming couple who had taken over her room. After the appointment was set, the two tired and hungry friends decided to go to the Pitt Grill for an early breakfast and a detailed discussion about Phoebe's desire to move back to Alexandria.

CHAPTER 8

Coffee ... Biscuits with White Gravy ... and an Unnecessary Justification

It was 4:30 a.m. Dylan and Phoebe were in Dylan's pickup truck on their way to the Pitt Grill. Phoebe complimented Dylan for cutting back on smoking cigarettes. He thanked her and then explained, "You know, I tried Chantix for two weeks, but I had to stop because I kept having a reoccurring nightmare where I was in a dirty kitchen, sculpting inappropriate sex tools out of butter with Paula Deen." Phoebe laughed at Dylan's excuse, and then the two had a discussion about Alexandria being the first city in Louisiana to pass the smoke-free law, which meant since 2012, no cigarette smoking was allowed in bars or restaurants. When they pulled in the parking lot of the all-night diner, they saw the fry cook and two of the waitresses in front of the restaurant smoking, as if each puff was a point scored in a basketball game.

Phoebe looked at Dylan and said, "Ahh, home sweet home."

They entered the restaurant, and after being instructed, followed by a coughing attack by one of the waitresses outside, to sit wherever they liked, they found a booth and took a seat.

Terri Seale, a tall, thin woman with a cleft lip, was their waitress. Terri was a big fan of Dylan's because he had such a positive impact in Sylvia's life. Sylvia, Dylan's unauthorized daughter-in-law and mother of his granddaughter, used to work the morning shift with Terri.

Because of the freezing room temperature in the diner, Terri was wearing a black hoodie over her uniform. She was excited to see the dashing, middle-aged rebel and rushed over to the table. Dylan stood up and gave the rather odd-looking waitress a hug. Before Phoebe was introduced to the animated server, she thought to herself how much Terri resembled the subject in the famous painting, *The Scream* by Edvard Munch.

After showing Terri all his pictures of his grandbaby on his cell phone, Dylan finally introduced Phoebe. The two ladies greeted each other, and Terri said, "I remember your mother. I voted for her when she ran for mayor years ago. Gosh, you look just like her. I always thought your momma looked like that gal who played Tina Turner in that show *What's Love Got To Do With It.*"

"Oh, you're talking about Angela Bassett," Phoebe interjected.

"Yeah her. I certainly can identify with Tina. My husband used to beat the tar out of me until I finally shot him dead in my kitchen," said Terri.

Phoebe was not sure if Terri was serious or if she was joking, so she smiled at the murderess holding the menus. She looked over to Dylan for help.

"She's not pulling your leg, Phoebe. Terri did take out her old man and is working here through the sheriff's department work-release program," explained Dylan.

"That's right, honey. The little prison van will be here at six thirty to pick me up, as well as two other waitresses who have done wrong but now serve Jesus Christ Almighty," Terri added.

Phoebe took the menu from the born-again husband killer and said to her, "It sounds as if you're a survivor."

"Oh, yes, honey, I am, after shooting that evil man in the back and seeing his wicked blood splattered all over my kitchen. Even my new, white George Foreman plate grill turned into blood-blister red," shared Terri.

"My goodness, I've never seen that color before. You know what? I've suddenly lost my appetite. I'll take a small bowl of grits and coffee," ordered Phoebe.

"I'll have the Cajun Boy Big Breakfast, and I'll also take some coffee," added Dylan.

Terri scribbled down their orders on her pad, looked at Phoebe, while pointing her pen at Dylan, and said, "I have to tell ya, Miss Phoebe, without Dylan's stepfather, the incredible Frankie Dubois, I wouldn't have made the first year of doin' time. I would listen to his song, "I Found Christ in K-Mart," every night behind bars before I went to sleep."

"How inspiriting. I must have been out of the country when that song was on Casey Kasem's *American Top Forty*," replied Phoebe.

Dylan snickered as Terri left their booth to turn in their order. Phoebe glared at Dylan, took a deep breath, and said, "This night has been a time capsule ride back to intense madness. And I must say, I've loved every minute of it."

"And this disturbing occurrence has made you want to move back here even more?" Dylan asked.

"I don't know, Dylan. We're fifty, and I consider the present to be our—well, actually my chance to make this second part of life spectacular," replied Phoebe.

"Although you may want to have your head checked for undiscovered mental disorders, I'm ecstatic for you to share this insane journey with not only me, but also with our fellow unstable travelers. Why? And why now?" asked Dylan.

"Oh, Dylan, where do I begin?" Phoebe sighed.

CHAPTER 9

Cane River Angel

Phoebe was the only child by her mother, Evelyn Werner. Unfortunately, her father was never in the picture. Evelyn had Phoebe at an early age and did a remarkable job as a single mother raising her. A petite woman, Evelyn, who wore wigs because of thinning hair, worked as a paralegal for years and became involved in local politics. She was a member of the Rapides Parish School Board and the president of the local chapter of the Women's Democratic Club. Evelyn was very strict mother, and her ultimate goal for Phoebe was for her to be independent and have the best education possible. Evelyn pinched pennies and made big sacrifices for her only child to attend private schools. Debbie, Dylan, Stuart, and John John used to call her Evelyn "Champagne" King, after the well-known post-disco singer. Shortly after Phoebe's seventeenth birthday, Evelyn left Alexandria and moved to Lake Charles, Louisiana, with Raymond Jones, a large gentleman who always dressed in the finest of men's apparel. Evelyn had met Raymond in Pineville at a Christian seminar led by Tommy Toomey, a famous preacher known for his best-selling book, *The God Hunters*.

The Christian couple married after knowing each other for only three weeks. Raymond was fifteen years older than his religious, political bride. He was a retired high school principal who had been married twice before he tied the knot with Evelyn. The two settled in Lake Charles, and Evelyn became part-owner of Raymond's spiritual bookstore, named Heaven Above Books & More.

Phoebe refused to move to Lake Charles, especially since she had only one year of Menard High School left. Despite her mother's disapproval,

Phoebe spent her senior year of high school living in the guest-house of Dylan's parents' mansion.

His parents, Brent and Norma, were still married at the time, and their beautiful family home was located on Georgia Lane, one of the most exclusive neighborhoods in the Garden District of Alexandria. Brent was able to keep the estate in the divorce settlement. Evelyn had always liked Norma and knew her daughter would be in good hands, but she was still not very happy with the situation because Phoebe's boyfriend, Garrett Sury, lived two houses down from Dylan and his family.

Garrett was adopted at birth by Dr. Michael Sury and his wife, Christy. The Surys were a very attractive Caucasian couple, and they were in their early thirties during the adoption process. Garrett's biological mother was a fourteen-year-old Caucasian female, and his father was a sixteen-year-old African American male. Both teens were from Natchitoches, Louisiana. Like his girlfriend, Phoebe, Garrett had movie star looks. He had dark-blue eyes and caramel-colored skin. In other words, he was Creole. Garrett was also an exceptional athlete; he played running back for the Menard Eagles. John John nicknamed him the Cane River Cheetah because he was born in Natchitoches and the fastest runner in central Louisiana.

It was an easy fit for Garrett to be a part of Phoebe's intimate social circle. No phony initiation was necessary. Dylan, Debbie, Stuart, and John John welcomed their new member as if he were that special ingredient in their already deliciously unique jambalaya.

Garrett loved Phoebe more than the LSU Tigers and life itself. They started dating the summer after their sophomore year of high school. It was love at first laugh. Garrett was a responsible, free-spirited individual who was intrigued by the comic relief Phoebe and her pals provided. Phoebe thought Garrett was an angel that was sent down from heaven or possibly an undercover teen-dating agency run by a brilliant female writer from *Tiger Beat* magazine. He was close to being the ideal boyfriend, though far above her expectations.

Garrett was almost too perfect. He always obeyed his adoptive parents and didn't find it necessary to partake in alcohol or nicotine. Peer pressure was never a problem for the idyllic teen. He did struggle in school and worked extremely hard to make Cs. A 2.5 grade-point average along with his phenomenal athletic talents were enough for him to be offered several football scholarships from top-notch universities across the States.

Unfortunately, before any decision was made, Garrett's opportunity was ruined during the state playoff game in Shreveport, when he broke both knees while being tackled by a 285-pound fullback from the opposite team. While lying in the hospital for weeks, Garrett struggled, trying to figure out what direction to go now that his college plans were shattered. He knew his parents could afford to send him to any university he desired, but he also was aware that he wasn't college material. Phoebe, Debbie, Stuart, Dylan, and John John visited the injured hero every day.

After Garrett was discharged from the hospital, he immediately started psychical therapy. In fact, Stuart and Phoebe took turns driving him to his sessions. Just about every evening after getting off from work at Winn Dixie, John John would come over and watch a movie with Garrett. One night, John John brought over the Kris Kristofferson movie, *Convoy*, which he had borrowed from Dylan's mom, Norma. Norma was a member of the Kris Kristofferson Fan Club and eventually named her youngest after the singer/songwriter.

It was this night combined with the multiple Diesel Driving Academy commercials that played every thirty minutes on television during his hospital stay that brought Garrett the answer to his occupation inspirations. He made John John watch the video twice with him on this mystic night. John John didn't have a clue that his movie selection would be such an important solution for Garrett's career fears. Who would have thought that the worst film made in 1978 along with a TV ad revealing a good ole boy waving cash from out the window of an eighteen-wheeler would be the answer to Garrett's profession uncertainties?

The decision to become a truck driver and having the support of the love his life, Phoebe, made the healing process from the tragic accident certainly more bearable for the former football star to accept. Although he recovered remarkably well, thanks to physical rehab, Garrett was limited in what he could physically do during the rest of his senior year of high school.

Two months after Garrett and Phoebe graduated from Holy Savior Menard Central High School, Phoebe discovered she was pregnant. The pregnancy put a major glitch in Phoebe's plans to attend Parsons School of Design in New York City. Her mother, Evelyn, was devastated. She had saved a fortune for her daughter's education. In spite of paying for Phoebe's private school tuition for twelve years, Evelyn managed to set aside over thirty-five thousand dollars in a college fund for her only child. When the disappointed mother found out her daughter, the southern black version of Hester Prynne, the protagonist in Nathaniel Hawthorne's novel, *The Scarlet Letter*, was pregnant, she ended up giving Phoebe the money and basically wrote her off.

Evelyn and her fairly new husband, Raymond, did show up for Phoebe and Garrett's wedding, which was held in the backyard of Dylan's family home. Norma and Garrett's mother did a wonderful job planning this unexpected ceremony. There were only 145 guests in attendance.

Debbie was Phoebe's maid of honor, and three members of the Menard cheerleading squad were her bridesmaids. Debbie kept on humming the Sesame Street song, "One of These Things Is Not Like the Others," because she felt so enormous compared to the other three slim bridesmaids. As the wedding party slowly walked down the aisle on the hot Louisiana day, Debbie couldn't help but think she was the gigantic Miss Piggy float leading the way while the beautiful, anorexic majorettes followed directly behind her in this miserable, make-believe Mardi Gras parade.

Phoebe asked Dylan's father, Dr. Brent Jacobs, to walk her down the aisle, but unfortunately, he had to attend a medical convention in New Orleans. Actually, the sex-addicted physician was spending the weekend in the Big Easy with one of his easy nurses. Phoebe ended up asking her Uncle Leroy to walk her down the aisle.

Leroy was an overweight Vietnam War veteran who was in a wheelchair. He had lost his legs in battle. He was honored that his niece asked him, and he did a decent job of escorting the beautiful bride. The only mishap that occurred while the bride and the handicapped usher were rolling and walking toward the preacher was that Phoebe's beautiful wedding gown, which she bought on sale at Gus Kaplan's Clothing Store, got caught in the left wheel of Leroy's wheelchair, and it made a sizeable rip at the bottom of the dress.

Garrett's father was his best man, and Dylan, John John, and Stuart were his groomsmen.

The beautiful oak trees and the sparkling swimming pool made a picturesque setting for the future married couple/parents. The ceremony was short and sweet.

Instead of a sit-down dinner, Norma and Garrett's mother, Christy, had heavy hors d'oeuvres catered by Molly Stagg, the number-one caterer in Alexandria at the time. The booze and bartenders came from Hokus

Pokus Liquors. Norma was one of their best customers and managed to get a healthy discount. The food, bars, DJ, dance floor, and tables were all under a huge white tent, and two gigantic fans were blowing from each side of the tent to keep everyone cool and comfortable on this sizzling hot August day.

The almond wedding cake was from Pouparts Bakery in Lafayette. Garrett's groom's cake was chocolate-covered doughnuts sprinkled with chopped pecans. The unique dessert was specially made for him by Harlow's Bakery in Pineville. As a kid, Garrett rode his bike two miles across the Red River to get a pecan chocolate doughnut from the legendary bakery. Because both cakes had nuts in them, Norma felt she had to bake something special for the mother of the bride, given that Evelyn was allergic to nuts. Norma had found out the hard way about Evelyn's severe allergy.

It was Evelyn's election results party when she ran for the Mayor of Alexandria in 1979. Instead of placing the pecans on top of the brownies, Norma added the nuts in the mixture; therefore, no one knew that there were pecans in the chocolate squares. The campaign party has held at the Plantation Manor restaurant, and the place was packed with Evelyn Werner supporters. Even Babs Zimmerman from KALB News was there with a camera crew, waiting eagerly for the results to appear on the thirteen-inch, black-and-white television. Norma nonchalantly made her way through the excited crowd and placed the silver platter of homemade brownies on the table right next to the hush puppies and avocado dip that had put the Plantation Manor on the map. Norma couldn't stay long because she had another function that night. She was going to a Mel Tillis concert at the Rapides Parish Coliseum.

Sadly, Norma attended both events alone. This was the time when Dylan's father, Dr. Brent Jacobs's, wandering eye was in full force.

When the votes from the last precinct were reported, Evelyn had lost by a landslide. She started eating everything on the table to alleviate her disappointment and had already shoved down two of Norma's brownies before Babs could get to her for an interview about the defeat. Right as the camera lights went on, Evelyn fainted. The swelling election loser, who also had green drool coming from her mouth from the avocado dip, was taken to the emergency room. She stayed overnight at the hospital so that the medical team could monitor her shortness of breath and tightening of the chest caused by her allergic reaction from the hidden nuts in Norma's deadly dessert.

Dylan was disgusted with how Evelyn was acting toward her daughter, the wedding, and the pregnancy. To fulfill his passive aggressive needs, Dylan found the perfect opportunity to seek revenge on the detached mother of the bride. The night before the wedding, Dylan walked into the kitchen and saw that his mom was making brownies.

"Damn, somethin' smells good, Norma. Who are the brownies for?" he asked.

"With both the wedding and groom's cake having nuts in them, I thought I would make an alternative treat for Phoebe's mother."

Dylan laughed and then said, "That's right! Shit! I forgot that you almost killed her four years ago!"

"That's not funny, you evil boy!" replied Norma.

While observing his mother stir the brownie batter, a brilliant idea blossomed in Dylan's devious brain.

"You know the Oak Ridge Boys are guest starring on *The Dukes of Hazard* tonight," lied Dylan.

"Oh, my Lord!" Norma shouted.

"The show is on in the den. You've already missed ten minutes of it; you'd better hurry," encouraged Dylan.

Norma told her scheming son that she would finish making the fudge brownies and put them in the oven during the first commercial break. When Norma bolted toward the den, Dylan ran upstairs to his brother, Steven's room. He opened the closet and grabbed an old baseball cap off of the top shelf. Inside the cap was a plastic sandwich bag with about two ounces of hashish in it. He hid the stash in Steven's room in case there was ever a raid at the wholesome Jacobs household. Dylan was eighteen at the time and at the peak of his drug excursion.

He ran back downstairs to the kitchen and placed three pinches of the illegal substance into the chocolate batter. He stirred the hash in well and then ran back upstairs to hide the evidence.

After waiting eagerly to see the Oak Ridge Boys (who never appeared) and several glasses of wine, Norma finished pouring the mixture into the pan and baked the fatal fudge cakes for thirty-five minutes. The only thing that Norma saw as rather odd was Dylan hanging out with her in the kitchen and begging to lick the batter bowl. Dylan had never been a big fan of sweets.

Everything seemed to be going well at Phoebe's reception. Guests were dancing, eating, drinking, and mingling. Evelyn was sitting between her husband and sister, Ruth. Ruth, a strong, full-sized woman, was Leroy's wife and LaToya's mother. They also had two other daughters named LaTokyo and LaTammera. All three daughters looked just like Ruth.

Norma brought Evelyn the nut-free brownies on a paper plate with the Virgin Mary drawn on it. Although Norma knew that Evelyn wasn't catholic, she wanted to express her appreciation for religion fanatics, and Evelyn was overjoyed.

"I thought you might enjoy these since you can't have nuts," Norma said to Evelyn.

"Oh, my lord, you're so thoughtful. My goodness, they look just like the brownies at Food Palace Bakery!" exclaimed Evelyn.

"It's my special recipe, honey. You've had these before, remember? I brought them to your fundraiser, the Women of God Chocolate Crusade," bragged Norma.

About twenty-five minutes later at the table where Evelyn was sitting with her husband, sister, brother-in-law, and nieces, the hashish kicked in. "My God in heaven! These are sinfully good!" shouted Evelyn.

"They sure do look good. It looks like she added more chocolate to substitute for nuts." her husband, Raymond, added.

Evelyn looked over at her sister, Ruth, and demanded that she take a storage bag out of her purse. The stoned mother of the bride knew that her sister and her three nieces were food hoarders. Ruth's defense to Evelyn's constant accusations about her being an embezzling foodie was she had to keep up her strength because of always having to lift up her legless husband, Leroy. Ruth discreetly took out a storage bag from her oversized handbag and gave it to her demanding sibling. As Evelyn was carefully storing her nut-free, chocolate-covered, happy pills into the bag, her husband had the audacity to ask if he could have one.

The euphoric woman of God angrily responded by saying, "Hold on, somebody take a picture of this. My husband is actually asking me for some sugar, which is ironic because he sure don't ask me for sugar in the bedroom!"

Everyone sitting at the table was shocked by Evelyn's statement. LaTammera and LaTokyo's mouths dropped as they stopped chewing the food that was neatly piled up high in front of them like poker chips on a high-stakes table.

"Oh no you di'int" was Ruth's response to her sister's attacking comment.

Raymond was very embarrassed and turned his head away from Evelyn and her family. To hide his humiliation, he acted as if he were interested in what the disc jockey was announcing.

Not knowing what to say or do about Evelyn's personal dig toward her old man, Leroy took out a flask from the side pocket of his tuxedo that he bought at Caplan's Men store (their tailor worked well with amputees) and took a big sip of fire water from it.

Inside the glassed-in patio, there was enough food for a failing class of Weight Watcher participants. Phoebe's cousin, LaToya, was in front of the table where the boiled shrimp tree was placed. She was having a healthy debate with a female who was part of the catering staff. LaToya insisted that the cocktail sauce was the recipe from Herbie K's Oyster House and Lounge, the famous Alexandria restaurant known for its humorous byline: "The World's Worst Service, with the World's Finest Food." The helpless woman could not convince LaToya that the catering company purchased the cocktail sauce on sale at Winn Dixie. John John, who worked in the produce department at Winn Dixie during this time, was walking past the two women having the heated argument about the dipping seafood gravy. He stopped in front of them when he overheard the name of his employer.

Meanwhile, back at Phoebe's family's table, her mother, Evelyn, had just returned from hiding the specially made brownies in the glove compartment of her Cadillac. She was sweating profusely as she took of her jacket and threw it over her husband's head. Right after she plopped down on the fold-up chair, she grabbed her sister's strawberry daiquiri and guzzled it down. With a blotch of whip cream on her forehead, she slammed the glass down on the table.

"What's gotten into you?" her sister, Ruth, asked.

"You don't worry about me! Isn't there a side of beef or a whole pig that you and your fat-ass daughters should be gnawing on?" screamed Evelyn.

Before Ruth could react to Evelyn mortifying remark, the disc jockey played the song "Shake a Tail Feather" performed James and Bobby Purify (the 1967 version). The spaced-out sister of Christ popped out of her fold-up chair as if she were shot out of cannon. With the whip creamed sign of the cross remaining on her forehead, she ran to the dance floor, kicked off her high heels, and proceeded to boogie. Dancing wasn't one of Evelyn's notable talents.

Waving her arms, kicking, and screaming, she looked more like a contestant who just won an RV on *The Price Is Right*. The more Evelyn twirled around, the more she perspired, which expanded the Reddi-Whip cross above her eyebrows. After her ill attempt to be a Hullabaloo dancer, Evelyn noticed the sparkling pool. She definitely needed to cool off, so she ran off the dance floor and then headed toward the swimming pool. Several of the wedding guests were in shock by the high-as-a-kite mother of the bride's actions.

Dylan, who was sitting on a lounge chair located next to the pool bar, encouraged two of the bridesmaids who were fighting for his attention to focus on Evelyn's psychotic behavior. Being in an altered state of mind himself, Dylan burst out in laughter as he witnessed Evelyn jumping into the pool. The guilty groomsman hallucinated that Evelyn was a demoniac, life-sized Milk Dud with a headband made of Cool Whip, diving into a pond of Hawaiian-blue holy water. Evelyn's wig instantly popped off her head when she hit the water.

Inside the glassed-in patio, La Toya had just finished telling John John that the only two good things about Winn Dixie were the S&H Green Stamps and the Check brand cola. John John really started getting mad when she said that instead of being known as the Beef People, the store's slogan should be the Cheap People.

While waiting for a smart-ass response from the proud produce manager of the chain food store, La Toya heard commotion coming from outside. She soon realized it was her Aunt Evelyn speaking in tongues. La Toya ran over to the front of the patio and then looked toward the pool. The first thing she saw was Evelyn's head bobbing up and down in the water with her wig floating beside her.

"Oh Jesus! Somebody get a lifeguard!" La Toya screamed.

John John ran behind the freaked-out Winn Dixie attacker and saw that Evelyn appeared to be having a wonderful time swimming around in her wig cap. Several children, Debbie, Stuart, and several other wedding attendees, all fully clothed, jumped into the pool to join Evelyn's bizarre water ballet class. Realizing that La Toya was still in a panic, John John attempted to calm her down.

"There's no reason to worry, La Toyota. It looks like the cocktails have taken effect and everybody is just having fun and cooling off," said John John.

"My name ain't La Toyota! It's LaToya! And my Auntie Evelyn don't drink alcohol!" shouted LaToya.

"Well, maybe she just had a bad Check soda," said John John.

"Get away from me!" barked LaToya.

LaToya, who was carrying a plate of jumbo boiled shrimp in her hands, dashed over to the swimming pool to see what the ruckus was about, leaving John John standing in place with a devilish grin on his baby face.

Oblivious to crazy activities that were taking place at their reception, Phoebe and Garrett were upstairs in Norma's Dottie West room. Garrett was sitting in the chair that had a slipcover with diamonds and cowboy boots printed all over it. He was waiting for his bride to get out of her wedding dress and change into something more comfortable. The patient groom was eating a plate of Molly Stagg's Spinach Madeleine and staring at the wall-sized poster of Dottie West, dressed in her finest sparkling western jumpsuit, when Phoebe came out of the bathroom in a white sundress. Garrett told Phoebe how beautiful she looked. Then he pointed to the poster of the country singer.

"Man, Miss Norma really likes that Dottie West. Now, I do have to admit that I like that song she does with Kenny Rogers," Garrett stated.

Phoebe walked over to her new husband, looked him straight in the eyes as she held both of his hands, and asked, "Are you sure about this?"

"I've never been surer of anything in my life," answered Garrett.

By the time the newlyweds made it back to the reception, Phoebe's frantic family had convinced Evelyn that it was time to go home. Phoebe was surprised to see her strict mother wrapped in a beach towel with her small amount of thin hair spiked up.

"What's going on?" she asked her soaking-wet mom.

Evelyn was too busy squeezing the water out of her wig cap to respond, so her family answered the million-dollar question.

"She was drugged!" hissed LaToya.

"I think she's having a little anxiety from the heat and all this wedding and baby stuff," explained Raymond.

"She drank my daiquiri like she was a thirsty child knocking back a pitcher of Kool-Aid," added Ruth.

Phoebe looked over at her cousins, LaTammera and LaTokyo, to hear their theories of her mother's condition. The sisters just stood there with blank looks on their faces. Both of them had a miniature chicken drumstick popping out of their mouths. Finally, Evelyn looked up at her perplexed daughter and gave an explanation for her toxic tango followed by the dip in the pool of the much-needed dreamland.

"Oh, my sweet baby girl, I was just living back in the day when I had all ten of my children and we would dance, play, and go swimming in Indian Creek. And when you and all your brothers and sisters would get a little bit out of hand, I would take a little, just a little sip of Martini & Rossi on the rocks. And yes, I would say, yes to Martini & Rossi on the rocks," slurred Evelyn.

"First of all, Mother, I've never seen you even taste an ounce of alcohol. Not to mention, I'm your only child," Phoebe responded.

Raymond put his arm around his wet wife and then convinced her that it was time to go home. Ruth ordered LaTokyo and LaTammera to fan their drenched, delusional aunt, and then she told LaToya to go get Leroy and wheel him over to their car.

As Phoebe's family slowly walked toward the front of the house where their vehicles were parked, Phoebe yelled out to her mother.

"I guess this is good-bye, Mom. Thank you for coming,"

Evelyn turned around, smiled at her baby girl, and said, "You're my greatest piece of work. God bless you and you're free to go. Tell Garrett to keep on truckin.'"

Phoebe was hurt that her mother didn't even give her a hug. She was also very confused about her mother's abnormal conduct.

Garrett saw Phoebe standing alone with a look of sorrow on her beautiful face. In the middle of having a conversation with some of his old high school buddies, Garrett excused himself and dashed over to his soul mate in distress. Phoebe embraced her angel and told him why her mother made her upset.

Garrett's mother, Christy, and Norma were having a discussion about Evelyn's whacky outbreak when Christy out of the corner of her eye saw her son comforting Phoebe. She asked Norma to go with her to see what the problem was. When the two concerned mothers walked up to the bride and groom, Phoebe was crying and laughing at the same time.

"What's the matter, baby?" Norma asked.

"My mother, I mean, I know that she's a distant woman who's always disapproved of everything I've ever done, but what was with her performance today? I mean, if I didn't know better, I'd swear that she dropped a hit of acid after the ceremony," said Phoebe.

Norma placed her arms around Phoebe and said, "Oh, honey, it's gonna be okay. I just can't imagine what got into her."

All of a sudden, the two women heard Dylan's "Tarzan" yell coming from the pool. When he saw that he had both Norma's and Phoebe's attention, wearing only his boxers, Dylan began doing the mash potato (a dance from the sixties beach party era). The two ladies stared at Dylan and then at each other. Without saying a word, both women knew that the evil Frankie Avalon had something to do with Evelyn's mermaid acid flashback.

Phoebe told Norma that she had some investigative work to do with a groomsman turned antagonist. She left them and walked over to the revelry going on in the swimming pool. Suddenly, Norma's oldest son, Steven, and his beautiful girlfriend, Lauren, strolled up to the bewildered hostess.

Before Steven expressed his dissatisfaction of having to attend this shindig, he looked around his family's backyard and saw older and younger guests forming a Soul Train dance line to the song "Goody Two Shoes," sung by Adam Ant. Because of the spilled liquor on the wooden dance floor, people were falling down and busting their behinds, as if they were participating in a break dance routine gone bad. Steven then gazed over at the pool area and watched Debbie, still in her bridesmaid dress, doing a cannon ball into the water as several of the wedding guests cheered her on with a chant led by Stuart. After his last observation of the circus, Steven looked at Norma and said, "Once again, Mother, you've managed to put on a blue-collar blowout instead of a respectful event." Norma was speechless as Lauren gave her a hug good-bye.

Evelyn's disturbing actions were never brought up again. The mother of the bride felt it was a sign from God Almighty to ease up on her daughter about Phoebe's life decisions.

Since Buddy Tudor had not reopened the Hotel Bentley yet, Garrett's parents gave the newlyweds a weekend stay at Pete Fountain's Buena Vista Hotel in Biloxi, Mississippi, for their honeymoon present. Garrett had to start truck driving school the following Monday, and the hotel was in the ideal location because Biloxi was so close to New Orleans, and both

Phoebe and Garrett wanted to be on the beach for this special occasion. Of course, Stuart, Dylan, John John, and Debbie tagged along, and the newly married couple wouldn't have it any other way. From joyriding on the Shrimp Tour Train to dining on seafood platters at Mary Mahoney's Old French House, the dysfunctional family of six had a wonderful time on their Gulf Coast getaway.

Because John John and Debbie married a month before Garrett and Phoebe, they treated this weekend as if it was their honeymoon as well.

John John and Debbie's wedding was far more white-trash conservative than Garrett and Phoebe's. They got married by the justice of the peace, followed by the reception, which was held in the Kiwanis Club Meeting Room at the Piccadilly Cafeteria.

Phoebe and Garrett moved to New Orleans the day after their honeymoon and lived in one of the luxurious apartments that Garrett's parents owned on Magazine Street. Garrett passed his truck driving school exam with flying colors, and Phoebe used her time wisely by studying and designing one-of-a-kind jewelry pieces. Many of Phoebe's designs were inspired by the extraordinary Barbara Westwood collection. Barbara Westwood was a brilliant, multi-award-winning, nationally known jewelry designer who was famous for creating beautiful pieces by using bold shapes and stunning sprinkles of sparkling diamonds that unquestionably produced a fashion-forward statement. Phoebe met Barbara when she had a showing at Schnack's Fine Jewelry in Alexandria.

Phoebe was just a freshman in high school at the time and instantaneously realized her life aspiration was to become a jewelry designer after viewing Barbara's astonishing art. Barbara was also appreciative of Phoebe's talent and eventually became her mentor.

The most traumatic circumstance possible happened in the seventh month of Garrett and Phoebe's marriage. Garrett was driving home from Shreveport, after dropping off his semi truck at the home base of the trucking company he worked for. He was about five miles past the Natchitoches exit when an eighteen-wheeler coming from the opposite direction hit Garrett's 1983 Dodge Ram pickup head on. The driver of the eighteen-wheeler had fallen sleep and lost control. Both Garrett and the truck driver were killed. It was ironic and extremely sad that the profession Garrett chose and loved actually destroyed him.

Phoebe was devastated. Her sweet angel had been taken from her, but she remained remarkably strong. Although she lost the love of her life, she conquered the overwhelming loss and realized that she was a better person for having loved Garrett. There would always be a huge missing piece of the Cane River Angel in Phoebe's heart.

Stuart, Dylan, John John, Debbie, and all of Phoebe's family and friends couldn't have been more supportive of her heartbreaking loss. Even her mother stayed with her for two weeks after the funeral. Everyone felt that she needed to move back to Alexandria to be closer to loved ones, but Phoebe wouldn't have it.

Phoebe inherited a small fortune from the national company that employed the truck driver who accidently killed her soul mate. Garrett also had 1.5 million-dollar life insurance policy. It was too painful for Phoebe to continue living in the apartment she had shared with Garrett, so she bought an old warehouse on Canal Street and turned it into a magnificent studio/home. The determined widow hired a personal assistant and a live-in nanny even before her baby was born, and she still found time to cry herself to sleep every night, yearning for Garrett.

On April 16, 1984, Phoebe gave birth to a healthy eight-pound baby boy. She named him Michael Nicholas Sury, after Garrett's father. Phoebe felt it was essential to pay tribute to the beautiful man who adopted the most incredible person she'd ever known. Michael was a fine-looking infant. He had his mother's distinctive cheekbones, and his skin tone was a little bit lighter than Garrett's. Strangers would stop Phoebe all the time and tell her how handsome Michael was. It was rare a combination of his sparkling blue eyes, curly blond hair, and the fact he was African American that got people's attention. Many times, strangers mistook Phoebe for Michael's nanny instead of his mother.

Michael was a resilient child, and all of Phoebe's family and friends instantly fell in love with him. Phoebe felt her son was her greatest achievement ever.

Michael worked hard in school and was an impressive football player. He played for LSU for two years and was let go because of a severe knee injury. He graduated from Louisiana State University with a BA in Business. At the age of twenty-two, Michael was discovered by an up-and-coming modeling talent scout named Logan Cage.

Logan was attending a cocktail party at Commander's Palace in honor of Phoebe's new line of charm bracelets when he first laid eyes on Michael. Logan was beyond astonished at Michael's stunning looks. The talent agent had never seen such a strikingly attractive black man with blond hair and dark-blue eyes. After observing the proud son interacting with his mother, Logan looked over to his girlfriend, who was also a jewelry designer, and said, "Baby, I think I've found the male version of the next Tyra Banks!" Logan was so overjoyed by his discovery he didn't even mind forking out $2,500 to buy one of Phoebe's bracelets for his girlfriend.

Michael had a successful international modeling career for three years, and then he retired and moved to New Orleans and put his LSU education to good use and became Phoebe's business manager.

Phoebe labeled her booming jewelry business Cane River Angel after her departed husband. John John had come up with the nickname Cane River Cheetah for Garrett, so Phoebe took out the word cheetah and replaced it with angel.

CHAPTER 10

Massage Gone Wrong

It was 6:45 a.m. back at the Pitt Grill. Dylan was on his fourth cup of coffee, and he had made a happy plate out of his Cajun Big Boy Breakfast. He listened intensely to Phoebe explaining how she intended to make her future Alexandria home at the Hotel Bentley, her jewelry studio/living quarters. After Phoebe finished clarifying how she planned to continue to keep her store open in New Orleans and start her new business journey in Alexandria, Dylan looked at his watch and said, "Oh my God, it's almost seven o'clock! I've got to be at the Special Ed Center in an hour." He paid the bill, and the two left the notorious Pitt Grill.

When they got to Dylan's condo, it was just as Phoebe remembered— no clutter whatsoever. Dylan definitely had inherited the obsessive compulsive disorder gene from his mother and older brother, Steven.

"And here we have it, the best suite any Hilton can offer," Phoebe announced as she looked around the condo.

Dylan told her that she would be sleeping in the guestroom, which had a queen-size bed with a mint placed on top. There was also a Bible as well as a *TV Guide* on the nightstand beside the bed. As they walked down the hall to the guestroom, Dylan informed Phoebe that there were miniature bottles of shampoo, mouthwash, and body lotion as well as new toothbrushes and tooth paste in the bathroom. Phoebe thanked and hugged the OCD innkeeper and sat down on the bed. Before Dylan closed the door, he told Phoebe there were clean nursing scrubs in the top drawer for her to wear to bed.

Phoebe washed her face, brushed her teeth, and changed out of her Valentino pantsuit into blue surgeon scrubs. She lay down on the perfectly made bed, pressed the number ten on the TV remote, and watched the tail end of KLFY's morning show, *Passe Patout*. She loved to see the news anchor, Bob Moore, report the weather in Cajun French. While Phoebe watched the charismatic French meteorologist, Dylan took a quick shower and headed over to volunteer at the Louisiana Special Ed Center.

For two hours, Phoebe struggled to fall asleep. She walked around Dylan's condo, hoping that his son's baby's momma, Sylvia, and little Maria would be home, but the two were spending the weekend in Forest Hill with Sylvia's family. Still wide awake, Phoebe began channel surfing and caught the beginning of the eighties classic movie, *St. Elmo's Fire*. She immediately called Stuart. Instead of "Good morning" or "Hello," "What!" was the response she got from Stuart, the eighties pop culture scholar.

"Hey, Prince Charming! I wanted to let you know that *St. Elmo's Fire* is on HBO," Phoebe said.

"So what?" responded Stuart. He was in bed alone. His wife, Mary Beth's, side of the bed hadn't been touched.

"Sooo, I thought you would like to know one of your favorite movies is now playing on TV," Phoebe explained.

"Why don't you and the old gang get some popcorn and all watch it together. Anyway, I have that movie along with *The Breakfast Club*, *Valley Girl*, and *Sixteen Candles* in my DVD collections," reported Stuart.

"Do you have the movie *I'm The Rudest Prick of the Century* in your collection?" Phoebe sarcastically asked.

"You have the audacity to say I'm rude? You all have left me out of everything this weekend, and I don't deserve that! I've worked my ass off for this reunion, and you four have shelved me away like you've always done! Enjoy the movie, Phoebe, and go straight to hell!" Stuart shouted as he hung up the phone.

After the hang up and harsh words, Phoebe hung up her phone and said to herself, "I guess asking him to come over to exchange friendship rings and watch *The Courtship of Eddie's Father* is out the question."

Meanwhile, back over at the Hotel Bentley, Debbie, wearing a hotel robe, was apologizing profusely to one of the massage therapists, as a team of housekeepers, who were wearing surgical masks and carrying cleaning supplies, walked back to the bedroom where the couple had their massages. Debbie gave the therapist a hundred-dollar bill and thanked her for being a trooper in the unforgiving incident.

Just as the health spa employee left, Debbie's youngest daughter, Savannah, entered the suite. Savannah was a drop-dead gorgeous sixteen-year-old with blonde hair and big, hazel eyes. She was holding a change of clothes for both Mom and Dad. As she walked further in the room, she sniffed something awful and said, "It smells like the grizzly bear cage at the Alexandria Zoo in here."

"Oh, baby girl, you don't know the agonizing episode that just happened," expressed Debbie.

Before Debbie could explain, she and Savannah heard John John screaming from the shower, "I will never, never drink Hot Damns again! Please believe me, sweet Jesus! I promise never again!"

Earlier that morning when John John and Debbie were each spread out on the massage tables, both wearing nothing but towels, lying on their stomachs, eagerly waiting for their massages, John John appeared to be fine. Once the rubbing started, the beyond embarrassing moment occurred.

The innocent masseuse began massaging John John's lower back when all of sudden, he yelled, "Wait! Wait! Stop!" John John passed a humongous amount of gas that sounded like a cannon ball being shot off during a Civil War battle, and then oil struck as a black liquid substance started firing out of the poor man's butt. It was as if John John's ass was an erupting volcano. Soft feces were splattered all over John John's backside, the massage therapist, the carpet, and a lampshade. Phoebe's thoughtful gift to the happy couple turned out to be a scene from the horror film, *The Exorcist*, only this time, the grotesque waste flew out from the other end of the subject. Thank God, Phoebe waited until late that afternoon before she returned to her suite.

After watching the sentimental movie in Dylan's guestroom, Phoebe called Dylan and asked if she could use Hunter's truck to run some errands. Since Hunter was off in rehab, Dylan told her that it would be fine and where to find the keys. Although her expensive high heels did not match the scrubs she was wearing, Phoebe was determined to take a drive.

The first stop on Phoebe's mission was Rick Ferguson Flowers to pick up a dozen blue roses to place on Garrett's gravesite. When she got to her departed husband's tombstone, she discovered that his plot was covered in a variety of green, white, and yellow flowers, which were Menard High School colors. In the center of the beautiful flowers was a football. Phoebe smiled, realizing that her classmates had gotten to Garrett's gravesite before she did. She set the roses right next to the football, sat down on the ground, and silently wept. She stayed for an hour, reflecting on the most incredible human who had ever come into her life. Phoebe wiped off the last tear from her cheek as she grinned and blew a kiss to Garrett. She walked slowly back to the pickup, got in, looked in the rearview mirror, and attempted to fix her makeup. As she reapplied her lipstick, she sang, "Mirror, mirror in this truck, who's the fairest of them all?" She put the lipstick back in her purse and took one more look at herself and mumbled, "Oh my God, Snow White lives." The displeased, evil queen drove off to take on mission number two, which was to make peace with Stuart.

Phoebe arrived at Stuart's house, which was off of Bayou Rapides Road. Most families who lived on Bayou Rapides Road were from Belgium and came from a long line of farmers. The area was very much like living in the country, but it was located just a few miles from the city. When she pulled into his driveway, she was surprised to see the new construction adjacent to his home. The building was too large to be a mother-in-law's quarters.

As Phoebe parked the truck, Stuart, wearing LSU boxer shorts and a worn-out Polo shirt, strolled out of his newly built man cave. As Stuart walked toward Phoebe, who was still in the pickup, she noticed how buff the once skinny runt had become. Stuart had a look of discontent on his face as he watched his betraying friend get out of the truck. Noticing her scrubs, Stuart asked Phoebe if she was there to operate on his hurt feelings.

"Oh, come on, sweetie, I'm here to apologize," answered Phoebe.

"Apologize for what? I suppose you and the others aren't able make to my reunion party tonight," Stuart voiced.

"I can't speak for the others, but I certainly will be here with bells on tonight. I'm so sorry we abandoned you last night. It was just that we're not as engrossed with the past as you are, Stuart, which is not a bad thing. I'm just saying—" Phoebe tried to explain.

Stuart interrupted her by saying, "Well, I'm just saying that you four have always treated me as a disregarded activity coordinator in this beyond problematic friendship, and I'm really sick of it, and I'm sick of all of you!"

Phoebe was speechless as Stuart continued.

"Phoebe, who was the one that always drove in high school? Who was the one always there during heartaches, bad decisions, and in John

John's case, bankruptcy? And not one of you has ever, ever been there for me when my life goes to hell in a hand basket! But boy when Dylan was strung out on drugs and basically became an irresponsible male slut, you, John John, and Debbie were right behind him, holding the support net. You all have each other, and I'm the isolated loser who's only called on when someone needs something!" stated Stuart.

Phoebe was stunned by Stuart's valid points, and an odd silence fell between them for about ten seconds before she nervously asked, "Would the lonesome loser mind fixing this selfish bitch a cup of Community Coffee before we go over more of this register of my regrets?"

Phoebe put her arm out for Stuart to escort her to the kitchen, and he apprehensively obliged. As they walked toward the front door of the house, the two eyed each other, and finally, Stuart's frown turned into a small smirk.

He opened the door for her, and as she sauntered in, he patted her behind.

"Watch it, Stuart. Although I'm dressed as a naughty nurse doesn't mean you're gonna get an apology performance," teased Phoebe.

After getting Phoebe a large mug of coffee and giving her a tour of his impressive home, he saved the new addition of his house to show her last. When most successful southern businessmen reach a certain age, they usually treat themselves to a hunting camp, a speedboat, or perhaps an RV, but not Stuart. He had a replica built of the legendary Bayview Yacht Club right at his backdoor. Stuart instructed Phoebe to close her eyes before he unveiled his idea of paradise. With her eyes tightly shut, Stuart held Phoebe's hand as he led her across the garage to the mysterious door. Phoebe giggled as she spilled a little bit of coffee on the garage floor while being guided by Stuart to his version of sentimental ecstasy. Stuart opened the door and then told Phoebe to open her eyes.

"Oh my God," she said as she looked around. Stuart was proud and felt as if he were Willy Wonka showing off his chocolate factory.

The enormous room was actually larger than Stuart's entire house. On each side of the unique lounge were huge windows with charming views of the cotton field. Twelve big flat-screen televisions were mounted on all four walls, and the music video of Duran Duran performing their song "The Reflex" was playing on each one of them. On the whole right side of the room was the bar itself. It was made of oak wood and sat fourteen barstools comfortably. Stuart's over-the-top tavern in the country could have definitely passed for a Dave & Buster's intended for adult products of the eighties in a midlife crisis who wished to relive their selective memories of freedom and fun. The proud bar owner had a large dance floor and a DJ booth custom made for his play room. Expense wasn't an issue for his project. Stuart had bought high-quality tables, chairs, sofas, glass refrigerators, name-brand liquor, a jukebox, and pool tables, and he had domestic and foreign beers on tap or in a bottle.

Phoebe couldn't believe her eyes. She asked Stuart if Wilbur Gutierrez, the original owner of the Bayview Yacht Club, had seen his backtrack to the eighties wonderland.

He laughed off her question and answered, "Yes he has, along with just about every one of our friends, except of course, you four."

"I must say you captured the Bayview to a tee, minus the mixture of cigarette smoke, Charlie perfume, and Polo cologne. You've nailed it," said Phoebe.

"Hey, I still wear Polo," Stuart stated.

"Yes, I know," bantered Phoebe.

Phoebe grabbed a pillow from one of the extended sofas, walked to the dance floor, lay down, and watched Duran Duran on the giant flat-screen television above the wall-sized mirror surrounding the dance floor. As she observed Simon Le Bon shake his butt, Stuart strolled behind the bar and prepared a Bloody Mary. He asked Phoebe if she would like an early afternoon cocktail, but she declined.

"Stuart, I haven't even taken a shower or been by my suite yet, so what's the deal with the early celebration?" Phoebe said.

Stuart topped his massive Bloody Mary with green beans and olives and suddenly developed a sad look on his face before responding to Phoebe's question. "It's a toss-up between everybody coming over tonight and Mary Beth leaving me for good."

Phoebe cheered, "Yes!" rose up from the dance floor, and performed a football touchdown victory dance. Stuart didn't find Phoebe's reaction amusing. He snatched a handful of olives, shoved them into his mouth, and made his way to the dance floor. The out-of-breath cheerleader was sitting Indian-style with a sofa pillow in her lap, waiting impatiently for Stuart to spill the beans on the sudden breakup from the uptight princess of doom. Stuart was not pleased at all about Phoebe's shallow and immature feedback. Not wanting to spill his drink, he carefully sat down on the floor directly across from his childish friend. The next music video that played was the Culture Club singing "Do You Really Want to Hurt Me?" Stuart stared into Phoebe's eyes for a few seconds before he spoke.

"Ya know, Phoebe, I realize that this is just an insignificant tale for you to share with our four other overly concerned friends, but it hurts like hell. Why is it that I'm like the irrelevant sidebar to everyone?" asked Stuart.

Phoebe was speechless while her hurt companion waited for a response. Stuart let out a brief snicker and answered for her, "Yeah, I thought so. No reply. See, I'm just Stuart, the ridiculous historian who hallucinates about having this eternal bond with you ungracious people. When have any of you ever come to my rescue? When my parents died? When I've been heartbroken? But boy, when one of your lives turned into pure shit, I was right there."

Tears rolled down Phoebe's cheeks as she cleared her throat to give Stuart his long-awaited response. "You couldn't be more wrong, Stuart. We all love you and know that you're actually the backbone of our malfunctioning family unit. I can definitely see where you're coming from, and I'm so sorry that you feel this way. Ya know, we have taken advantage of you, but I promise you that it's been unintentional. You're the one who makes us better, if that's possible," justified Phoebe.

Stuart struggled not to shed a tear. Phoebe shoved the pillow into his lap and rested her head on it. They formed a capital letter T on the wooden dance floor, and together, they watched the end of the Boy George video. All of a sudden, Phoebe raised her head from the pillow, looked at Stuart, and said, "I love you and appreciate you very much."

He grinned at his sincere sister from another mother and replied, "That's all I needed to hear."

Phoebe fluffed up the pillow, placed it back in Stuart's lap, and lay her head down on it again, and they continued to watch the music video. About one minute into the next video, which was ironically "Love Stinks" by the J. Geils Band, Phoebe asked Stuart what happened with him and Mary Beth. He took a long sip of his tomato cocktail and went into detail about their imaginary love affair. It was unfortunate that the two people involved never even liked each other. The marriage was a counterfeit connection that died from resentment and false hope. Both his wife and stepson were detached almost immediately after the wedding ceremony. Stuart admitted to Phoebe that it was a marriage of convenience to prevent his fears of being alone and left out. She held his hand and said, "I saw a commercial on TV this morning for Farmers-Only-Dot-Com; it might be better than eHarmony-Dot-Com to meet that Mrs. Right."

"Ya think so?" Stuart asked.

"I'll tell ya what. I'll make a deal with you. You try this online dating service for lonely field hands, and I'll try my luck with Black-People-Meet-Dot-Com," Phoebe sarcastically suggested.

They both cackled, and then Stuart asked her the million-dollar question. "How come we never hooked up? I know back in high school, you made out with Dylan, not to mention, you let John John feel you up at Charlene Vanderhoven's eighth-grade graduation party …"

"We were playing Truth or Dare!" interrupted Phoebe.

"So have you ever been attracted to me?" Stuart inquired.

"You were cute. Skinny and small but cute. You kinda reminded me of Scott Baio," Phoebe replied.

"Oh yeah, that good-looking actor who played in *Charles in Charge*," Stuart bragged.

"No, actually, it was before he it hit puberty; you looked more like him when he was Chachi before falling for Joanie on *Happy Days*," corrected Phoebe.

"Gee, I'm beyond flattered. Incidentally, in real life, Joanie is homeless and suffers from mental illness," reported Stuart.

"Stuart, you have become a gorgeous man! Look at you, all buffed up and swagged out. I would definitely go for you if I didn't know you and had low self-esteem," encouraged Phoebe.

"Really?" asked Stuart.

"Yes, really," Phoebe answered.

Stuart beamed from ear to ear as he placed his hands behind his head and stared up at the ceiling. Suddenly, the pillow on his lap with Phoebe's head on it began to rise as if it were a hospital bed being controlled by a remote. Phoebe rapidly realized that the sudden elevation was a result of Stuart's seldom-used erection tool. As Phoebe's head continued to rise, she calmly said to her horny buddy, "If you're doing what I'm thinking you're doing, in about three seconds, Chachi is getting castrated." Phoebe jumped up and punched the pillow. Stuart screamed in pain as he held his groin area. After the guilty snake groaned in agony, the two burst out in laughter. When it was understood that there would be no more funny business coming from Stuart's midsection, they both lay back down on the floor in their same position as before and viewed more music videos from the eighties.

Two hours had passed, along with multiple music videos from artists such as The Police, Toto, Men at Work, Kajagoogoo, Pat Benatar, Prince, and several more. Phoebe and Stuart were sound asleep. Stuart was exhausted from stress, and Phoebe had only two hours of sleep the night before. The two were cutting some major Z's while sharing the same large pillow. All of a sudden, there was banging on the door. It was Denise Wood, owner of Landry's Catering, and Tracey Gwinn, co-owner of Spirits Food & Friends. Both ladies were extremely attractive, successful businesswomen. They were also Menard High School graduates and were tremendously tolerant of Stuart's peculiar demands. Of course, he wanted all the food to symbolize the 1980s. From taco-flavored Doritos to petit fours made into Rubik's Cubes. The caterers had a challenging time, but they made it happen.

The loud knocks woke up the two sleepyheads. Stuart was startled from the noise and knocked over what was left from his Bloody Mary. Phoebe looked at her watch and then shouted, "Oh my God, it's five o'clock!"

Denise discovered that the door was unlocked, and she and Tracey walked in. Stuart and Phoebe were staggering to make it to the door and met the two curious caterers at the halfway mark. The innocent intruders didn't know what to think when they saw the tense twosome.

Phoebe had drool dripping down the right side of her mouth from sleeping so hard, and Stuart had a bad case of bedhead, along with a big, bright-red stain surrounding his mouth from the Bloody Mary.

"What the hell were ya'll doing?" asked Denise.

Phoebe and Stuart, still drowsy from their long nap, took a while to respond. Both ladies could have cared less what might have happened. They were just ready to get the show on the road. Before Stuart or Phoebe could speak, Tracey interjected, "Honestly, it really doesn't matter what you two were up to. What matters is I have pounds of boiled shrimp with corn, potatoes, and onions all dyed Menard-green in my van, and we only have two hours to get our act together for this reunion slash eighties flashback bash or whatever you want to call it." Stuart would have loved to be able to serve crawfish, but unfortunately, they were not in season. Tracey and Denise already felt Stuart was off his rocker because of his request to dye the shrimp green, gold, and white, which was an impossible task.

CHAPTER 11

Let's Just Forget

At a quarter past seven, Phoebe was sitting at a table, sipping a glass of white wine in the Mirror Room of the Hotel Bentley. She was waiting on John John, Debbie, and Dylan to have a drink with her before they headed out to Stuart's Yacht Club for the second night of their high school reunion. The night's dress code was totally eighties. Phoebe was going to take the suggestion from the waitress with the disfigured face from Pitt Grill and wear a leather skirt, a blue jean jacket, and a spiked-out wig and go as Tina Turner, but that would have been too much trouble, so she settled for a white Izod cardigan sweater and Gloria Vanderbilt jeans that she purchased at a vintage store in Lafayette. Phoebe was the type of woman who could wear a worn-out housecoat and still look like a million dollars.

Phoebe was answering texts on her iPhone when Dylan and Debbie entered the lounge. Debbie was wearing a pink Esprit sweatshirt and tight Chic jeans. Dylan was feeling less nostalgic; he had on a black, button-down shirt, jeans, and cowboy boots. Phoebe noticed that John John was missing in action and asked, "Where's the king of the cinnamon shots?"

As Dylan and Debbie took a seat at Phoebe's table, Debbie answered, "He's at home, still in recovery from last night. I'm tellin' y'all, that man has our toilet seat imprinted on his fat ass."

"Our bodies aren't what they used to be," Phoebe announced.

"Tell me about it. The only food that John John could get down today was Popeye's Chicken, and of course tater tots from the Sonic. They have to be from Sonic, 'cause somehow the grease they're fried in coats his disturbed stomach," added Debbie.

"I don't feel that great myself. I have a headache. I think it's from the fumes in my suite. Housekeeping overdid it today with the Lysol," reported Phoebe.

Debbie developed a look of shame on her face while hoping that the subject would quickly change.

"I love the smell of Lysol, especially the Sparkling Lemon and Sunflower Essence," proclaimed Dylan.

Phoebe rolled her eyes and asked Dylan, "Were you conceived at a Procter & Gamble Plant?"

"Honey, he and his whole entire family are clean freaks," Debbie teased.

Phoebe laughed as Dylan replied to Debbie's accusation by saying, "My apologies, Your Highness of Hoarding."

"Hey, I've never claimed to be the best housekeeper in Louisiana," Debbie retorted.

"Well, for one thing, you live in a trailer," snapped Dylan.

"It's a doublewide, you overly domestic dick!" defended Debbie.

Dylan giggled and asked Debbie, "Didn't you get fired from Merry Maids years ago?"

"I don't recall that," answered Debbie.

Phoebe looked over to Dylan and said, "It's a shame Stuart isn't here. He could give us the exact date and the reason for Debbie's departure from her promising career in house cleaning."

Debbie flipped her middle finger at Dylan and Phoebe and said, "All right, you two, I've had enough. I'm saving myself for the rude comments and harsh judgments from our classmates."

Phoebe noticed Debbie's fake long nails and then remarked, "Are you wearing Lee press-on nails?"

"No, they're Broadway nails. I got them on sale at Walgreens. Hey, we're supposed to wear what we wore back in the day, aren't we?" asked Debbie.

Before Phoebe could respond, Dylan stood up and took beverage requests. Phoebe told him that she was still sipping on her wine, and Debbie couldn't make up her mind. Phoebe placed her glass of wine in front of Debbie and suggested, "Try my wine. It's Broken Road Chardonnay."

"No thanks, I had a box of cheap wine before I left the house—I mean trailer," Debbie replied.

Dylan continued to wait patiently for Debbie's drink order, and after three agonizing minutes of Debbie debating what type of alcohol her stomach could handle, she decided on the old faithful Crown and Coke. As Dylan moved toward the bar, Phoebe leaned over to Debbie and asked her why she had a box of wine before she left the house, better known as the double-wide.

Debbie explained that she was a bit nervous and really disliked the "back to the past" weekend. The only reason why she was taking part in the night's festivities was because it was Stuart's party and she would never hear the end of it if she were a no-show. It was bad enough that her hung-over husband would not be in attendance. Phoebe understood and assured Debbie that she also felt a three-day weekend with classmates who didn't relate was not on the top of her bucket list. Not to mention that they would be missing a new episode of *Saturday Night Live* because of Stuart's poor planning efforts. Dylan brought back Debbie her mixed drink and had ginger ale for himself. He appeared tired and worn-out as he sat down.

"Dylan, I know you have to be exhausted," Phoebe commented.

"I am. It hasn't been the greatest day," answered Dylan.

Debbie took a sip of her Crown and Coke, glared at Dylan, and jokingly asked, "Ah, did some nasty person go in your kitchen cabinet and steal your Glade oil diffusers?"

"Debbie!" scolded Phoebe.

"Hey! He's the one that brought up my horrible experience with the damn Merry Maids!" protested Debbie.

Debbie looked over at Dylan and realized that he really wasn't having a good day. She gently scratched his back with her counterfeit nails and apologized. He smiled at her as he held her right hand and kissed it. Debbie smiled back at him and said, "Be careful, honey. I paid good money for them nails."

After the brief altercation ended on a sweet gesture, Dylan described the rotten day he had to his two best girl buds. "First, the day started off with me having no sleep whatsoever, and then one of my favorite kids at the special education center had to be taken to the emergency room. The little guy was standing on top of a chair and fell down, face first, and busted his forehead. While I was waiting in the emergency room lobby, I got a call from one of the cashiers at my store, saying that Heath, my weekend manager, who apparently was off his medication, started hallucinating and went psychotic on Neal Lambert. Y'all know who Neal Lambert is?" Dylan asked.

"Yeah, he's the pastor of the First Assembly of God. I see him on TV all the time during the Christen Corner on Channel Five's *Morning Show*," answered Debbie.

Dylan drank a sip of his ginger ale and resumed with his awful day report. "Well, Heath—by the way, I failed to mention he's a paranoid schizophrenic and suffers from Tourette's syndrome—"

"What the hell is Barrette syndrome?" interrupted Debbie.

Dylan didn't respond. He closed his eyes and shook his head in disbelief at Debbie's ludicrous question.

Phoebe took it upon herself to correct her naïve girlfriend and said, "It's not barrette. It's Tourette. You know, it's when someone can't control themselves from swearing."

Debbie hooted and replied, "Hell, this Heath fella sounds like my kind of guy."

"May I get back to why my day and life sucks at the moment, or do you two want to continue your in-depth conversation on inaccurate hair clip diagnosis?" asked Dylan.

"Ouch," Debbie uttered.

"By all means, please continue, Dylan," said Phoebe.

Dylan cleared his throat and stared at both ladies to make sure that he truly had the floor and continued on with his story. "Neal was at the register and placed a box of Aunt Dewy's Venison Jerky on the counter. We give him a discount because he buys the jerky in bulk for his youth group. I think they put a meat stick in the lunch bags of each youth member who's attending this Praise Jesus workshop or somethin' ..."

"It's for their annual Deep South Holy Land in Our Own Backyard Youth Retreat. I told ya, I see that slick man of Christ on TV all the time," interjected Debbie.

Once again, Dylan didn't respond to Debbie's useless commentary and went on with telling his story. "The innocent preacher asked Heath for his regular discount, and Health flips out and calls the man a child-molesting metrosexual and accused the poor bastard of being sent to Norma's Cajun Rage Quick Stop from Satan's camp to recruit the store clerks and deli workers into his perverted cult! Wait, that's not all. Heath then jumped on the counter and started throwing those little plastic bottles of 5-Hour Energy all over the store while screaming every cuss word imaginable at the top of his lungs. At this point, he thinks the traumatized pastor has let out hundreds of Russian rats to invade the entire store. Agnes, ya know the sweet, older lady with no teeth?" asked Dylan.

Phoebe nodded her head, but she really had no idea who the hell Dylan was talking about.

Debbie informed him that she knew who Agnes was and asked him to please give them the *Reader's Digest* version of the story because he was starting to take on Stuart's drawn-out way of storytelling.

Dylan couldn't care less about Debbie's criticism and wrapped up his insane report.

"Agnes is my store clerk who all my customers think is the original Aunt Dewy, and she's the only one of my employees who actually knows the right way to clean the Icee machines—"

"Focus, Dylan! Get to the point!" demanded Debbie.

Dylan shot his middle finger at Debbie and continued explaining the mental health breakdown at register two. "Agnes tried everything she could to calm Heath down. In the past, she would impersonate an old out-of-work Muppet by giving the manic young man a big smile, showing nothing but her gums …"

"Gosh, who would have thought that displaying a bad case of gingivitis by way of improvisation could prevent a psychotic episode?" interrupted Phoebe.

All three burst out in laughter. Dylan paused for Debbie and Phoebe to settle down and carried on with his real-life *One Flew Over the Cuckoo's Nest* experience.

"At any rate, Agnes's attempt as the toothless, swollen-gums puppet didn't work, so she called me first, and when I didn't answer because I was dealing with my little friend in the emergency room, she had to call my wonderful brother, Steven. Steven called the police as he hauled ass to the store. Long story short, Steven had the cops arrest Heath. I bailed him out and took him to the psych hospital," Dylan explained.

"Jesus, Dylan, you really have had a rotten twelve hours," Phoebe uttered.

"Wait, that's not all. While I was waiting for Debbie to come pick me up, I called Hunter's counselor to see what time I needed to be at the treatment center for family therapy next weekend, and his therapist told me that my son was still angry with me and not ready to see me. So, instead of me, his father, participating, my parents and Sylvia are all going. Oh, and my little brother is also taking the ride to Florida," added Dylan.

"Let's all get shitfaced," suggested Debbie.

Debbie signaled for the cocktail waitress to come to their table. When the server arrived, she ordered another round for herself and Phoebe and added a beer for Dylan. She also requested a basket of fried crawfish tails. As the waitress walked away, Debbie looked at Dylan and assured him that everything was going to be okay. She took a big sip of her Crown and Coke, followed by a major belch.

"Excuse me, y'all. All I've done this whole weekend is eat and drink. It's like I've been reliving Thanksgiving dinner over and over, minus John John's god-awful family," clarified Debbie.

As Debbie chuckled at her own statement, she saw Dylan's brother, Steven, and his wife, Lauren, enter the room. Steven was still extremely handsome and in good physical condition. Although Steven was fifty-four, the gorgeous blond-haired and blue-eyed gynecologist could have easily passed for a thirty-five-year-old. His former college sweetheart and present wife, Lauren, was also easy on the eyes. She had blonde locks and a toned body, just like her husband. Debbie warned Phoebe and Dylan that the perfect couple of the parish had arrived.

"Damn it to hell! It's abundantly clear that family torture doesn't end at happy hour," blurted out Dylan.

"Well, maybe if Debbie stopped glaring at the poisonous pair, they won't come over," Phoebe advised.

It was too late. In a matter of thirty seconds, Lauren spotted Phoebe from across the room. Lauren was a huge fan of Phoebe's line of jewelry. It always had been a mystery to Lauren why a stunning, successful, and wealthy woman such as Phoebe would be such good friends with such common individuals as her brother-in-law and Debbie, the unfiltered mouth of the South.

Lauren, who was dressed in a beautiful, off-white dress, left Steven, who was wearing a Seersucker suit, behind as she rushed over to the queen of fine jewelry and her two ill-mannered court jesters. "Hey, girl" Lauren said to Phoebe as she arrived to her table. The doctor's wife completely ignored Dylan and Debbie. Her attention was on Phoebe's brooch because she was wearing the same exact piece, which was a wing-shaped, white gold pin, showered in 1.56-carat diamonds.

"Oh my God, you're wearing your Cane River Angel brooch too!" Lauren screeched.

"Yes, I am," Phoebe answered.

"I was just at your jewelry store in New Orleans last week. My God, you've raised your prices. I didn't get anything because Steven wouldn't go with me. He hates shopping. I had my eye on a gorgeous black diamond ring, but unfortunately, Steven's black American Express card was in his black leather wallet in his pants pocket back at the Royal Sonesta," bragged Lauren.

Phoebe smiled and waited for Lauren to stop laughing at her "black American Express" comment before she attempted to respond. Right before Phoebe could speak, Steven came up to the table. He said hello to Phoebe, and before he could acknowledge his brother and Debbie, Lauren dominated the conversation by reminding her husband that she still would like for him to go by Phoebe's store and purchase the extravagant ring for his well-deserving wife.

"Honey, you know I don't care for black diamonds," Steven told his superficial bride.

Debbie snorted out loud at Steven's remark as the waitress placed the basket of fried crawfish tails in front of her. She looked at Steven and lectured, "Honey, don't ever tell the best African American jewelry designer in the world that you disapprove of black diamonds!"

Nobody understood Debbie's joke, including Debbie. After fifteen seconds of awkward silence, Debbie confessed, "Okay, that box of cheap wine and the Crown and Cokes are kickin' in."

Steven spotted the basket of fried tails in front of Debbie, his patient, and shook his head in disapproval.

"How's that diet working for you, Debbie?" Steven asked.

"Well, I have to tell ya, Doc, earlier today, I waited to eat my McDonalds french fries until got home instead of scoffing them down in the car on the way to the trailer. So, I'm definitely practicin' self-control," confessed Debbie.

"I see that," Steven sarcastically replied back to Debbie.

"Well, Doctor Steve, ya'll look nice tonight. Ya kinda have that Andy Griffith in his *Matlock* days look goin' on. Where ya'll headin' to?" Debbie inquired.

"We're attending a surprise birthday party for the mayor that's being held in the ballroom," Lauren answered for her husband.

As Debbie went into detail with Lauren about how her mother's side of the family was related to Mayor Roy's family in Marksville, Louisiana, Steven grabbed Dylan's shoulder from behind and demanded that the two of them have a brief meeting at the bar. Dylan excused himself and walked with his wicked brother to the bar. Not listening to a word Debbie was saying about her family tree in Avoyelles Parish, Lauren cut off the babbling country girl by asking Phoebe if she ever gave discounts on her jewelry to family and friends.

The first question Steven asked Dylan was, "What the hell are you doing?"

"I'm not in the mood, Steven," Dylan replied.

"You never, ever change, Dylan. Jesus H Christ! Here you are, an addict drinking a beer with not a care in the world, right? Let's just forget the fact that your son is screwed up and in treatment. Let's just forget the fact that you allow a paranoid schizophrenic to manage our store, which is your only income, due to the fact that you've lost your nursing license.

Let's just forget the fact that your main concern in life is to play God for special needs children in order to escape from your real train wreck of a life!" criticized Steven.

Dylan had a blank stare on his face while Steven eagerly waited for his carefree brother's reaction.

"Thoughts?" Steven asked Dylan.

"I'm trying to think of anything that you may have *just* forgotten," answered Dylan.

CHAPTER 12

Fist City

Phoebe, Dylan, and Debbie were waiting at the side entrance of the hotel for the valet parking team to bring them their vehicles. Phoebe decided to ride with Debbie so that Dylan could take back his son's truck. Both ladies, yes, even Debbie, were trying to make light of Dylan's sensitive situation with his older sibling. Debbie went into detail about how much better the fried crawfish tails were at her restaurant than the ones she managed to devour. Dylan didn't hear a word of Debbie's "how to fry a good crawfish tail" story. He was in another world of silent passive aggression. Phoebe and Debbie had known the hurting rebel for so long that they knew to let Dylan marinate in his older brother's harsh words. Thank goodness, just in time to off trigger Debbie's "how to batter seafood" theory, all three of them got a text on their cell phones. The message was from Norma. She wanted everyone to come over for a good, ole home-cooked (actually catered) Sunday dinner. Norma felt that it would be nice to have an intimate gathering of family and friends after the tribute mass for those members of the class of '83 who were no longer with them, such as Garrett. Right after the three read their messages, a large man dressed in a worn-out tie-dyed T-shirt and cutoff jeans staggered up to Debbie.

"Ma'am, I need a big favor. I was on my way to the hospital and ran out of gas about two blocks down, and my mother is in the car. She's very sick. Could you loan me a few bucks?" the man off the street pleaded.

Before Debbie responded, she instantly developed her Nancy Grace look on her face.

"Listen, honey, your story smells just as bad as you do, and I love fat, stinky men! You need to try somethin' else. I heard this pile of shit from you in Walmart's parking lot, and then again at Super One Food's parking lot, and then again in front K-Mart! Look at us! We're wearing the same damn clothes we had in high school! Do we look like we have money to give to you? You probably have a college education and a condo in Galveston!" scolded Debbie.

"Forget it," the man replied.

As the homeless impersonator turned around and walked away, Dylan shouted for him to stop. The man turned around, and Dylan walked up to him and gave the panhandler a twenty-dollar bill. The professional beggar thanked Dylan and went away.

When Dylan turned around, he saw that the valet workers were driving Hunter and Debbie's trucks up to the entrance. Phoebe tipped the young lady who drove Debbie's pickup and grabbed the keys from Debbie. She definitely didn't want the tanked-up, ex-Merry Maid behind the wheel.

The ladies told Dylan that they would see him at Stuart's flashback bash. As Phoebe playfully pushed Debbie into the passenger seat of the truck, she looked over to Dylan and winked at the lost soul, assuring him that everything was going to be all right.

Stuart was beyond excited with the turnout of his totally eighties celebration. In fact, there were more classmates at his function than the get-together that took place the night before. The once conservative accountant had set aside his feelings of losing his wife and nerdy stepson for an evening of make-believe memories. For one night only, Stuart was going to be the most popular man on campus, the grand marshal of his own Mardi Gras, the proud captain of his own Bayview Yacht Club, and nothing and no one was gonna rain on his parade. All of the fellow students of the self-appointed cruise director couldn't believe their eyes. Stuart's add-on den for reminiscing was the spitting image of the lounge where everyone once played. From the classic eighties music videos that played on every flat screen to the cocaine cakes, which were actually French Quarter beignets covered in powdered sugar. The powdered sugar represented the American crack epidemic that started in 1984.

The guests were very much awestricken with the gracious host and the hard work that went into planning this one-of-a-kind event. The only minor glitch of the spectacular affair was that the platters of hot, red boiled shrimp, loaded with the green potatoes, onions, and corn, looked more like Dollar Store Christmas wreaths than shrimp covered in Menard High School's colors.

Dylan, Phoebe, and Debbie entered Stuart's fabulous tavern and saw that the celebration was in full force. Dylan and Debbie were amazed at their best friend's bar. The music video of The Producers singing "What's He Got?" was loudly playing, and the members of the class of '83 were having a blast. Debbie leaned into Dylan and said, "This is the damn Bayview! How in the hell can Stuart, the cheapest bastard on this side of the bayou, afford his own freakin' Bayview?"

"I don't know. Maybe the former penny-pinching trust fund baby is now a big spender in midlife crisis," Dylan answered.

Stuart spotted his three friends from across the bar and ran over to them. He was extremely excited to see his inner circle. The enthusiastic host looked at Phoebe standing in the middle between Dylan and Debbie and said, "You three look like an inside-out Oreo!"

Stuart chuckled at his own lame comment and suddenly realized that he wasn't receiving any type of positive response from the jaded threesome.

Phoebe waited for Stuart to stop his nervous laugh and said to him, "Comedic timing is not one of your better attributes, Stuart." Stuart disregarded Phoebe's remark as he grabbed Debbie and Dylan's hands and led them to the bar. Phoebe was left behind to greet her past classmates, who were three females and one gay male. The three were also big fans of her jewelry. The three ladies were dressed as Madonna during her "Like a Virgin" period, and the male looked just like Mike Score, the lead singer for the new-wave band, A Flock of Seagulls. The Madonnas and the lone seagull were wearing customized pieces from Phoebe's jewelry line. Phoebe was flattered the small group of admirers was so happy to see her.

"Feelin' fine, feelin' free! We are seniors eighty-three!" was what several of the guests chanted when they saw Dylan, the original Jackson Street Cruiser, and Debbie, the better half of the Rowdy Rachels, make their way to the bar.

"If they only knew how repulsive we thought the class cheer was," Dylan said to Debbie.

Debbie agreed with Dylan by letting out an obnoxious laugh. As the Debbie Downers of school spirit waited for the bartender, several former members of the girls' softball team came up to Debbie. The state champs of '83 all looked wonderful. They had turned into older, beautiful, large women just as their old captain, Debbie, was. They all screamed for joy as each took a turn hugging their once fearless leader.

While Debbie received the warm welcoming from the Menard Lady Eagles, Stuart, who was wearing a light-blue Izod shirt with the collar turned up, Khaki shorts, and penny loafers, told Dylan that he really needed to talk with him. Dylan agreed, and Stuart gave him a strong hug.

"What's with you?" Dylan asked Stuart.

"I'll be fine. I just need my true friends tonight, that's all," answered Stuart.

Stuart gave Dylan a brief recap of his recent breakup with his miserable wife, and Dylan wasn't listening to a word of what his brokenhearted buddy was saying. His focus was on Linda Juneau, a hungry divorcee who was the head booster back in high school. Dylan couldn't remember her name, but he did remember that she could do a hell of a lot more with a drumstick than just beat a drum. At the midpoint of Stuart's whining, Dylan excused himself and traveled toward his prey. As the rebel strutted over to the multitalented booster, Stuart shouted to him that they would definitely talk later. Stuart then moved closer to Debbie and asked her where John John was.

"Oh, sweetie, he still has the backdoor trots from all those cinnamon shots," answered Debbie.

"That figures," Stuart snarled.

Debbie didn't hear Stuart's remark because several of her softball chums were asking her the same question about John John. Stuart was very disappointed about John John's absence. He desperately wanted John John to see the massive accomplishment of his duplication of the Bayview. His depression quickly dissolved when Marie Sylvester, the 1983 homecoming queen, asked him to dance to the tune of "Weird Science" by Oingo Boingo.

Debbie immediately took her iPhone (covered in a rhinestone case) out of her purse and called John John. It took a while for her hung-over husband to answer because his cell phone was left on their bed while he remained glued to the toilet. It took seven rings for John John, wearing a XXX large *Duck Dynasty* T-shirt and tight-whities, which were down to his knees, to answer the phone. He looked like a huge, life-size version of the popular egg-shaped toy figure from the seventies in the "Weebles wobble, but they don't fall down" television commercial.

After a serious struggle, John John finally answered Debbie's call. The poor man had difficulty figuring out how to use the Face Time on his cell as he rapidly wobbled back to his porcelain throne. He plopped back down on the commode and was finally able to see Debbie on the confusing technical device. Debbie realized that her pitiful companion was in their bathroom because of the sign that read *Daddy's Thinking Room*, over John John's head.

"Hey, baby! Are you still glued to that damn latrine?" Debbie yelled into the phone.

"Yes, I am. I'm startin' to think that them pizza bites at Sweet Daddy's were laced with some kinda fatal fiber," answered John John.

"Yeah, maybe the bits of pepperoni were poisonous," joked Debbie.

While Debbie and John John went back and forth about the different possibilities causing his loose day on the toilet seat, two of Debbie's old teammates, who lived out of town, were waving their hands for Debbie to give them the phone. Debbie told John John that there were two people excited to talk with him.

"Don't you dare put anybody on the phone! I'm not playing with you! I'm dying here!" begged John John.

It was too late. Debbie passed the phone to her eager girlfriends. The deceiving dame of the swamplands leaned against the bar and grinned, knowing her husband was crashing from humiliation.

After a few minutes of talking with one of Debbie's old teammates about the photo she placed on Facebook of a huge deer she shot last fall, it appeared John John had forgotten that he was even on the crapper. Therefore, the joke was essentially on Debbie.

As the female hunter handed Debbie back her phone, a handsome man dressed in an executive suit walked up to Debbie and her group of softball legends.

Debbie was the only one who didn't know who this stranger was. The mystery male had divulged his identity to the others earlier that evening. Debbie observed the Wall Street-type of guy from head to toe and then said, "Well, hey, good-lookin'. Who are you supposed to be? Michael J. Fox during his *Family Ties* days?"

"Actually, my intention was to be Robert Chambers," the man answered.

"Who in the hell is that? Some old porno star?" Debbie replied back.

Before the stranger could reply, one of the old teammates answered for him. "Robert Chambers was the dude who murdered that eighteen-year-old girl in New York's Central Park back in the mid-eighties. The media gave him the name Preppie Killer," reported the teammate.

"Oh, my Lord! I remember that!" Debbie shouted.

Debbie took a closer look at her anonymous classmate and quickly remembered who the fella was.

"Oh, my Lord! Rebecca Vercher! Is that you?" Debbie asked.

"I'm Ricky now," the man kindly corrected Debbie.

"Well, you look just as good as—or even better than Chaz Bono," Debbie remarked.

"Go ahead and ask me millions of questions. Everyone else has," Ricky instructed.

"I only have two for ya," stated Debbie.

"Go for it," encouraged Ricky.

"Okay, number one, do you still have a mean pitch? And question number two is can you now get jock itch?" Debbie asked.

Ricky gave the curious softball captain a big smile, and they both laughed and hugged.

Meanwhile, the celebration for the midlife partiers continued as the prior disc jockey from Murphy's (the hot spot for LSU students in the eighties) played one hit after another from the decade that made them. It actually took a while for the classmates, who were not considered Generation X but were too old to be Generation Y, to break out of their comfortable cliques. Stuart was the only one who appeared to be preoccupied. He was panicking because he couldn't find Dylan. He ran over to each concealed circle.

After all the years that had passed, people ultimately migrated to the company responsible for their approval. Those who were not characterized in any particular grouping back in the day were heading straight to the bar to gain liquid courage.

Stuart's first stop was past jocks. These good, ole country boys were all friends of John John's. Stuart interrupted the old athletes, who are having a debate on who had the worst mullet, by asking if they had seen Dylan, and their answer was no.

The flustered host then walked over to the food area where the "in crowd" was. Out of Stuart's close network, only Dylan and Phoebe might have been considered part of this superficial society. He asked several of the aging A-list guests where Dylan was, and they didn't know.

Stuart didn't bother asking the geeks, scholars, or those in recovery if they had seen the missing rebel. He also avoided the possibility that any of the husbands or wives of his classmates would have known where Dylan was.

He saw Debbie and Phoebe boogying on the dance floor with the women's softball team and an overly dressed dude. Stuart recognized all the ladies, but for the love of God, he couldn't figure out who the sharp-dressed man was. The only thing Stuart knew about the fetching fella was that he was trying to put the moves on Phoebe. He worked his way through the poor excuses for dancers, and when he got closer to Phoebe and Ricky, Stuart realized that the strange man Phoebe was dancing with was indeed Rebecca Vercher. He nonchalantly said, "Holy shit," to himself, and then he clutched Debbie's hand and led her to the side of the dance floor. The two had to shout at each other because of the loud music.

"Where's Dylan?" Stuart asked.

"I don't know! Ask Phoebe!" Debbie answered.

"She's too busy doing the hermaphrodite hustle right now! Does she realize her Prince Charming is Rebecca Vercher?" asked Stuart.

"Bless her heart, she doesn't have a clue!" replied Debbie, followed by a wicked laugh.

Before Stuart could say anything else, the DJ played the song, "Kids in America" by Kim Wilde, which was one of his all-time favorite tunes. Stuart smiled as he had a flashback from the date of Thursday, September 3, 1981. That was the day when he found out that he was elected student council representative of the junior class. He fondly remembered getting into his Volkswagen Rabbit after school, turning on the radio, and hearing that song. The catchy melody combined with his election win made for a wonderful drive back home. Debbie was confused by why Stuart was just standing in place, smiling from ear to ear.

"What's up with you? I bet cha it's either the Viagra or the Ecstasy kickin' in," Debbie said.

Stuart remained smiling and then explained, "It's this song,"

"Well, I was kinda hoping for a song that everyone could slow dance to. I'm just dying for Phoebe to make a love connection with the Preppy Murderer. Hey, do ya think the DJ has "80's Ladies" by K. T. Oslin?" Debbie requested.

Stuart was oblivious to Debbie's joke. He left her and sauntered back on the dance floor to the wall-size mirror. Stuart then looked into the mirror and danced with himself. He was celebrating the victory that made him feel significant back when he was seventeen. That was not an unusual characteristic for Stuart, particularly if he had been drinking. His classmates, including Phoebe, and Ricky, a.k.a. Rebecca, began to leave the dance floor one by one. They all thought Stuart was getting ready to give them a spectacular solo performance. However, Stuart was so into himself that he was unaware the dance floor was clear.

While Stuart performed his interpretation of Kevin Bacon's dance finale from *Footloose* in the mirror, Debbie walked over to the sofas that were located in front of the nostalgic candy table. She was exhausted from the physical activity and sat down on one of the sofas.

Meanwhile, Phoebe and Ricky were at the entrance. They exchanged phone numbers, hugged, and Ricky left.

On her way back to the bar to get a glass of water, Phoebe saw Debbie sitting on the sofa. Debbie yelled out, "Phoebe Cakes! Get me another Crown and Coke!"

Phoebe got their drinks, as well as some napkins for their sweaty foreheads, and strolled over to her lazy friend. She placed the beverages on the table and proceeded to give Debbie one of her best "go to hell" looks. Debbie asked Phoebe, "What's wrong?" Phoebe refused to respond. She stared at Debbie for about fifteen seconds, and then they both burst out in laughter.

"Why didn't you tell me that Ricky was once Rebecca?" Phoebe shouted to Debbie.

"When did you finally discover who your sex stalker was?" asked Debbie.

"Just a few minutes ago when Ricky told me he had to leave because his ex-husband was babysitting their twelve-year-old son!" Phoebe yelled.

"That's right! Rebecca married that ole boy from Tioga. I think she was in her late thirties before she tied the knot," confirmed Debbie.

"I don't even remember Ricky or Rebecca or whoever he-she was in high school!" Phoebe shouted.

The two laughed so hard that they started to cry.

"I'm going to have to go to the ladies' room before I pee all over myself," announced Phoebe.

"You better make sure that it's a unisex restroom," said Debbie.

Both ladies were drawing attention from others by laughing so loudly. Once they caught their breath, Debbie requested a small favor from Phoebe before she went to the bathroom.

"Before you hit the john, walk behind me and get me a mint or somethin'. I'm starting to taste those crawfish tails," ordered Debbie.

Phoebe walked to the table with every type of retro candy on it and grabbed a handful of little, green pebbles out of a green bowl. She thought the pebbles were Nerds, but they were actually Pop Rocks. Phoebe placed the candies in Debbie's hand, turned around, and headed toward the restroom.

Debbie popped the whole handful of the tiny, green candies into her mouth and chased them down with a big sip of Crown and Coke. All of a sudden, she began choking and coughing.

Phoebe, who hadn't even made it to the ladies' room yet, heard Debbie gagging. She turned around and ran back over to check on her friend.

Vines Reed, a veterinarian, and Cathy Brown, a registered nurse, were standing by the candy table talking about how annoying pharmaceutical salespeople could be when all of a sudden they saw Debbie struggling. The two health professionals dashed over to Debbie to find out if she was all right. Debbie coughed up a large amount of green liquid into a napkin, looked up at her two classmates, and told them she was fine.

When Phoebe arrived to the scene, Cathy, the nurse, asked Debbie what happened. Debbie smiled and pointed to Phoebe.

"I'll tell ya what happened! Rebecca Vercher's girlfriend here tried to kill me!" Debbie playfully bellowed.

"What?" shouted Phoebe.

"Now listen here, you voodoo queen! You purposely gave me them damn Pop Rocks when you know damn well that popping candy mixed with cola can cause a heart attack!" Debbie barked.

"You can't die from eating Pop Rocks!" Phoebe yelled.

"Well, honey, you just ask the parents of that child actor who played Mikey in those Life Cereal commercials! That cute little boy's stomach exploded from mixin' Pop Rocks with a Dr. Pepper!" explained Debbie.

Phoebe, along with Cathy and Vines, cackled at Debbie's story, which was actually an urban myth.

Out of the blue, Stuart staggered upon Phoebe, Debbie, Vines, and Cathy. He looked at Phoebe and slurred, "Tell Dylan he's a prick." He then looked at Cathy and asked, "Hey, Cathy Brown, remember me?

The loser you turned down in high school." Cathy didn't know how to respond. Last but not least, Stuart turned his attention to Vines and mumbled, "You wouldn't go out with me either."

Phoebe redirected the dialogue by telling Stuart that he missed Debbie's deadly candy episode. Stuart fell down on the sofa next to Debbie and gave her a hug. As the plastered host consoled his feisty victim of Pop Rock shock, Cathy moved closer to Phoebe and showed the jewelry designer the Cane River Angel pin that her husband gave her on their last anniversary. Once again, Phoebe was flattered that so many of her old schoolmates were supporters of her work. Vines left the group when he noticed his wife waving for him to come dance with her to the beat of "She Sells Sanctuary" by The Cult.

On the Looney Tunes sofa sat sloshed Stuart and drunken Debbie.

"I've made a totally ass out of myself, Debbie," Stuart revealed.

"How, sweetie?" Debbie asked.

"Ya know, the pouting dance of self-pity and all," replied Stuart.

"Oh, honey, I'm sure everyone thought it was more like a self-indulgent presentation than a low, self-worth act," corrected Debbie.

"You always know the right thing to say," cried Stuart.

"Listen, Stuart, nothin', I mean nothin', not even a fancy bar and all this food dyed in Menard High School's colors, could ever match the love I have for you!" Debbie stated.

"I love you too. I'm gonna get us a drink," said Stuart.

"I better take it down a notch. Get me a White Russian, and I mean white, not green, Stuart!" Debbie ordered.

Stuart got up from the sofa, looked over at Phoebe, who was still talking with Cathy, and asked her if she would like anything from the bar. She told him that she was sticking with water because she was the self-appointed designated driver for Miss Debbie. Stuart stopped and visited with a few classmates on his way to the bar, which was located about fifteen feet from the candy table.

As Phoebe continued to carry on a pleasant conversation with Cathy, Debbie started loudly singing, "Ricky, don't lose her number—you don't wanna call nobody else …" The song was really titled "Rikki Don't Lose That Number" by Steely Dan. Although Debbie was butchering one of the best ballads ever sung by Steely Dan, Phoebe understood exactly what her asinine friend was trying to accomplish. Phoebe struggled to keep a straight face while listening to Cathy. Debbie knew she was getting on Phoebe's nerves and sang even louder.

Once Debbie started losing her voice, she finished off her Crown and Coke and sat back and giggled. She was thinking to herself that out of all the eligible men at the reunion, the only person that gave her beautiful friend attention was the former Rebecca Vercher.

Suddenly, she heard the voices of two of her worst enemies from back in the day. They were Jill Flynn and Sandy Thomas. The ladies were known as the spoiled, rich girls back in high school. Jill and Sandy looked good. They had both kept their girlish figures, and their faces had no expressions at all, thanks to the precious Botox needle.

With all the noise going on, it was amazing that Debbie could hear every word her frienemies said. Jill and Sandy were standing behind the sofa where Debbie was seated. The two insensitive women were chatting about how Stuart went overboard by building an authentic nightclub to impress everyone. They also felt that he overdid it with decorations and food, all highlighted in Holy Savior Menard Central High School's colors. With each negative statement said about Stuart by the ruthless Junior Leaguers, Debbie pulled off one of her fake nails. "What a loser," "It's a shame he tries so hard," and "No wonder Mary Beth is leaving him; he's married to his past" were just a few of the negative comments that were broadcast by Sandy and Jill. It did not take long for Debbie to tear off all her cheap nails.

Phoebe, who was patiently listening to Cathy Brown talking about her couponing addiction, looked over at Debbie. Phoebe immediately panicked because she realized that Debbie was on her way to kicking somebody's ass. The look on Debbie's face was the same look she had many years ago when she beat up girls at the Lighthouse Bar for flirting with John John. Debbie jumped off the sofa and instantly turned into a mean drunk. She turned around and glared at the two idiots.

"I see you two bitches are up to the same old shit!" Debbie shouted at Jill and Sandy.

Sandy turned her back while Jill faced Debbie, the fired up, nail-less Wonder Woman.

"Really, Debbie, what are you going to do? Hit me?" Jill snarled.

As Debbie slowly walked up to the brave female, Stuart, who was holding a Flaming Volcano, a tropical cocktail in a ceramic bowl, strolled past Sandy and got behind Jill. He didn't see that Debbie was in front of

Jill and the two ladies were having a tense moment, because he was too busy concentrating on not spilling a drop of the specialty drink that he and the gang used to consume at the China Restaurant when they were only fifteen years old.

"Did you just ask me if I was gonna hit you?" Debbie asked Jill.

"I'm not going to take part in your little game show here to get attention," replied Jill.

Phoebe saw that Debbie was making a fist in her right hand. She ran over to the two heated women, and right before she could grab Jill's left arm, Debbie said, "Oh what a shame, Jill Flynn, cuz you just won the grand prize."

Phoebe pulled Jill away just in the nick of time, preventing her from receiving Debbie's right hook. Sadly, Stuart got the hit across the face, thanks to Phoebe being a Good Samaritan. And what a hit it was. Debbie's beautiful blow to Stuart's left eye caused him to fall back and hit the floor. The festive bowl of alcohol spilled all over Stuart's chest, and the flame, lit from the 151-proof rum, burned the tip of his chin. Debbie was shocked that she socked Stuart instead of the gossiping witch. A large crowd gathered around as Debbie knelt down on the floor to check on her injured pal. "Oh my God! Stuart, I'm so sorry," Debbie said.

A few of the classmates stomped out the flames burning on the floor beside Stuart. With his left eye swollen and chin burned, Stuart slowly rose and looked directly at Debbie and uttered, "Last call for alcohol. I'm done. Get everyone out of here."

CHAPTER 13

A Tribute to Angels Leads to Inappropriate Goat Stories

After the last class member left Stuart's infamous gathering, Phoebe called LaToya to pick up Debbie, and then she brought Stuart to the emergency room. He was fine. The unsuccessful event planner's left eye was swollen, and he had a minor burn on his chin. Although Stuart was appreciative of Phoebe's help, he was very distant to her. The one night that he wanted validation turned into a morning of mortification.

Phoebe asked Stuart if he was okay. He told her that he would be fine and thanked her once again for her help. Stuart got out of the truck and walked to his front door. Phoebe backed out of Stuart's driveway and drove down Bayou Rapides Road. On her way back to her suite, Phoebe ignored her phone calls from Debbie and LaToya. She speculated that the two were chowing down at the Pitt Grill and they wanted her to meet them. Phoebe's prediction was accurate. She felt badly for Stuart during the entire drive to the Hotel Bentley.

It was nine o'clock on Sunday morning and the last day of all the reunion mess. Phoebe was still in bed and felt refreshed because she actually got in seven hours of sleep. It was a bittersweet day for her because Garrett and eleven other classmates who had passed on would be honored at a special Mass held for the class of '83 at the high school chapel. Stuart had worked extremely hard on the ceremony. It took him several months to get photos and home videos from the families of his deceased colleagues. Stuart hired Arceneaux Productions, the best production company in central Louisiana, to produce a touching video that paid tribute to those who had departed. He also spent a small fortune on flowers by Rick Ferguson to make sure the observance would definitely be one his follow students would never forget.

Phoebe, who looked gorgeous in her black, sleeveless dress, pulled up to the Rachel's humble double-wide. Both John John and Debbie, dressed in their Sunday's best, were on the front porch, or as John John would say, "Their redneck veranda." As Phoebe drove up in Debbie's truck, John John was sashaying around as if he were a GQ model working the runway. It was rare that the big man ever had on a coat and tie. Debbie was spraying her whole head with hairspray while laughing at her plump bundle of fun prancing like a peacock. Phoebe got out the truck and smiled as she looked at John John strutting his stuff.

"Howdy, Phoebe! I bet you've never seen a finer man!" John John shouted. Phoebe continued to grin as she shook her head no.

"Hey, Phoebe cakes, we're ready!" Debbie yelled. Phoebe tossed the keys to John John, and all three got into the truck. Phoebe, sitting in the middle, was squished between the rather large rumps of the two lovebirds. John John noticed that Phoebe was uncomfortable.

He looked at Debbie and joked, "Someone has completely ignored the calorie content listed on the back of their Lean Cuisine box."

As Debbie laughed at her husband's remark, John John started the pickup, and the full-size couple, along with their petite friend, headed off to Menard High School.

When they arrived, the school parking lot was half full, which indicated that Stuart's memorial had a decent turnout. John John parked along the side of a white BMW. It was Aaron Flynn and his wife, Jill. Debbie didn't notice that the woman she wanted to kill the night before was standing right beside the truck. She was too busy looking in the mirror, touching up her lipstick. Phoebe saw Jill and said softly to herself, "Oh please, God, not today."

Debbie turned to the side and realized that the Flynns were right next to her. John John politely demanded his wife get out of the truck and be a Christian. Debbie told him to go to hell and then opened the door. Jill was surprised to see her. Aaron, a tall, slender, pretty boy, stood in front of his wife as if protecting her from an angry momma bear. Debbie walked up to the timid couple, looked at Aaron, and uttered, "Hey, Mr. Lawyer-Man. You look just as good in person as you do stretched out on that billboard ad."

"That's right. I am an attorney, and you're lucky that I'm not slapping you with a huge lawsuit," Aaron replied.

"I understand you're defending your wife, and if you don't mind, I'd like to take this time to apologize to her," requested Debbie.

Aaron looked at Jill, and she nodded her head okay. He then walked over to John John and stood next to him. Both men had their arms crossed as they waited for their lovely wives to make up.

Phoebe saw Michael and Christy Sury (Garrett's parents). She didn't waste any time running over to her in-laws to avoid a possible confrontation between the Rachels and the Flynns.

Jill's head was slightly shaking from nerves as she waited for Debbie to speak. Debbie grinned at the Nervous Nellie and said, "Jill, I'm very sorry for my behavior last night."

"I'm not a psychiatrist, but you may need to get help with your anger management," Jill replied.

"Bourbon does that to me, especially when I hear others babbling bullshit about my friends. But let's just leave it alone. Shall we?" Debbie suggested.

Debbie put her hand out for Jill to shake, and Jill obliged.

After the two shook hands, Jill felt brave and asked Debbie if she wished to hug it out. Debbie graciously told her no.

When the men saw that the women had resolved their issue, Aaron laughed and nudged John John, then said, "I can't figure out these petty-minded women."

"Must be the season of the witch," replied John John.

Aaron had an odd look on his face while trying to make sense of John John's comment.

The chapel looked beautiful. Stuart, with a black left eye and a bandage on his chin, along with his classmate, Danielle Myers, a blonde, natural beauty, did a wonderful job making the special ceremony happen. Back in the day, Danielle was known as the queen of the bikini contests, which were held every Saturday night during the summer of 1982 at the Light House Bar. Danielle had become a nun. She taught religion at Menard High. Father Stephen Morris, a tall, handsome male, who was also a classmate of Danielle and Stuart, was standing up front at the podium waiting for silence. When the chatting stopped, Father Morris began with his sermon.

As Father Morris delivered his sermon, Stuart and Danielle were standing off to the left side of him. John John and Dylan were sitting beside each other in the front pew, along with Debbie, Phoebe, and Garrett's parents. They were listening intensely to Father Morris's dynamic speech about how each of the classmates who had gone on to a better place played such a significant part of everyone's lives. The heartfelt address made everyone in the chapel realize how losing loved ones enhanced the positive powers within. All through the meaningful speech, Dylan stared at Stuart, hoping that Stuart would look at him and give him a wink or some other gesture to let him know that his rapid departure the night before had been forgotten. Stuart did not respond. He was very much familiar with Dylan's work.

After Father Morris wrapped up the sermon, he introduced Stuart and Danielle. They walked up to the podium, and Stuart gave a presentation about the video he and Danielle had produced. Stuart directed the audience to look at the huge, flat-screen television and requested that the lights be dimmed. The video played, and it was a phenomenal tribute to Garrett and the other eleven departed classmates.

There was not a dry eye in the chapel. The tearful crowd applauded when each of the honorees were introduced, followed by their back stories being told by way of running footage of precious photos and clips from old home movies.

The video tribute was a major success. The work of Stuart, Danielle, and Arceneaux Productions received a standing ovation. After the prolonged applause, Danielle announced that the reception would be held in the gym.

Inside the school gymnasium, tables and chairs were set up with a divine flower arrangement on each table. The food, cratered by Robbie G's Seafood, was displayed buffet-style on a long table. Father Morris, Stuart, and Danielle were standing at the entrance, greeting people as they came in. Stuart appeared distracted. Although he was pleasant and thankful to all for complimenting his video project, Stuart was sad. His failed marriage combined with the lack of concern from his close friends had dispirited his heart.

Phoebe was the only one who Stuart greeted. He avoided Debbie, Dylan, and John John by giving other classmates his full attention. Dylan and John John could detect Stuart's cold shoulder. Debbie, on the other hand, was clueless of Stuart's behavior as she was having an in-depth conversation with Ricky (a.k.a. Rebecca Vercher). She was more concerned with how the artificial penis was added in a sex change procedure than Stuart's hurt feelings.

Stuart was talking with Rita Howard. Rita graduated from the class of '85, and she was there to pay tribute to her late husband, Jim. Jim died six years ago. He was struck by lightning while coon hunting in Bastrop, Louisiana. Rita was a short, stocky woman. She was wearing a coonskin cap, a camouflage skirt, and a sweatshirt with a photo of a squirrel on it. The quote embroidered on her shirt read: *You Had Me At Let's Go Hunting.*

John John walked up to his buddy and Rita. He looked at Rita and said, "Is this Miss Rita Howard or Davey Crockett in drag?" Stuart turned away as Rita gave John John a hug. John John asked Rita why she and her mother hadn't been in Johnny Boy's Bistro for quite some time.

"Ya know, Mother has irritable bowel syndrome," Rita explained.

"Oh, I feel her pain," interrupted John John.

"Well, your menu is inappropriate for Mother's constant constipation. So, we've been going to the Golden Corral. Speaking of Mother, I better go check and see that she's not sneakin' any fried foods from that there buffet table," stated Rita.

Rita then looked at Stuart and said, "God bless you for having this wonderful memorial service for your classmates and hunter widows like me."

As Rita darted toward the food, John John and Stuart looked at each other. Stuart knew that John John was going to make a joke about his black eye and burnt chin.

"You don't look half as bad as I usually do after receiving an ass whippin' from Debbie," John John said to Stuart.

"Gee, how lucky can you get?" replied Stuart.

John John realized that Stuart was not in a joking mood. Stuart excused himself by telling John John that he had to settle up with the caterer from Robbie G's Seafood. John John tried to tease Stuart about using another restaurant to cater the event, but Stuart wouldn't budge. He walked away from his old pal without even saying good-bye.

As John John watched his annoyed buddy walk, he said himself, "He's pissed."

Meanwhile, Debbie and Dylan were in line at the buffet table. In front of Debbie was Carol Harris. Carol, a lanky, unattractive brunette with a rather large nose, was a medical psychiatrist. Carol turned to Debbie and complained, "They really didn't cater to vegetarians like me."

"Well you could pick the pork out of the beans and make yourself a coleslaw sandwich," snarled Debbie.

"Debbie, you're hiding a lot of anger by protecting yourself with that comedic shield of yours," Carol stated.

"Is this where the big-shot therapist from Bunkie, Louisiana, is gonna analyze me? The jolly, fat woman from Alexandria?" asked Debbie.

"Your actions last night were unacceptable; you really may want to seek help," suggested Carol.

Dylan giggled while waiting for Debbie's response to Dr. Carol's suggestion. Debbie gave her plate full of fried seafood and smoked meats to Dylan to hold and then looked at the Cajun psychoanalyst directly in her eyes, pointed in her face, and replied, "Who in the hell do you think you're talking to? Do you not remember? I was in all the same honors classes with you all through high school, and if my memory serves me right, I made better grades than you."

Debbie looked at Dylan and stated, "Oh God, I'm startin' to sound like Stuart."

She looked back over at the stunned shrink and said, "I was defending my friend last night, just like I defended you our freshmen year when the rumor was that you were caught being aroused by a billy goat at your grandpa's farm in Evangeline Parish."

"You're atrocious!" Carol shouted at Debbie. Carol then stormed off.

Debbie turned to Dylan, took her plate back, and said, "Well, I'm waitin' on you to tell me how screwed up I am."

Dylan placed his arm around Debbie and said, "Debbie, don't worry about her. She's just a confused vegan in our meat-lover's pizza world. By the way, did you see the strange look on her face when she saw the celery stuffed with goat cheese?"

Debbie and Dylan both burst out in laughter.

Phoebe, finally getting away from all her loving classmates who had nothing but kind things to say about Garrett, was able to talk with Stuart. She thanked him for his hard work and also reminded him about Norma's dinner party, which started at seven. Stuart told her he would be there, and then he hugged her. Phoebe knew Stuart was embarrassed about his appearance. Before they could actually end their conversation, more classmates came up to Phoebe and shared their wonderful memories of Garrett. The interruption couldn't have come at a better time. It was Stuart's chance to escape from having to see and talk with anyone else, particularly Debbie and Dylan. His mission was accomplished. No one knew that Elvis (a.k.a. Stuart) had left the building.

In the school parking lot, Dylan suggested to John John that both of them needed to check on Stuart. The men were aware that they had disappointed their cantankerous chum. John John told Debbie and Phoebe that he was going to go with Dylan to see about Stuart. The ladies had no problem with John John and Dylan's kind gesture. Debbie and Phoebe informed the men that they were going home to take a nap before they all went over to Norma's. In fact, the last sentence to come out of Phoebe's mouth was, "You two better be on time for dinner tonight." Dylan and John John promised they would, and the southern gentlemen and ladies went their separate ways.

CHAPTER 14

Fandango, Done Country-Boy Style

Stuart, still dressed in a coat and tie from the memorial ceremony, was sitting in an oversized chair in the middle of the dance floor of his over-the-top playroom. He was drinking a stout vodka and tonic in a thirty-two-ounce LSU Tiger glass as he watched the movie *Fandango* on the largest flat screen of the many televisions that were hung throughout his bar.

Fandango came out in 1985, and it was the first film released where Kevin Costner had a lead role. The movie took place in 1971. It was about five college pals who took off on their last road trip the night of their graduation. The five young men left their frat house on the University of Texas campus in Austin and headed off to Mexico to dig up a magnum of Dom Perignon champagne that they buried during their heyday of youth and freedom. The spontaneous joyride to their past was obviously an escape to avoid the Vietnam War, a wedding, and just growing up in general. Stuart fell in love with the movie the first time he watched it, which was in his dorm room back in 1986. During his college years, Stuart was told on several occasions that he had a strong resemblance to Kevin Costner. Stuart could still remember when and where women told him that he looked like the handsome actor. He bought the VHS version of the motion picture and brought it over to Dylan's condo for him and John John to view on Thanksgiving Eve of 1987. The men felt *Fandango* was a decent movie, and there were some scenes that reminded Dylan and John John of themselves. Clearly, Stuart felt differently. He believed that *Fandango* was the story of their lives. He tried making it a tradition for him and his two best friends to watch *Fandango* every Thanksgiving Eve, but the mandatory meetings failed after two years. John John and Dylan thought it was ridiculous to watch a video every year where they were assigned to be the characters in Stuart's fictional recollection.

Stuart remained seated on his throne in the center of his royal dance floor of false hopes. He had the TV remote in his hand and was repeatedly rewinding back to an essential scene of his favorite film. It was the part of the film where Kevin Costner's character, Gardner Barnes, asked Judd Nelson's character, Phil Hicks, if he had ever been in love. When Phil told Gardner that he didn't know, Gardner said, "Of course you know. If you ever thought you loved a woman, you loved her … That's all love is—mostly thoughts." Stuart felt that the line from Kevin Costner's mouth was the most profound statement he had ever heard.

As the king of sentimental flashbacks continued to play the (Have you ever been in love?) scene over and over, Dylan and John John snuck in. Stuart left the door unlocked, and he had the volume up so loud that he was unaware that his two devious friends had entered his big-ticket dungeon of doom.

When Dylan and John John entered, they saw Stuart watching *Fandango* on the big screen. Stuart's back was turned away from the entrance of his bar. Right away, the intruders recognized Stuart's sappy memory of male bonding caught on film.

"Oh my God, he's watching *Fandango*," Dylan whispered to John John.

"This is gonna be one long afternoon," John John whispered back.

As the two strolled toward the dance floor to comfort their disheartened buddy, John John was oblivious to how spectacular Stuart's party mansion was. Stuart had no reaction whatsoever when his two friends walked in front of him.

"Okay, let's get this over with. I'm a selfish whore, and John John is just selfish," Dylan said to Stuart. Stuart didn't reply as he continued to stare at the screen.

John John grabbed the remote from Stuart's hand and then lectured, "All righty then, I'm takin' the shortcut from Dr. Phil's remedy of how to fix the relationship between three egotistical dicks." John John fast-forwarded the movie until all five main charters, who call themselves the Groovers, were all in the same scene. He paused on Dorman, who was the big and silent Groover, and said, "This guy is me, right? The token fat guy with not much to say." John John waited for Stuart's reaction and didn't get one.

He then fast-forwarded to Lester Griffin, the Groover that was passed out during the whole journey, and said, "See this guy? He's supposed to be Jeremy Armstrong, ya know, the fella that we only let hang out with us because he would steal us Old Crow from his daddy's liquor store … I wonder what ever happened to that drunk enabler?"

Stuart remained silent as Dylan remarked, "Gee, John John, I wonder where you learned such big words like enabler."

John John chose to ignore Dylan's sarcasm and fast-forwarded to another character on screen. He paused on Phil Hicks. Phil was the responsible, geeky Groover who felt it was time to grow up and stop playing adolescent games. Phil was definitely a follower—not a leader. Secretly, John John and Dylan always felt that Stuart was the Phil Hicks out of their clique, but John John said that Garrett was this borderline-loser character to appease Stuart because he knew that Stuart honestly thought that he was Gardner Barnes, the cool Groover with the lost soul played by Kevin Costner. John John blew smoke up Stuart's behind by basically assuring him that he was the Kevin Costner of their close-knit tribe. Suddenly, Dylan interrupted John John's idiotic pitch to butter up Stuart.

"Wait, wait, I'm the Kevin Costner Groover! I'm the lone wolf … the king of corruption … the mystery man afraid of love! Stuart was the wimpy follower—not Garrett. Garrett was the Groover who was madly in love and believed the only other Groover who would be competition for him, was me … Kevin-freakin-Costner!" Dylan shouted.

"Damn it to hell, Dylan, work with me here!" John John yelled back.

Stuart stood up and announced, "I've had enough of you two patronizing me for one day."

"And I'm tired of feeding your bullshit. Hey look, Stuart, I apologize for my wife's right hook and for me not being here for you last night. And I'm sure Dylan is sorry for picking up a loose woman, who apparently was blind, and leaving you out to dry," John John said.

"Go to hell!" Dylan shouted at John John.

John John and Dylan saw a tiny smile coming from Stuart's roughed-up face, and then John John said, "Stuart, we're sorry. Come on and be a man, accept our apology, and give your brothers from several different mothers some love."

John John and Dylan extended their arms for Stuart to give them a hug, and he did. While the three men embraced, John John got a good look at Stuart's bar.

"Jesus H Christ! This is the damn Bayview Yacht Club!" John John yelled.

Dylan and Stuart laughed at John John, who was running to the bar. John John couldn't believe that Stuart had six types of domestic beer on tap. He took a pitcher and filled it with each type of beer. He grabbed three mugs and shouted, "Let's get this male-bonding crapola out of the way! Y'all come sit here at this fine-ass bar and let's end the world's problems by playin' an old-fashioned game of quarters! Come on now! Let's loosen up our ties and take our funeral jackets off!" John John ordered as he took his sports coat off and threw it on the floor.

Stuart and Dylan took off their blazers and placed them on the chair that Stuart was sitting in, and then they both walked up to the bar. Stuart couldn't believe that just the three men of their once tight-knit alliance were getting ready to relive a young gangster moment, while Dylan was apprehensive about John John's pubescent problem-solving solutions. Stuart and Dylan sat down at the bar as John John set up for the quarters game.

"What we're gonna do, ladies, is each time one of us bounces the quarter in this here glass, you choose the one you want to drink, but before the chosen one guzzles the brew, he has to tell the appointee why he has a problem with him," John John explained.

"I don't think Dr. Phil would approve of this ice-breaking tactic," Dylan uttered.

John John took a quarter out of his pocket and shouted, "Let the problem solving begin!" He bounced the coin into the glass of beer and told Stuart to share his number-one drawback with him.

"You're irresponsible and extremely immature," replied Stuart.

As Stuart downed the glass of beer, John John said, "Hey, that's two flaws; you're supposed to only mention one."

"Okay, I'll start with irresponsible. You have a horrible sense of business. Johnny Boy's Bistro at one time was the best seafood restaurant in Alexandria, but now you've turned it into a common cafeteria for future heart attack victims," Stuart stated.

"Hey, if it ain't fried and all-you-can-eat, we ain't comin' … that's our city's mantra … now, what cha got to say?" said John John.

"Your failing restaurant is suffering from a lack of creativity, consistency, and dedication, and not to mention poor management, hiring, and training skills. Shall I go on?" Stuart asked John John.

"Who the hell are you? The business manager for the Iron Chief?" barked John John.

Before Stuart could answer John John's question, Dylan said, "Besides your fried catfish, everything else is mediocre. It's as if you buy truckloads of seafood frozen dinners on the black market and then fry them all up and shovel the premade chow that's protected by a sneeze guard on your greasy buffet."

John John was flabbergasted by Dylan's option. The suffering restaurant owner grabbed the pitcher of beer, consumed every bit of it, and let out a loud belch. Stuart shook his head and said to John John, "I guess that's your response to my accusation of you being immature."

John John passed the quarter and empty glass to Dylan. He then took the empty pitcher and filled it back up with beer.

"Wait a minute, John John, aren't you supposed to have two more turns?" Dylan asked.

"Yeah, there's a three-turn limit, but I lost my chances once I downed the pitcher. So go ahead and continue your attack on me," John John ordered as he poured beer into the glass.

"Good deal," replied Dylan.

Dylan took the coin, bounced it off the counter, and missed the glass.

"Are you gonna chance it?" Stuart asked Dylan.

"No, I'm not. I've always sucked at this game," replied Dylan.

"Dylan, you've always sucked at taking chances," Stuart added.

As Dylan passed the quarter and the full glass of beer over to Stuart, John John yelled out, "This is your chance, Stuart, to deep fry Dylan's ass like you did mine!"

Stuart effortlessly bounced the coin into the glass and told Dylan to drink. After Dylan guzzled the alcohol, Stuart instructed him to pick a person and give his outlook on their major flaw. Dylan picked John John and said, "We haven't finished with John John. Tell us, Stuart, do you honestly feel John John is heading toward bankruptcy?"

"This is so like you to escape and take the focus off of you ... and yes, I feel John John is in financial trouble," answered Stuart.

"I'm switchin' to hard liquor," said John John.

Dylan glared at Stuart and asked, "Is this what you want—all three of us to tear each other apart? Is this what's gonna make you stop being a pouting, self-indulging, living-in-the-past prick?"

"Hey, it wasn't me who wanted to play this truth serum game," defended Stuart.

"This whole reunion crap has been nothing but a giant pain in my ass. I don't have time for this nonsense. There's no need for me to compete anymore, Stuart! We're all grownups now! And if you think I'm gonna sit here and participate in this absurd examination of everyone's failures, then you're even more of a bitter asshole than we all think you are! I mean, except for you, we're all middle-aged parents who are living and providing the best way we know how!" Dylan screamed.

"And how's that working for you?" asked Stuart.

"How's what working for me?" Dylan replied back.

"The parenting part of your notable speech," answered Stuart.

Dylan's face was actually turning red from anger, and before he could return an attack back to Stuart, John John roared, "Enough! Enough! This is bullshit! I should have never tried this make-amends approach induced by alcohol therapy on you two! And I'm sorry as hell!"

As John John poured himself a Jack Daniels on the rocks, Stuart looked over at Dylan and said, "I didn't mean what I said."

Dylan stared at Stuart's bruised-up face for ten seconds and replied, "No worries."

John John took a large sip of whiskey and stated, "Face it, men, we're all good people, but we're not perfect. He then grabbed two mugs for his amigos and poured each of them a beer.

After the men gulped down their cocktails, Stuart said, "Mary Beth wants a divorce."

"Yes!" shouted Dylan.

"That's dancin' words!" shrieked John John.

Stuart couldn't believe John John and Dylan's reaction to his disturbing news. He watched them run to the DJ booth to find some good music to dance to. Even though Stuart didn't receive the type of support from his two best friends that he expected, he was happy that John John and Dylan were ready to party like it was 1999. He saw that his buddies didn't know how to play the music, so he jumped off the barstool and ran over to the booth. Stuart listened to several song requests from his rowdy friends and then ordered them to the dance floor. Dylan and

John John stood in the center of the floor and waited impatiently for the music to begin. The first song that Stuart played was "Head Over Heels" by the Go-Go's. John John was amazed that the popular music video from 1984 was also playing on all the television screens throughout Stuart's over-the-top saloon.

Immediately, he and Dylan attempted to dance. Stuart, who was still in the DJ booth, couldn't stop laughing at the redneck Chubby Checker and the awkward rebel trying to take on Belinda Carlisle's (the lead singer of the Go-Go's) dance moves. As the two new-wave ballerinas made jackasses out of themselves, Stuart sprinted to the bar and filled two more pitchers of draft to bring to the ugly dance off.

It was 6:55 p.m., and for three and a half hours, the three mischievous musketeers danced to every one of their favorite pop, rock, and country songs from the seventies, eighties, and nineties. During their performance from the very selective playlist, they also managed to consume several pitchers of beer and smoke an entire pack of cigarettes. All three men were shirt-less and sweating profusely as they sat Indian-style on the dance floor and sang the last verse of "Old Man" by Neil Young. When the song ended, Stuart looked at John John's bare chest and blurted, "Damn, John John, you've got some gigantic man-boobs. Your tits are a lot bigger than Mary Beth's."

John John hid his chest with his arms and shouted, "Don't be a hater!"

As Stuart and John John playfully argued back and forth about who had the better body, Dylan grabbed an empty pitcher, stood up, and walked to the bar. While filling up the pitcher, he heard John John's cell phone ring. The men had left their phones on top of the bar while they celebrated on the dance floor. "Oh, my God!" yelled Dylan as he looked at the cell phones.

"What's wrong?" John John shouted from the dance floor.

"This is Debbie calling on your phone, and all three of us have hundreds of missed calls and texts!" Dylan shouted back.

"Well, answer it, dumb ass. She doesn't bite," John John ordered Dylan. John John looked over at Stuart and said, "She does punch, but she won't bite."

Dylan answered John John's phone, and the voice coming from the other side sounded like Charlie Brown's teacher with a strong southern twang.

"Sorry" and "okay" were the only words coming out of Dylan's mouth as Debbie ripped him a new one. Finally, she hung up, and Dylan told his grown playmates that all three of them were in big trouble.

"What did she say?" asked John John.

"She said that we're already late for Momma's dinner party, and she can't believe the three of us are trashed, and she and Phoebe are already there, and then she cussed me out some more, and the last thing she said was, she's sending someone to come pick our drunk asses up," Dylan reported.

John John looked at his watch and shouted, "Sweet Jesus, it's fifteen minutes after seven! We are late! Men, be prepared for the biggest ass whippin' of your sorry lives!"

John John snatched his and Dylan's shirts from off the dance floor and told Stuart to fix a pot of coffee or pour them all a fountain coke so that they could be somewhat sober. John John recommended that Dylan go with him to freshen up. The two rushed over to the bathroom located in the master bedroom of Stuart's house. While Dylan and John John were giving themselves a speedy sponge bath, Stuart picked up his shirt and remote from the floor and stood up. He turned on the *Fandango* DVD and fast-forwarded to the wedding scene where Kevin Costner's character was dancing with the bride, who was actually the woman that he let slip away and marry his best friend. Stuart's smile never left his face as he watched the cherished scene twice.

John John and Dylan, who had cleaned up well, entered the bar and saw Stuart watching the finale of the man flick dedicated to friendship. Before they yelled at him to get it together, they patiently waited for Stuart to finish basking in a memory of immature innocence.

Suddenly, there was a knock at the door. "Oh, no," Dylan said to John John.

"I got this. It's probably my youngest comin' to deliver us to this Last Supper. Honestly, I don't give a rat's ass who it is. Ain't nobody gonna mess with this Groover," stated John John.

John John opened the door, and it was Phoebe's cousin, LaToya, who was dressed for church, hat and all. "Good evening, gentlemen. I'm your driver, LaToya," LaToya proudly announced.

John John glared at Dylan and said, "Show her in while I run to the bathroom and hang myself."

LaToya strolled in and took a look at Stuart's lounge. "This place looks just like that old white club, the Bayou View Bar," uttered LaToya.

"You mean the Bayview," corrected Dylan.

"Whatever, I only went to Bone Shaker back in the day … ya know, the only club for us black folk," LaToya said.

Before John John or Dylan could comment on LaToya's past hot spot, Stuart, who was still shirt-less, turned to John John, LaToya, and Dylan and shouted, "Wait a minute y'all, please just be quiet for a minute and watch the ending with me."

The three walked closer to the big screen, and surprisingly, they were silent as they watched along with Stuart. It was the last five minutes of the film where the wedding reception and the journey were over and there were only two of the Groovers left from the last escape before growing up and being responsible. The scene revealed the geeky Groover, Phil, shaking hands with and saying good-bye to Dorman, the big, quiet Groover. After Dorman told Phil to have a nice life, the next scene was Kevin Costner's character, Gardner, who was standing on top of a cliff overlooking the town where the Groovers' journey ended, lifting up his beer to salute his friends. Stuart held up his beer at the same time Gardner held up his, and the credits rolled on the screen while the song "Can't Find My Way Home," sung by Blind Faith, played. Stuart, who was smiling and still holding up his mug to the screen, turned around to see the expressions on Dylan and John John's faces. He was pleasantly surprised that his buddies had just as big of a grin on their faces as he did. At that moment, Stuart could definitely feel the love from the real-life Groovers in his life.

"I guess it's time to go," Stuart suggested to John John and Dylan.

Before Dylan or John John could respond, LaToya shouted, "You three better get your asses in gear! Come on, it's time to go!" She then ordered the three Groovers to line up and start marching toward the door. As the men marched to LaToya's healthcare transportation van, LaToya, the drill sergeant, sang, "Bad boys, bad boys … Whatcha gonna do, whatcha gonna do when they come for you …"

The guilty men were sitting in the back of LaToya's van, because she would not allow any one of the three tanked-up troublemakers to sit up front with her. As Stuart put his shirt back on, LaToya popped in a gospel CD and ordered the men to buckle up and shut up. Once LaToya saw that her passive passengers were cooperating, she turned up the music and drove off.

On their way to Norma's condominium, LaToya passed Johnny Boy's Bistro and there were only four cars in the parking lot for the Sunday all-you-can-eat buffet. She turned down the music with the sinner prevention message and yelled back to John John, "Look at that! Your restaurant is sinkin' as fast as a Hoochie Mama goin' down on a NFL player."

John John looked at his fellow offenders and said, "We're being escorted to hell by an overly religious hospitality consultant."

Chapter 15

The Last of the Good Chicken Fried Steak

Norma, Phoebe, Debbie, and Phoebe's mother-in-law, Christy, were sitting at the island in the kitchen of Norma's immaculate condominium. The ladies were watching Frances, who was an ex-employee of the Piccadilly, prepare chicken fried steak.

Frances, a light-skinned, older, African American woman with dyed blonde hair, was let go from the Piccadilly Cafeteria years ago for being too stern with the customers. She had a bad habit of letting patrons know which foods were fresh and which ones were not. The immoral dietitian would also stare down overweight individuals who would order fattening food items. Her final act that caused her employment dismissal was when Rosalyn Duggan, who was president of the Alexandria Newcomers Club at the time, requested another dinner roll. Rosalyn, a rather large lady, was mortified when Frances refused to give her a second roll. Frances told the pleasantly plump woman that she didn't even need the first roll to begin with. The rejection for the demand of more yeast and butter given by a fat, famished, well-known Welcome Wagon woman triggered an early retirement for the chicken fried steak specialist. Norma knew that Frances's steak was definitely a favorite of Phoebe's father-in-law, Dr. Sury, and Debbie. In fact, the only meat that Debbie wanted on the menu for her small wedding reception held at the Piccadilly was Miss Frances's chicken fried steak.

As the ladies watched Frances load the last batch of the chicken fried steak onto a platter, Debbie said, "Now, that's the way to do chicken fried steak. My God in heaven, they're as big as a city bus hubcap!"

Everyone laughed, and all of a sudden, Norma saw Loretta Lynn performing on her kitchen television. The music video of Loretta was from *The Best of Country's Cuties* DVD that Christy had brought to Norma as a gift for hosting the dinner party in honor for her late son, Garrett. Loretta was singing her 1971 hit titled "One's on the Way." Norma scrambled to find the remote. When she realized that the remote was actually in the pocket of her apron, she took it out and turned the volume up. Immediately, Norma, the eccentric honky-tonk fan, sang with the First Lady of country music.

Debbie grabbed two large spoons and gave Norma one to use as a pretend microphone. They both sang as loudly as they could along with Loretta.

Suddenly, Kris entered the kitchen and saw the Sweethearts of the Rodeo wannabes attempting to carry a tone. Kris, who was wearing a vintage T-shirt with the theatrical release poster of the movie *A Star Is Born*, starring Barbra Streisand and Kris Kristofferson (his namesake), on it, also took a large spoon and joined his mother and Debbie in the sing-along. Phoebe, Christy, and Frances enjoyed the untalented trio perform.

As the concert continued in the kitchen, Christy's husband, Michael, and Norma's ex-husband, Brent, were in the living room, oblivious to the Loretta Lynn Chicken Fried Steak Show that was going on in the next room. The two physicians were in the middle of conversation about a new drug to cure internal hemorrhoids when Steven and Lauren Jacobs entered the front door.

Steven had a bottle of red wine in his hand, and Lauren was carrying a bowl of salad and a bottle of Lilli Courtney's Delightful Palate salad dressing. It was the *Wild Mayhaw Berry*. Lilli's salad dressings were famous throughout Louisiana. Lauren was famous for bringing her own meals to Norma's dinner parties. Steven and Lauren hugged his father, Brent, and then they shook hands with Dr. Michael Sury. After they greeted both doctors, the stuffy couple headed toward the kitchen where there seemed to be an all-star karaoke blast going on.

Steven and Lauren walked in the kitchen and saw Norma, Kris, and Debbie singing their hearts out into the large spoons.

"Here in Topeka the flies are a buzzin' ... The dog is a barkin', and the floor needs a scrubbin' ... One needs a spankin', and one needs a huggin' ... Lord one's on the way ... Oh gee I hope it ain't twins again!" Norma, Debbie, and Kris all sang together.

Frances, the gifted fry cook, along with Phoebe and Christy, applauded as the amateur singers took their bows. During the ovation, Steven looked over at his superficial wife and whispered, "Well if it isn't the inbred trio performing for the common folk."

"Bingo," agreed Lauren.

The fun-loving kitchen crowd welcomed Dr. and Mrs. Steven Jacobs, and Norma politely ordered Kris to find another Loretta Lynn song on the DVD. She wanted to sing along to Loretta's controversial hit, "The Pill." Steven shook his head in disgust at his mother's request, and Lauren placed the bowl of salad on the granite countertop of the gigantic kitchen island.

Steven got a whiff of the grease the steaks were fried in and said, "Ah, there's nothing that can beat the smell of the beginning of congestive heart failure."

Nobody was listening to the condescending physician. Debbie and Norma were having an in-depth chat about how brave Loretta Lynn was to record a song about birth control, especially back in the early seventies.

Lauren didn't bother to say hello to Phoebe and Christy; right away she held out her right wrist to show the ladies her new Tiffany diamond bracelet. After the ladies complimented her new piece of jewelry, Lauren pulled Phoebe to the side and asked her what the true retail value was of the gift given to her by her generous hubby. Phoebe told the shallow doctor's wife that she made it a point to never appraise jewels during her off time.

Steven walked up to Frances and told her that he would like a scotch with a touch of water.

"That does sound good. I'd like Malibu rum and Coke myself," replied Frances.

Steven wasn't pleased with the past Piccadilly professional's remark. It was quite sad that he didn't remember Frances from his childhood when the whole family would go to the Piccadilly in MacArthur Village to eat every Sunday after church.

"Boy, you sure have changed from the pretty, little man who used to order a drumstick, mash potatoes, and green Jell-O on the children's satellite plate," Frances told Steven.

Steven didn't reply. Forgetting a lot from his innocent childhood, Steve had a bewildered look on his face as he stared at Frances. Suddenly, Norma strolled up to her befuddled son and the cafeteria legend and said, "Steven, you remember Miss Frances,"

"Yeah, I recall Miss Frances ... it took me awhile to recognize her without a hairnet on her head," answered Steven.

"I think your baby boy here has me confused with one of the wait staff at the country club or possibly an Aunt Jemima with a mixology degree," Frances said to Norma.

"Steven, you know where the liquor is. Fix yourself and your lovely wife a drink," commanded Norma.

"Ah, we brought our own wine," said Lauren.

"Of course you did," replied Norma.

Steven exited the kitchen with the bottle of wine that he and Lauren brought and went to the living room where Norma had set up a card table for a bar. Kris followed behind his oldest half-brother. As Steven prepared his and Lauren's cocktails, Kris glared at him and asked, "Why are you here?"

"What do you mean?" Steven asked.

"You don't even like anybody here ... well, except for yourself, your father, and Dr. Sury," Kris replied.

"This is ludicrous. I will not stand here and listen to false assumptions from a teenage punk!" Steven barked.

Kris stared directly into Steven's eyes and calmly said, "Your entire existence is false."

Kris walked back to the kitchen while Steven, who had a sour expression on his face, finished making his and Lauren's beverages. As he searched for the wine opener, his father and Dr. Sury were still talking about the latest medicine. All of a sudden, the doorbell rang. It was LaToya, John John, Stuart, and Dylan. LaToya darted straight for Norma's hors d'oeuvres, which consisted of bowls of Aunt Dewy's Duck and Garlic Jerky Bites, Zapp's New Orleans Kettle Style Voodoo Potato Chips, along with the leftover deli spiral delights piled on a paper Power Ranger platter. The odd combinations of munchies were placed on another card table next to the set-up bar. The hungry chauffeur grabbed

116

several cocktail napkins (with the Gilley's mechanical bull's logo printed on each one) and looked at Steven. "Hey, Doctor Jacobs, you are so much better lookin' than that foolish brother of yours," said LaToya, as she snatched a big handful of the jerky bites.

"Ah, hello," Steven replied, not having a clue who the bold church lady was.

LaToya discovered that the several napkins she grabbed were from the original Gilley's Bar when it was located in Pasadena, Texas. As she admired the rare napkins, Stuart sauntered up to her to find out what the big deal was. He looked at the napkin in LaToya's hand and said, "Gilley's, the honky-tonk that became famous for being in the movie *Urban Cowboy*."

"Aren't you just the walking dictionary of useless knowledge," replied LaToya.

"I'd have to say that *Urban Cowboy* is probably my favorite Debra Winger film," stated Stuart.

"Who the hell is Debra Weiner?" LaToya inquired.

Stuart chose to ignore LaToya's mispronunciation of the movie star's last name and asked, "You don't know her from *An Officer and a Gentleman* or *Terms of Endearment?*"

While LaToya struggled to remember who one of the biggest actresses of the eighties was, Steven was in disbelief that he was actually listening to this senseless discussion between his brother's friend with the battered face and the large stranger with a duck jerky compulsion.

"Oh! I know who Debra Weiner is!" shouted LaToya.

"It's Winger, woman! Not Weiner!" corrected Stuart.

"I remember her! She played Drusilla, Lynda Carter's younger sister, in *Wonder Woman*," LaToya proudly announced.

"Yes, LaToya, you are correct, Debra Winger was Wonder Girl," Stuart cheered.

"Well, now that we've got that straight, I need to go to the kitchen and find some Food Club paper towels or somethin' cause I sure don't want to waste any of these valuable napkins," LaToya said.

Steven's facial expression remained sour, as if he was constipated, while he watched LaToya walk to the kitchen. Steven looked at Stuart. Stuart smiled and winked at the uptight gynecologist with his black eye and threw out another film title, *Guess Who's Coming to Dinner*. Steven remained speechless and sickened while he observed Stuart strolling to the kitchen.

Steven then looked over to the living room where Dylan and John John appeared intoxicated as they took turns hugging his fellow physicians in the condo. "God, help me," he mumbled to himself as he watched John John give Michael Sury a bear hug.

Meanwhile, back in the kitchen, Kris and all the ladies (except for Lauren) greeted Stuart and LaToya. Norma told LaToya that she was so happy that she would be joining them for dinner, and she also thanked the tolerant taxi driver for safely delivering her three mischievous men. LaToya conveyed to Norma that she was happy to be invited. Frances walked up to LaToya and gave her a hug. The two attended the same church. Frances recognized Stuart and said, "Hamburger steak, mac and cheese, two hushpuppies, and red Jell-O,"

Stuart was not only impressed that Frances remembered him, but he was even more awestruck that she recalled his favorite Piccadilly meal when he was a child. Frances noticed Stuart's face and asked, "What happened to that beautiful face of yours, my baby?"

"Debbie would be the one to answer that million-dollar question," replied Stuart.

Frances looked at Debbie, who was smirking, and then looked back over to Stuart and asked, "You mean to tell me that cornbread-fed heifer hammered you like you were a cheatin' husband?"

"It was an honest mistake," answered Stuart.

"That's why I'm lettin' this joker off the hook for bein' so late. Now the other two stooges in the living room won't be sittin' down for a long time!" shouted Debbie.

Everyone laughed, and suddenly Kris placed his arm around Stuart and said, "I'm sorry to hear about the split from your disdainful mate and slow-witted stepson. Believe me, Stewy, it's for the best. I'm not sure about your ex old lady, but her son is definitely heading toward an insane asylum for social vegetables."

Stuart removed Kris's arm from around his shoulder and cynically replied, "Thank you, Kris, for your sincere condolences."

"Ah, Kris, honey, why don't you go up to your room. I'm sure there's an underprivileged village or something you can blow up on one of those video games," suggested Norma.

Kris grinned, winked at his mother, and spontaneously hugged Stuart. During the embrace, Kris whispered into Stuart's ear, "You're gonna be okay." Stuart was touched by the amusing adolescent's gesture. Kris obeyed Norma and left the kitchen.

When Kris arrived in the living room, he ran into Dylan and greeted, "Hey, my brother from the same mother."

"Just the man I want to see. How are Phoebe and Debbie? Do the evil sisters want us dead or alive?" Dylan asked his younger brother. Kris didn't have a chance to reply because of Steven's interference.

"The evil sisters, don't you mean the enabling supporters?" Steven asked Dylan.

"And there it is, the anticipation is over from the man of the hour to spread joy and love to all of us disappointing underdogs," snapped Dylan.

"For God's sake, grow up, Dylan," replied Steven.

Kris looked at Dylan and said, "I've already asked our Honorable Brother Steven here why he feels the need to even grace us with his blissful manifestation."

Dylan snickered at Kris's remark while Steven glared at his youngest sibling and asked, "Shouldn't you be in your bedroom sexting a slut or hacking into somebody's computer?"

Kris didn't respond to Steven's rude comment. He looked at Dylan and said, "As much as I would like to hang out with the cultivated physicians and the lost frat boys, I really do need to finish up some homework. Call me when dinner is ready."

"Will do," said Dylan.

As Kris ran upstairs, Dylan left Steven and strolled over to his father, Dr. Sury, and John John. Steven consumed his last sip of scotch as he watched his distant brother walk away.

John John was in the middle of explaining why he felt the red dye in the cinnamon liquor from the night before last was the cause of his severe nausea and life-threatening diarrhea. Dylan giggled to himself, knowing that the doctors, who were tolerantly listening to John John's line of crap, didn't believe that red dye had anything to do with the big man's overindulgence of alcohol.

While John John was struggling to persuade Dr. Jacobs and Dr. Sury that the color of the Hot Damn shots activated his mysterious virus, Steven was at the bar, pouring another scotch.

All of a sudden, LaToya, who hadn't had enough chips and dried meat bites, joined him. He witnessed the famished female empty both bowls of snacks and sarcastically mentioned, "I think you accidently missed a crumb out of the bowl of chips."

LaToya snatched the last potato morsel and said, "Thank you. Hey, you wouldn't know how to fix a Beyoncé, would you?" Steven looked at her as if she was crazy, and LaToya explained, "It's a Shirley Temple but with more fruit in it."

"I don't know what you're talking about," replied Steven.

"Oh hell, Doc, just pour some cherry juice into a Sprite and add a lot of cherries. Jesus, you can perform surgery, but you don't know how fix a lady a fruity drink!" LaToya fussed.

Meanwhile, back in the kitchen, Frances insisted that Debbie stay away while she was taking out the last pan of cornbread sticks (Debbie had managed to put away three of the Piccadilly's most popular bread item). Phoebe, Stuart, Christy, and Lauren were sitting at the island. The ladies (excluding Lauren) were complimenting Stuart on his hard work with the ceremony for the departed. Norma waited for Christy's final words of gratitude to Stuart then announced, "All right, everyone, it's time to eat. We're going buffet style tonight."

Lauren's fresh green salad appeared to be out of place next to Miss Frances's chicken fried steak, white gravy, mash potatoes, fried okra, fried pickles, fried green beans, cornbread sticks, and the two three-layer red velvet cakes. The uptight doctor's wife saw the Power Rangers paper plates and napkins placed at the end of the kitchen island and asked Norma, "Are we eating on paper plates this evening?"

"Oh yes, I found them yesterday. They're left over from Kris's birthday party when he turned seven," answered Norma.

"It's a shame you didn't find the Power Ranger piñata to go with your paper party items," proposed Lauren.

"That reminds me, Lauren, I did find a gift for you that I've been meaning to give to you," Norma stated.

Debbie elbowed Phoebe and whispered, "Hopefully, it's a personality." Phoebe agreed by giving Debbie a wink followed by a giggle.

Norma took off her apron and then said to Lauren, "I know how much you love southern authors, and I'm still enjoying that book you give me many years ago by Paul Aertker …"

"Paul went to school with us. I just bought book one in his *Crime Traveler series*, which reminds me I need to get it back from my soon-to-be ex-wife," interrupted Stuart.

"Lauren gave me his first book that he and his wife wrote. It was right after she and Steven got married," stated Norma.

"Was it an action-adventure?" Stuart questioned.

"No, the tittle is *Write After the Wedding*. It's a clever etiquette book, basically explaining the correct way to write thank-you notes," clarified Norma.

Debbie, once again, eyed Phoebe and mumbled, "That figures."

Lauren noticed that Norma was wearing the green, chic blouse and black leggings that she bought for her at Kathy Ward Apparel last year for Christmas. She said, "I'm so glad that you're wearing the outfit I gave you."

"It's one of my favorites," replied Norma.

"I guess her movie theme costumes must be at the cleaners," joked Debbie.

Norma told everyone that she would be right back and headed upstairs to get Lauren's gift. As Norma left, LaToya entered the kitchen.

"Are we about ready to eat? Them Aunt Dewy Jerky bites and chips ain't cuttin' it for me. This big woman is hungry," broadcasted LaToya.

"Amen, sister!" agreed Debbie.

Lauren looked at Christy Sury, who was sitting next to her at the island, and asked, "Is it just me or does anyone else feel that it's rather bizarre to have a lovely antique table in the dining room and we're going to be eating on old, kiddy tableware? I know for a fact that Norma has beautiful china."

"I don't feel it's bizarre at all … tonight, we're all just dining in Norma Jean Dubois style. And I love it," replied Christy.

While Debbie stole another cornbread stick and shoved it in her mouth, John John and Dylan apprehensively entered the kitchen. John John tried to hide behind Dylan when Debbie and Phoebe spotted the late birds.

Everyone chuckled at the cowardly lions, except for Lauren and Debbie. John John realized that his wife's mouth was full of bread, and he roared, "Thank you, Jesus! Her mouth is occupied with a heavenly corn stick, and she's unable to chew the hell out of my sorry ass!"

"Yeah, that's the only stick that will be in her mouth for quite some time," blurted out Frances.

Everybody was shocked by Miss Frances's statement. Lauren, who was extremely offended, stood up and rushed out of the kitchen while the rest of the odd crowd continued to laugh.

LaToya pointed her finger at Frances and then shouted, "Gurrrl, talkin' dat filth and you went to church today!"

"Which reminds me, it's Pastor Rodger and Janet Williams's anniversary at the church tonight, and I need to get out of here." Frances took off her apron as she asked LaToya, "Are you goin' tonight?"

"Nah," replied LaToya.

"I'm not surprised. They're only serving punch at the reception," said Frances.

Out of everyone in the kitchen, John John laughed the hardest at Miss Frances's accurate observation of LaToya's desire to eat anything as long as it was free. He put his arm around the retired fry chef and declared, "I love this woman!"

Back in the living room, Dr. Jacobs and Dr. Sury were having a serious discussion about Obama Care while Lauren was pleading with Steven to leave the disastrous gathering.

"Maybe if I would have put deep fried pork cracklins in the salad instead of rye croutons, your family and their vulgar acquaintances would be a lot more hospitable to me," Lauren said to Steven.

"Believe me, sweetheart, we're not going to stay long," Steven assured his wife, who was obviously drowning in misery.

Steven kissed Lauren and took her by the hand to lead her back to the kitchen. As the perturbed couple entered, Norma had a pink book in her hands, waiting to give it to Laruen. She gave the book to her uncomfortable daughter-in-law and said, "I got this for you months ago."

Lauren thanked her generous mother-in-law and read the title out loud, "*Secrets of the Southern Belle: How to Be Nice, Work Hard, Look Pretty, Have Fun, and Never Have an Off Moment* by Phaedra Parks ... oh, you shouldn't have, Norma,"

"Phaedra Parks, the Real Housewife of Atlanta's Phaedra Parks?" shouted LaToya.

"That's her! She was signing books at Barns and Noble when I was in Atlanta for a Roy Clark Fan Club meeting," Norma proudly answered.

LaToya ran over to Laruen and hollered, "I love Phaedra! I have her stun gun and all her Donkey Booty workout videos!"

John John glared at LaToya's behind and then said, "Good Lord, woman, why the hell do you need a workout tape to make your ass even bigger than it already is?"

LaToya ignored John John and asked Lauren if she would be willing to sell her gift from Norma. Lauren looked at Norma to see if she would have problem with her giving LaToya the book and then expressed, "I'm really not in the habit of re-gifting, but since you seem to adore the author …"

"Oh please, I would love for LaToya to keep the book. The guide on southern manners can be her tip for picking up my three tanked-up musketeers and delivering them to us safely.

I don't think it would be too difficult to change the name from Lauren to LaToya where Ms. Parks signed the book," insisted Norma.

"Thank you so much, Miss Norma," cheered LaToya.

"Oh, it's my pleasure, honey," Norma told LaToya, and then she announced, "All right, everybody, thank Miss Frances for preparing her famous chicken fried steak, and then it's time to eat!"

Dylan, John John, and Stuart had red eyes as they were coming down from their major buzz. All three men said thank you to Frances as if she were their kindergarten teacher. As Norma called Kris, Dr. Sury, and her ex-husband, Brent, to dinner, the rest of the guests formed a line, took a Power Ranger plate, and started loading up. During the help-yourself buffet activity, Lauren and Steven stood back and observed the adult trick-or-treaters savor in glory from the southern fried feast.

CHAPTER 16

Home-Style Humiliation

In Norma's dining room where a beautiful hand-cut, crystal chandelier hung above the long elegant table, which was an heirloom of Norma's that Lauren had been eyeing ever since she married into the Jacobs family, everyone (except for Steven and Lauren) was seated with their paper plate piled high with deep-fried steak and batter-fried vegetables in front of them. A small serving of salad and half of a cornbread stick were placed on Lauren and Steven's cartoon hero dish. Norma was sitting at one end of the table, and Kris was seated at the other. On the right side of the table sat Dr. Brent Jacobs, Dr. Michael Sury, Christy Sury, Phoebe, Stuart, and Dylan. Sitting on the left side were John John, Debbie, La Toya, Lauren, and Steven.

Norma held up her wine glass filled with Miss Scarlett's Sweet Muscadine and made a toast. "I want thank all of you for being here tonight, especially Michael and Christy, because without you all, we wouldn't of had the pleasure of having your amazing son, Garrett, in our lives." Everyone held up their glasses in honor of Phoebe's late husband. Phoebe and Christy's eyes teared up.

John John looked up and toasted, "Here's to you, my brother, better known as the Cane River Cheetah. You'd love what we're gettin' ready to dig into. Hell, the only thang missin' from this Piccadilly feast is your favorite chocolate doughnut from Harlow's—"

"I prefer Shipley do-nuts, myself," interrupted La Toya.

John John gave La Toya a dirty look and continued, "Please excuse the cuisine commentator over there who needs to shut her pie hole—"

Then Debbie interrupted her babbling husband by finishing his toast, "I'm not gonna sit here and watch this chicken fried steak that I've been dreaming about for years get cold by listing to Punch and Judy debate about freakin' damn doughnuts! We all love Garrett and miss him dearly, but it's time to eat!"

Norma, Phoebe, Stuart, Dylan, Christy, and Michael giggled at Debbie's remark, and then Kris yelled, "Amen! Let's eat!"

Ten minutes into Norma's farewell banquet for Garrett, Christy Sury took a break from the home-cooked meal to monitor her deceased son's very alive companions in action. First, she looked across the table to the right where LaToya was begging Debbie to retell her story about being kicked off the *Momma Swap* reality show. Debbie was shaking her head no as her mouth was full of fried okra and green beans followed by a cornbread stick.

Christy then glanced over at John John, who was sitting next to Debbie. Just as his wife, John John was stuffing himself like a Thanksgiving turkey as he listened to Norma talking about how wonderful the movie *The Sterile Cuckoo* was, which she had watched the night before while waiting for Kris to get in. Supposedly, Kris was attending a classmate's birthday party, but he was actually at the boating dock on Kincaid Lake, making out all night with his girlfriend, Sky. That night would be one of the last nights that the two young lovebirds could be together because Sky was arrested a few weeks ago for shoplifting at the Acadiana Mall. She was caught trying to steal a box of Nicki Minaj's Pink Friday perfume at the cosmetics counter at Macy's. Kris's shoplifting sweetie was court ordered to attend an all-girls juvenile delinquent facility for three months. Kris did confess to his mother what really happened that night, and Norma let him use her theater makeup to cover up his hickeys. After Norma went into detail about Liza Minnelli's incredible performance in the coming-of-age film, John John swallowed his last bite of steak and told Norma, "I'm not too familiar with Lisa Minnelli's work, but I did like her in the movie *Arthur*."

Stuart, who had been eavesdropping on Norma and John John's conversation from across the table, corrected John John. "It's not Lisa—it's Liza with a Z. I mean she's *only* an Academy Award–winning actress."

"Well, excuse my lack of theatrical knowledge on gay icons!" barked John John.

"Speakin' of heroines admired by homosexuals, I really need to start sending out thank-you cards to all my daughter-in-law's family who gave my baby girl wedding gifts," added Debbie. She then looked at Norma and said, "I may need to borrow that book on proper manners that your daughter-in-law gave ya." Norma chuckled at Debbie's request.

Lauren, with an unpleasant sneer on her face, said, "My goodness, Debbie, I did not know your daughter was married."

"Oh yeah, it was a small ceremony, and instead of a reception, we all went to the Bunkie Corn Festival," Debbie replied.

"I love the corn festival. I remember when Frankie performed there. As an alternative for cigarette lighters being lit, the crowd held up ears of corn to show their appreciation for my wonderful man's performance," Norma bragged.

Christy Sury was surprised that the conversations among the others continued, even though shade was spontaneously being thrown throughout the dinner.

The wallflower then eavesdropped on Steven and Dylan's argument about coffee. Steven strongly felt the convenience store should sell Mello Joy, which was known as the original Cajun coffee, instead of Community Coffee. Dylan believed their customers would hate the change and disregarded Steven's point that it would be cheaper and more profitable to change brands.

When Steven realized he was losing the battle, he pounded his fist on the table and bellowed, "Damn it, Dylan, the only reason why we sell Community is because you feel sorry for our local distributer's young daughter who suffers from panic attacks!"

"Let's not do this here," warned Dylan.

"And while we're on the subject of mental disorders, this time, we're not paying for psychiatric treatment for the manager, whom you've already given a million chances to. He continues blaspheming our customers!" yelled Steven.

"Nice, what a wonderful bedside manner you have, Doctor Jacobs. Go in for the brother whose son is off at rehab camp. You're such a coward," said Kris.

Norma was feeling tense as she witnessed her sons battling it out and lectured, "Okay, let's not dive into each other's shortcomings. We all have them, you know."

Debbie looked down at John John's lap and stated, "Some of our inadequacies are shorter than others."

While John John defended his small package, Christy leaned over to her husband, Michael, and whispered, "This dinner party is like being in a scene of a Woody Allen movie."

"Unfortunately, this dialog is poorly written," added Michael.

The other topics discussed in length leading up to dessert were: country singer Randy Travis's last DWI arrest when he was found buck naked, the disadvantages of having Blue Cross Blue Shield insurance, the different forms of social media that Phoebe used to promote her jewelry, and Kris's mild acne problem. During the in-depth deliberations, Steven and Lauren felt nauseated from the absence of insight shown by Norma, John John, Debbie, and LaToya. The peevish couple was silent throughout the main course.

Norma and LaToya entered the dining room carrying the massive red velvet cakes. After they placed the cakes on the table, Norma asked if anyone would like coffee. They all declined, and Dylan said, "I'll take a cup, as long as it's not Mello Joy." Norma hushed her belligerent son as she cut everyone a piece of cake. The gracious hostess ran out of Power Rangers plates, so everyone received their slice of heaven on a Hulk Hogan disposable dish.

The only person who turned down dessert was Lauren. Everyone else devoured a large portion of Louisiana's most popular sweet course.

By not participating in dessert, it was perfect timing for Lauren to bring up the white elephant in the room. She waited for everyone's mouth to be full, and then she popped the damaging question to Norma.

"So, I hear that Hunter asked for only a few chosen family members to participate in his first family session. I know Steven hates that he has prior comments. Now what part of Florida is this treatment center located in?" asked Lauren.

"Destin," answered Norma.

Dylan understood what the wicked wife of his older brother was seeking to accomplish and said, "Yeah, it's about two hours away from that eating disorder facility you attended years ago."

"That's my boy, go in for the kill," Kris mumbled to himself.

Everyone was silenced by his surprising comeback. To break the tension, John John looked over at Debbie, who was munching on her last bite of cake, and teased, "All I can say is get me the name of this eating disorder clinic, and do they accept the Sears MasterCard?" Kris and Stuart are the only ones who laughed as Debbie took her fork and gently stabbed her hypercritical husband's leg under the table. Lauren and Steven were furious.

"How dare you, Dylan! For your information, my anorexia was triggered by depression from not being able to have children! How dare you go there!" Lauren cried.

"Ya know, it's sometimes a blessing from God that some people don't have children," Stuart whispered into Phoebe's ear.

Steven stood up and yelled, "All right, I've had enough!" He glared at his mother and said, "Thank you so much for the dinner soaked in grease and the stimulating conversation. We're leaving. Come on, Lauren. The only guests who Steven and Lauren said good-bye to were Michael and Christy Sury.

"Oh no, ya'll are gonna miss the after-dinner charades games Mother has planned. It's a shame because one of the categories is the top megalomaniac married couples in Rapides Parish," uttered Kris.

"Hush, Kris. Honestly, I did not plan for any games this evening. Now, I do have the Jeopardy electronic game," replied Norma.

Lauren stood up to be by her husband's side, and all of a sudden, Dr. Brent Jacobs, who hadn't said a word during the entire dinner, demanded that the two sit back down, and they obliged.

"Oh, child, look at the old doc over there. Now he's the true engineer of this train wreck., Go ahead, Doc!" LaToya hollered.

Brent smiled at his ex-wife and said, "I guess you could say I'm the boss of all this family madness."

Dr. Jacobs reached under the table and patted Norma's left thigh with his right hand. Norma decided to take Debbie's approach and jabbed her ex-husband's hand with her dessert folk. He quickly took his hand off her thigh and tried to remain calm and keep a straight face while hiding the pain caused from the fork stabber.

Dylan, who was stunned that Steven was asked to attend his son's therapy session, looked at Norma and asked, "What the hell? Why was Steven asked to participate in Hunter's family day and I wasn't?"

"I'm not sure, honey. You know that your father here was also requested to attend," answered Norma.

"This is ludicrous!" Dylan shouted.

"Well, we did all watch him a lot during your bar-hopping days," uttered Lauren.

Before Dylan could respond to Lauren, John John jumped in and defended his best friend. "Hunter knows exactly what he's doin'. He wants to punish his daddy by using the one person who's been nothin' but a deceitful prick to Dylan his entire life, to get back at him for his past mistakes. Yeah, Hunter knows that the sweetest revenge to hurt his daddy is to bring in Steven," John John explained.

"Look, big man, I'm not gonna sit here and listen to this nonsense. I'm not the one who's avoided any form of parenting responsibility to fulfill my selfish desires," said Steven.

"You may be the better-lookin' brother, but you sure play dirty," LaToya uttered to Steven.

"Shouldn't you be on your way to pick up a handicapped senior citizen at the casino or something?" Steven asked LaToya.

"No, but I do need to go. They're showing all eight episodes of ex-Governor Edwin Edwards' reality show tonight on the Arts and Entertainment channel," responded LaToya.

"Ya know his wife is from Alexandria, and he was born in Avoyelles Parish. I'm tryin' to think how I'm related to the former governor," Debbie uttered.

"As much as we would like to stay and hear about your impressive family tree of scandalous political figures, my wife and I have to leave," Steven said to Debbie. He then looked at his father and uttered, "We are leaving, and I mean it." He grabbed his wife's hand, and they walked out of the room.

LaToya shouted, "Thanks for my book!" to Lauren as she and Steven walked out.

Everyone sitting at the table was quiet for ten seconds, and Kris announced, "Mommy Dearest and I wish thank everybody for attending the Jacob Family Dinner Theater, where there's always plenty of drama and tension served to perfection."

CHAPTER 17

Housekeeping before Healing

It was back to the everyday grind for the folks who attended the brutal reunification of lost memories. Dylan started his Monday off by having a serious conversation with his son's girlfriend, Sylvia, about replacing the Glade Plug Ins without asking his permission. She also messed up the alphabetical order that the scented oils were placed in. Still in a rotten mood about the Plug In problem, Dylan faced an even more crucial issue when he arrived at the store. He had to rearrange the employees' work schedule because of his manager, Heath's, mental breakdown. Room freshener adversities along with psychotic disorder dilemmas would be extremely difficult for anyone to handle, particularly for a man who was already suffering from his son's rejection. To top off Dylan's problematic Monday, Kelly Manganaro, the manager of the deli, put in her two weeks' notice. Kelly, a single mother of three, accepted a job with Dairy Queen's corporate office as a troubleshooter. She would be the person who traveled to all the Dairy Queens located in Louisiana and Texas to report steak finger fallacies and Blizzard blunders. Dylan was happy for Kelly, but he was sad to lose her. Norma and Dylan invested a lot in each of their employees. Norma's Cajun Quick Stop was one of the only convenience stores in the state that offered decent health insurance, 401K, and continuing education scholarships. Clearly, Steven was against all the benefits that his mother and brother continued to provide for their store staff.

John John and Debbie also felt the back-to-reality blues. The long weekend was not profitable for Johnny Boy's Bistro. The once popular restaurant, known for the best fried catfish in the city, was descending as fast as a politician's promise. John John was fearful that he could barely make payroll and had exhausted all possibilities of getting any more bank loans.

Stuart was slapped in the face by true life on Monday as well. His eye remained as bruised as his expectations for an incredible reunion. He was feeling let down from all the work and buildup he did to justify his strong presence in a previous life that he could never let go of. Oddly enough, Stuart was more upset about the outcome of his class get-together than the end of his marriage. He didn't go to his office because he had made plans to have lunch with Phoebe before she went back to New Orleans.

Phoebe wasn't detoxing from depression like her friends were. She was ready to get back to her jewelry business and expand her brand. She and Stuart decided to have their early lunch at Sentry Grill, which was located in a historical drugstore from across the Hotel Bentley.

They both ordered the daily special, and then the recap began.

"Last night's dinner at Miss Norma's was definitely the cherry on the cake of my weekend," stated Stuart.

"Come on, Stuart, even though your aspirations have taken a wrong turn, it's just temporary. Remember that, okay? It's just temporary," Phoebe said.

Stuart smiled at Phoebe, and they continued talking about the disasters from their three-day tragedy. Phoebe, being the optimistic person she was, focused on the humorous parts of the weekend, such as: John John's cinnamon shot misfortune, Debbie's near-death experience with Pop Rocks, Dylan's forever promiscuous ways, and last but not least, the only romantic interest shown toward her, from the class transgender disguised as the Preppie Killer. Purposely leaving out the marriage breakup and Dylan's troubles with his son, Phoebe managed to get a few hard laughs out of Stuart. After the two finished lunch, Phoebe ended the visit by saying, "Can't wait to see what Thanksgiving's gonna bring."

It was Thursday evening, and Dylan was sitting on his sparkling clean carpet with his beautiful granddaughter, Maria, in his lap. They were watching *Dora the Explorer* while Sylvia packed for her trip to see Hunter. Initially, Hunter wanted to see his daughter at the first family therapy session, but he had changed his mind. The young father felt he couldn't take the pain of seeing his child during this time.

Hunter knew that he would pack up and leave treatment because of his overwhelming desire to be with his baby girl. Sylvia's mother agreed to watch Maria at Dylan's condo while he was at work.

Maria was getting sleepy as Dylan softly rubbed her head. Sylvia entered the room and said, "I'm all packed, and it's bedtime for my little princess." Dylan kissed his granddaughter before Sylvia took her. While Sylvia got her daughter to bed, Dylan grabbed a pen and pad and wrote a list of house rules for Sylvia's mother.

It did not take long for Maria to fall asleep. Sylvia tiptoed out of her daughter's room into the living room. Dylan looked up from making his list and asked Sylvia, "How do you say, there's no eating burritos or chili rellenos on my brand-new carpet in Spanish?" Laughter was Sylvia's response as she sat down on the sofa next to the mistrustful clean freak.

"Come on, Papa. You know my mother is a spick-and-span spic," joked Sylvia.

Dylan almost fell off the couch from laughing so hard at Sylvia's remark.

After the two shared a hearty cackle together, Dylan put his hand on Sylvia's shoulder and said, "I'm really sorry for being such an ass about my Plug In obsession."

"No worries. I didn't take it personally. I know you're stressing out about Hunter," replied Sylvia.

"It just really hurts me that he doesn't want to see me," expressed Dylan.

"He refuses to see his daughter too, ya know, Papa. Maybe Hunter can't face the people he loves most right now," revealed Sylvia.

"Good try, sweetie, but if that were the case, you and my mother wouldn't be going," Dylan stated.

"All I can say is we must have faith in Hunter. He's a beautiful, smart man like his father," declared Sylvia.

Dylan, touched by Sylvia's opinion, smiled at her and teased, "Okay, your momma can have a Mexican fiesta on my expensive carpet if she wants to."

"You're loco," responded Sylvia.

As the germaphobe granddad and the wise mother continued to laugh, Dylan noticed how abnormally bright the red dye was in Sylvia's hair. It was the same color as his Norma's.

"Ya know, Sylvia, I love my mother more than anyone else in this world, but not enough to bleach my hair flaming hot red. You look like a Hispanic Sharon Osbourne," stated Dylan.

"It's just hair," replied Sylvia.

"I wish I had your optimistic outlook," said Dylan.

"You do, Papa. Right now you're fighting a war of emotional madness, so it's hard finding peace, but when you do, own it," instructed Sylvia.

Dylan grinned at his bright daughter-in-law and said, "I appreciate you."

It was Friday morning. In front of Norma's condominium, Kris was helping his mother's first husband, Brent, load luggage into Brent's brand-new Range Rover. Norma, Sylvia, Maria, and Sylvia's mother were standing on the side of Dr. Jacobs's lavish vehicle. Sylvia was holding Maria and couldn't stop kissing her while Norma talked with Feliciana Carrillo (Sylvia's mother).

Feliciana was the spitting image of her daughter except for a few more wrinkles and many more pounds due to a thyroid problem; at least that was Feliciana's story. Sylvia knew her mother's weight problem was triggered from an overindulgence of beef burritos and Baskin Robbins' Pralines 'n' Cream ice cream.

Mrs. Carrillo, having a limited understanding of the English language, smiled at Norma as the gracious woman of sanitation explained to the clueless babysitter the perks of having a Swiffer Wet Jet Mop.

Suddenly, Dylan, dressed in his work attire, which was a white polo shirt with the words Norma's Cajun Rage Quick Stop monogrammed above the right pocket and khaki pants, walked up to the ladies.

"Are y'all ready for your big trip?" Dylan asked the ladies.

"Hey, honey. Look, Feliciana is gonna watch the baby at my house instead of yours," Norma reported to Dylan.

"Why's that?" asked Dylan.

"The Spanish soap operas are not on your cable, so you'll pick up Maria at my condo after work," answered Norma.

"Miss Norma here has already given my mother tidiness tips and the no eating on the carpet rule," added Sylvia.

Dylan snickered and said, "That works for me." He then looked over at Kris, who was placing a guitar case in the back of the SUV.

"Why are you bringing your guitar? Are ya gonna be singing some jailhouse blues on the drive to Florida in honor of your kleptomaniac girlfriend?" Dylan teased Kris.

"Ha, ha, very funny, Dr. Steven Jacobs," barked Kris.

"Let's not talk about your older brother. You two already put him through hell Sunday night," ordered Brent as he loaded the last suitcase into the vehicle.

Dylan and Kris ignored their elder as Norma rolled her eyes at her first husband's attempt to take charge. Kris and Dylan continued their conversation.

"Actually, I just might have the chance to perform for some attractive female addicts in need of my spiritual guidance," Kris told Dylan.

"You're an idiot," responded Dylan.

"Kris, hug your brother and then get your smart ass in the car," ordered Norma.

Kris obeyed Norma and hugged Dylan. During the embrace, Kris muttered into Dylan's ear, "I got your back on this one, brother. Hunter will listen to his wiser Uncle Kris here."

Dylan thanked his little brother for the encouraging words, and when they looked over at Sylvia, she was crying because she didn't want to leave Maria. As the sad mother handed over her toddler to her mother, Kris shouted, "My God, Sylvia, it's not as if we're courageous soldiers being deployed to Iraq. We'll be home in three days!"

"Sweet Jesus! That reminds me. I forgot my Lee Greenwood *Proud to Be an American* CD! Dylan, be an angel and go get it for me. It's on my kitchen counter," requested Norma.

CHAPTER 18

Therapy American Express Can't Buy

The dysfunctional family arrived at the Marriott Courtyard in Destin at three o'clock. They could have arrived a lot earlier, but Brent had to stop every forty-five minutes to urinate because of his overactive bladder. Since Norma had Marriott Platinum Elite status, everyone was able to have their own room. Norma would only stay at a Marriott property. She earned thousands of Marriott points each year from traveling all over the United States, attending concerts and fan fairs promoting the biggest and the has-been stars of country music.

After they each received their room card from Norma, the group decided to meet in the lobby at five o'clock to make dinner plans. They didn't stop for lunch, and the only snack Norma brought was the Nancy's Deli spirals that she got at Sam's Club (apparently no one but Debbie and Norma enjoy these store-bought appetizers).

It was 7:45 p.m. when the group got back from eating at Buster's Oyster Bar and Grill. They stopped in the middle of the hotel lobby to discuss their agendas for the rest of the night. Sylvia wanted to get back to her room and talk with Maria on Skype. Brent was going to have a few cocktails at the bar. Kris told everyone that he was going to his room to work on a song he wrote for Hunter, and Norma planned to give herself a facial and watch the QVC shopping network. As soon as everyone's plans were made clear, Norma told her crew to meet back in the lobby at seven the next morning so that they could eat breakfast and then head out to the treatment center.

Two hours later, Brent was still in the bar, scoping out two middle-age women who were in Destin for a state floral convention. Suddenly, the electric doors to the lobby opened, and in walked a tall Korean woman dressed in a very short, pink, cocktail dress. The lady of the evening was wearing a red pageboy wig, and she had a tattoo of a tiger on her left arm.

The lonely doctor focused on the mystery woman's buttocks as she limped to the elevator. When the elevator door closed, Brent said to himself, "Ah, to be sixty again."

Kris was nervously waiting on his guest to arrive. He was stretched out on the bed and wearing nothing but the New Orleans Saints boxers that Phoebe gave him last Christmas. All of a sudden, there was knocking at the door.

"Come in, it's open," shouted Kris.

When the hobbling hooker entered, Kris immediately grabbed a pillow and placed it over his groin. The first thing he noticed on the woman was her tattoo of a tiger.

"That wouldn't happen to be Mike the Tiger tattooed on your arm? You know the LSU mascot?" Kris asked.

The hooker realized that Kris was underage and said, "You not twenty-one."

Kris didn't respond because he was distracted by the shiny gold teeth grill in the angry woman's mouth. She stared at him, waiting for a reply.

"Um, it said on the website that you're a video vixen," stated Kris.

"I work for Korean rapper long time ago. You not twenty-one!" shouted the hooker.

"Actually I am. I'm German, so I don't have much body hair," uttered Kris.

"You better not tell lie," scolded the hooker.

She took off her high heels, and Kris was in shock to find out that there was no big toe on her left foot.

"What happened? A foot fetish gone wrong?" asked Kris.

"You no worry, it none of your business," she answered.

As the annoyed escort took a condom out of her handbag—it was too late, Kris had just undergone a premature ejaculation. With the condom in her hand, the hooker limped over to the bed. Kris held his hand up and said, "Ah, stop right there. I'm sorry but I've already struck white gold."

Since Kris had already paid the escort service with his credit card, the woman decided to wait for him to recharge, with the understanding that he would pay her a substantial tip.

Meanwhile, across the hall from the unsuccessful sex experiment, Norma, with wrinkle cream covering her whole face, dressed in black satin pajamas and her hair wrapped in a towel, was sitting on the bed watching the QVC shopping network. Joan Rivers was showing her clothing line, and Norma had her eye on a midnight-blue sequined blazer. Although Norma adored the apparel designed by Ms. Rivers, she was not a big fan of Joan Rivers herself. Many years ago, while watching a talk show on television, Norma was appalled when she heard Joan say, "When I look at my crotch ... I see Willie Nelson staring back at me."

Right before the comedienne and the QVC host displayed the sparking blazers, Norma reached in her purse for the American Express card. She only used the credit card for infomercial purchases. She discovered that she must have left the card at home on the nightstand when she ordered the Meaningful Beauty set (the anti-aging lotion endorsed by Cindy Crawford) the night before. Remembering that Kris had an American Express card, Norma grabbed her son's room card and rushed to the bathroom to get her robe.

Norma made it a habit to always get an additional key to Kris's room when they traveled because of an incident that occurred three years ago at the Hilton in Baton Rouge. On Kris's fourteenth birthday, Norma treated her son and five of his friends to a day at Blue Bayou Water Park. The thoughtful mother had booked a suite for the juvenile delinquents and was fined two hundred dollars because the boys broke the no-smoking rule in their room, and they cleaned out the minibar, which was an extra one hundred and fifty dollars that Norma had to pay.

Norma tied the belt of her robe and walked across the hall to Kris's room. She entered the room without knocking and couldn't believe her eyes when she saw the hooker pushing up and down on Kris's deflated canopy while singing, "Grow little mushroom, time to grow, little mushroom ..."

Norma startled the naughty nurse and her immobile patient by shouting, "Oh, my Lord!"

"Oh shit!" yelled Kris.

"I knew you not twenty-one!" the woman screamed at Kris.

The humiliated hooker leaped off of the bed and wobbled around the room, searching for her high heels.

"You need to apologize to this lovely young lady, and you will pay her for her services!" Norma ordered Kris.

"I know better, he too young," the hooker said to Norma.

As the hooker continued to search for her shoes, Norma noticed the bright nail polish on her ten fingers and nine toes.

"I love that color of green. It's the same shade of green Liza Minnelli wore on her nails in the movie *Cabaret*," stated Norma.

"Thank you," responded the hooker.

"Ah, Mom, my wallet is on the dresser there. Would you give the *Pretty Woman* with the pretty nail polish a tip. I don't want to get out from under the covers right now," pleaded Kris.

Norma took a hundred-dollar bill from Kris's billfold and handed it over to the hooker, who had just slipped on her heels. The hooker placed the bill in her bra and wished Norma and Kris good-bye as she left. When the door shut, Norma glared at her son, who remained lying in the bed of shame, and scolded, "I can't believe this! Well, there goes your hard-earned money from working at the store—limping out the door!"

"Oh, you made a little rhyme, Norma," replied Kris.

"It's not gonna be so funny when you can't afford to go to the House of Blues next week and see Cowboy Mouth! I mean it, Kris! Instead of going to see one of your favorite bands, you've blown your money by having some kinda crazy CPR penis procedure!" shouted Norma.

Norma took the American Express out of Kris's wallet.

"Why are you taking my credit card?" Kris asked.

"You're buying me a Joan Rivers Blazer! I'm giving you fifteen minutes to lay there and think about the consequences of having your private parts served by Miss Saigon, and then you will report to my room and sleep on the sofa tonight!" shouted Norma.

Kris responded with a smile.

"Why are you smiling? I'm serious, Kris Dewy Dubois!" Norma roared.

Norma slammed the door as she left. Kris stared at the ceiling for five seconds and said to himself, "A semi-witty dig followed by the calling of my full name ... yep, I'm in deep shit."

An hour and a half later, Norma was awake watching television as Kris was sound asleep on the sofa. Suddenly, there was banging on the door. It was her ex-husband, Brent. The tipsy physician was feeling lonely after watching *Gilligan's Island* on the TV Land channel in his handicapped room. Because of the floral convention, the only room available for Brent when Norma made the reservations was the handicapped one. Seeing Ginger Grant on television in a leopard print swimsuit reminded Brent of how pretty and sexy Norma was.

"Who is it?" asked Norma before she opened the door.

"It's your charming ex-husband," answered Brent from the other side of the door.

Norma opened the door and asked, "What on earth do you want?"

"I was just sitting in my handicapped room thinking you might want some company," explained Brent.

The knocking on the door woke Kris, but he pretended to be sleeping while listening to the conversation between Ginger Grant and her frisky first husband.

Hoping that Norma would let him in, Brent stood in the hall panting while waiting for his ex-wife's response.

Norma handed him the Do Not Disturb tag and said, "Tomorrow is gonna be a long day, so I suggest that you go back to your handicapped room, sit on the shower chair, run the cold water, and cool down." Before Brent could respond, Norma shut the door in his face. As she walked back to the bed, she heard Kris giggling.

"What was that all about?" the amused son asked his mother.

"It was a bottom-ring attempt from Brent," replied Norma.

Kris burst out in laughter then corrected Norma, "You mean a booty call, Mother."

Norma was not in a jovial mood as she got back in bed. She took the remote and turned off the TV and said to Kris, "The men in my life are driving me crazy."

"We keep you young, Norma," joked Kris.

"One more word from you and I'll turn the TV on the Home Shopping Network and go to town with your American Express!" warned Norma.

Kris continued to laugh as Norma turned off the lights.

It was Saturday morning, and Norma, Sylvia, Brent, and Kris were sitting in semicircle in the family room of Ocean Breeze Recovery Center. They were waiting on Hunter and his counselor. Respecting Hunter's therapy, Kris decided to make this day about his older nephew; therefore, the guitar was left in the SUV.

Hunter, who looked fantastic, and Stan, his counselor, who resembled a middle-aged Jesus in recovery, entered the room. Stan immediately told the family to remain seated and said they would all have a chance to hug Hunter later in the day. Tears ran down Sylvia, Norma, and Kris's faces as they watched Hunter sit down in front of them. Brent was the only one of the family members who was actually listening to Stan's introduction. Everyone else was in awe of how good Hunter looked. Kris, Norma, and Sylvia also realized how much they had missed Hunter. During the next forty-five minutes, Stan shared his life story of being an addict.

As the counselor explained his struggles to stay sober, Hunter took turns making eye contact and smiling at each loved one except for grandfather, Brent. After Stan wrapped up his history of overdoing barbiturates and booze, the addiction counselor then asked each future Al-Anon member to express how Hunter's addiction had affected them. Stan pointed to Sylvia to be the first one to share her experience of being with the "high" Hunter.

Sylvia took a breath and said, "I feel Hunter's substance abuse issues were caused by his parents' dismissal of him. It's like his mother rejected him because she had better children to raise, and his father abandoned him for liquor and loose women …"

"Oh, honey, I know for a fact that Hunter is the love of Dylan's life," interrupted Norma.

"Liquor and loose women … this sounds like it should be one of dad's songs," joked Kris.

"I mean no disrespect," Sylvia uttered to Norma.

"She's only tellin' the truth," said Hunter.

Stan told Norma that it was her turn to talk. Norma looked over at Hunter for approval. He smiled at his grandmother and nodded his head for her to proceed.

"Well, as I was saying, Dylan may not have been the best father back then, but believe me, there's no instructions that come with the duties of being a parent," defended Norma.

Before Norma could say another word, Kris chimed in, "That's bullshit! There are instructions, books, pamphlets, and guides on how to parent. I feel that's the lamest excuse when a mother or father says that to their child!"

"Remember this mother still has her son's American Express card," cautioned Norma.

Hunter smiled as he took in every word from his eccentric relatives. The counselor asked Kris to share his thoughts because apparently he had a lot to say.

"Okay, let's move this session right along, shall we? Hunter's father, who is my brother, Dylan, didn't exactly hit the lottery when it came to having positive male role models in his life. In fact, Dylan's father, Dr. Brent Jacobs, here, and his older brother, Dr. Steven Jacobs, are two of the most narcissistic people on the planet ..."

"Now you just wait one minute!" Brent shouted to Kris.

Stan ordered Brent to please let Kris finish. Brent folded his arms and pouted. Kris looked at everyone to make sure they were silent before he took back the floor.

"Please continue, Kris," instructed Stan.

"Hunter knows exactly what he's doing. He didn't want his father here because he's enjoying being able to control the pain Dylan is going through by using his exceptional manipulation proficiencies. Let's face it, the only reason the old doc is here, and the hypocritical invitation for his Uncle Steven to be here, is nothing but a slap in the face to his father!" shouted Kris.

"What do you have to say, Hunter?" asked Stan.

"Kris is partially right. I invited my grandfather and my uncle here to ask them why they made my father a distant, selfish man," clarified Hunter.

"Dr. Jacobs, how do you feel about what Hunter has just said?" asked Stan.

Brent stood up and yelled, "I'm not going sit here and listen to this garbage! I have been good to all my sons and grandson! I thought this assignment was supposed to be all of us explaining how Hunter's addiction has affected us!"

Before Stan could address Brent's complaint, Kris intervened. He looked at Stan and said, "Honestly, experiencing your long, drawn-out biography of being an addict distracted us from listening to the actual task."

"I'm sorry my story bored you, Kris," uttered Stan.

"No need to apologize," responded Kris.

"Well I'm sorry ... I'm sorry that I came," declared Brent. The wounded doctor then stormed out of the room.

After Brent left, Hunter sang the Sister Sledge song "We Are Family." Kris and Sylvia laughed at Hunter's sarcasm as Norma hastily walked out to check on her ex-husband. Stan tolerantly waited for the young people to stop laughing, and when they finished, he informed them the session had ended.

Norma was unsuccessful at getting Brent back in the facility. He decided that he was going to the pro shop located in the Indian Bayou

Golf and Country Club to shop for new clubs while Norma, Sylvia, and Kris took a tour of the recovery center.

Once Hunter gave the family a tour around the center, they had lunch, and afterwards he showed them the arts and crafts room where his pottery class was. As Kris, Norma, and Sylvia admired the other residents' ceramic pieces, Hunter walked to the shelf, grabbed a box, and brought it to Norma.

"What's this, honey?" asked Norma.

"I made it for you. Open it," answered Hunter.

Norma opened the box and pulled out a red clay pig that was very similar to the pig on the roof of Norma's Cajun Rage Quick Stop. She immediately cried.

"Oh, Hunter, it's absolutely beautiful. I'm beyond touched," whimpered Norma. She then hugged her big-hearted grandson.

Although it seemed absurd that Norma kept the life-size counterfeit farm animal (that caused the death of her husband) on top of the convenience store, the heartbroken widow strongly believed the fake killer pig was a symbol of her true love, Frankie's great achievements. She even rebuilt the historic symbol and added an interior light after the tragedy. Unfortunately, the pig hadn't lit up for nearly two years. From mentally challenged employees to the demanding job of keeping the reputation of being the cleanest quick shop in town, a burnt-out light bulb was not on Dylan or Steven's top priorities list.

Suddenly, Stan entered the arts and crafts room. He requested that everyone go to his office. When they arrived, Stan sat at his desk while Kris, Norma, Sylvia, and Hunter sat down in front of him.

"I just got off the phone with Hunter's father, and he has agreed with the treatment plan that the staff here has worked on for Hunter," Stan informed them.

"Okay," replied Norma.

"We're gonna discharge Hunter to Bayou Peace Recovery Center on Monday morning. He has agreed to continue his therapy there. This way, he'll be closer to home," Stan added.

"This is wonderful news!" cheered Sylvia. Kris and Norma were also overjoyed with the decision.

"Do you need us to stay until Monday to take him to the recovery center?" Norma asked Stan.

"No, I'm gonna take him. Hunter has requested that Sylvia stay here and come with us." Stan looked at Sylvia and asked, "Are you okay with this, Sylvia?"

"Oh yes," replied Sylvia.

"You can stay at the Marriott. I have enough points for several nights. And you have the American Express I gave you for emergencies, and I can't think of a better crisis than this," Norma said to Sylvia.

"When in the hell did you give your Latino clone an American Express?" teased Kris.

It was three o'clock, and Family Day was officially over at Ocean Breeze Recovery Center. Norma, Kris, and Sylvia waited outside of the entrance for Brent to pick them up. Norma had already informed her ex-husband that they would need to drop Sylvia off at the Marriott so that she could check back in.

Brent remained silent, as Norma, Sylvia, and Kris got in the vehicle. As they drove off, Norma asked Brent, "Are you all right?"

"I'll be fine," answered Brent.

There was silence during the first six hours of the drive back home. Brent was listening to talk radio while Norma stared at the clay pig in her lap. Kris was in the backseat sleeping with a *Rolling Stone* magazine on his chest. As they entered Lafayette, Brent asked Norma if she would mind stopping at the Cracker Barrel because he hadn't had anything to eat since the continental breakfast at the Marriott. Understanding that the family session wasn't a good experience for her starving ex-husband, Norma agreed to stop and eat, even though Cracker Barrel didn't have a wine list. As Brent took the exit to get to the chain, home-style cooking restaurant, Norma woke up Kris.

After they ordered, Kris attempted to figure out the notorious peg game that was placed on each table. Brent and Norma watched him struggle with the brainteaser surrounded by golf tees. After several tries, Kris shouted, "Screw me! Screw me! Screw me running!" He then knocked the perplexing puzzle to the side. No one said a word for a few seconds, and then all three burst out in laughter.

"I remember when Dylan had the same reaction when he tried to figure out the Rubik's Cube," Brent said to Norma.

"Actually, that was Stuart who went into a rage from the Rubik's conundrum—not Dylan," corrected Norma.

Kris's tantrum made it more comfortable for the three stressed travelers to make small talk during their meal. Once they were done eating, Norma informed the men that she was going to browse the gift shop.

While Brent waited in line to pay the bill, Norma and Kris browsed through the classic television DVDs. All of a sudden, Norma screamed, "Oh my sweet Jesus! I can't believe this!" Brent stepped out of the line and rushed over to his ex-wife, who was holding a DVD to her chest and hysterically crying. Kris consoled his mother by putting his arm around her shoulder and telling her to let it all out.

"What is it, Norma?" Brent asked.

"She found this," Kris answered while taking the DVD out of his mother's hands and giving it to Brent.

Brent saw that the DVD was *The Best of the Hee Haw Honeys*. The confused doctor looked at Kris and stated, "I don't understand." Kris instructed Brent to look on the back of the DVD. Brent read the episode guide, which was listed under a photo of Kathie Lee Gifford (when she was known as Kathie Lee Johnson, the wannabe Christian country music star) and discovered that Frankie Dubois was the musical guest in episode fourteen.

Brent held Norma's hand, looked directly into her eyes, and said, "I understand, Norma. Genuine love never fades. Maybe, just maybe, Hunter's gift and this DVD are indications from your guardian angel letting you know he's watching over you." Norma smiled and thanked her ex-husband for his kindheartedness. Brent looked over at Kris and requested, "Kris, take your mother out and let her gets some fresh air while I pay for dinner and this special DVD."

"Good deal. I saw a lovely LSU rocking chair outside that would love to have Norma's sentimental derriere rock in it," responded Kris. The two men then grinned at each other as if they were friends.

During the rest of the trip back to Alexandria, Dr. Brent Jacobs and his newfound pal, Kris, debated over the best quarterback in the NFL. While Kris dominated the conversation with Brent by expressing his opinion as to why Andrew Luck was better than John Elway, Norma continued to have wonderful flashbacks of Frankie as she stared at the bright-red pig and his name on the *Hee Haw Honeys'* box.

CHAPTER 19

Forgiving a Jackson Street Cruiser

The transfer from Ocean Breeze Recovery Center to Bayou Peace was a smooth one for Hunter. During his stay at Bayou Peace, Hunter's hard work and dedication to therapy was quite remarkable. On the fifth day at the new facility, Hunter decided to ask his father and only his father to come for Family Day. Dylan was touched by the invitation. The anxious rebel called the special education center to inform the program supervisor that he was proud to say that he would not be volunteering Saturday because he was spending the day with his son.

It was a hot September Saturday at the Bayou Peace Recovery Center. Hunter was sitting on the swing attached to the oak tree in front of the antebellum style mansion located in Cheneyville, Louisiana. As he waited for Dylan to arrive, Hunter was thinking of all the concerns he wanted to discuss with his father. Suddenly, he saw Dylan's pickup slowing down to turn into the entrance of the facility.

As Dylan drove up the gravel road leading to the treatment center (that very well could pass for a bed-and-breakfast), he noticed a sign that read Expect Miracles. "I hope," Dylan said to himself. Dylan parked in the visitors' parking area and was met by his son. Dylan opened the door and saw Hunter standing on the side of truck, smiling.

"You look great. You've gained some weight," said Dylan.

"Ya know us addicts love sweets," replied Hunter.

Dylan looked around, observing the beautiful eighteenth-century home, the majestic oaks trees, the ten-acre pecan grove, and the bayou.

"It's nice, isn't it?" asked Hunter.

"I didn't realize how nice," replied Dylan.

Hunter noticed the cardboard box his father was holding and questioned, "What's in the box?"

"Oh, ah, I stopped by Lea's Lunchroom on my way here and picked up thirty ham sandwiches. There are twenty-nine other people in treatment here, right?" inquired Dylan.

"Yeah, there is. That was really nice of you," answered Hunter.

"Speaking of ham, I really liked the pig you made Momma," Dylan stated.

"Who knows, maybe I'll be the family's first pig artist. Come on, let's take those sandwiches to the kitchen, and then I'll give you a tour," said Hunter.

Hunter gave his apprehensive dad a grand tour of the plush substance abuse treatment plantation, and they ended up sitting on the same swing that Hunter sat on while waiting for Dylan. There was an awkward silence between the two for many seconds, and Dylan announced, "It's really strange seeing you in person, I know we've talked on the phone and all, but it's odd to see you. I mean, it's been what? Ah, a little over a month?"

"Yeah, it's been thirty-three days," replied Hunter.

"I was gonna bring you some Glade Plug Ins—, I know you like the holiday scents—but ah, I figured that they wouldn't allow you to have them in here," explained Dylan.

"Yeah, it would be kinda hard to smoke an apple-cinnamon air freshener," joked Hunter.

Both men were laughing as Janis Presley, an older woman wearing a lab coat, walked up.

"Hey, fellas, you have about forty-five minutes until the volleyball game starts," Janis told Dylan and Hunter.

"Hey, Miss Janis, I'd like for you to meet my father, Dylan Jacobs," said Hunter.

Dylan stood up, shook Janis's hand, and said, "Very nice to meet you."

"Hi there, I'm Janis Presley, the clinical supervisor," she proudly announced to Dylan.

"Janis Presley, you say? Are you named after the king and queen of rock and roll?" teased Dylan.

"Let me tell ya somethin', Mr. Jacobs, Bayou Peace is not a rock concert. We take addiction issues very seriously here, so get out of the ha-ha land of lame jokes, wake up, and be a part of your baby boy's recovery!" snapped Janis.

"Will do," responded Dylan with a smirk on his face.

"That's what I like to hear … remember, volleyball in forty-five minutes," reminded Janis.

As the lovely Nurse Ratched marched off to find another patient's family member to announce the volleyball game time, as well as a possible speech on substance abuse, Dylan looked at Hunter and said, "Boy, is she a breath of fresh air."

"Bitterness must be one of the aftereffects of a recovering man hater," stated Hunter.

Both men chuckled as Dylan sat back down on the swing next to his son.

"We're not gonna play volleyball, Dad. We're gonna sit here and discuss our defective relationship," said Hunter.

"Okay, where do we start?" asked Dylan.

"First, let's get the drug problem out of the way," suggested Hunter.

"Okay, um, I know my self-centeredness caused you to feel rejected, and by feeling rejected, you want to numb yourself," said Dylan.

"Well, you're right on with the self-absorption and rejection points, but I honestly feel I have an addictive personality like you and just about everyone in our family. I mean, I love getting high. I love it! And yes, I'm sure that my love for being in a euphoric state of mind stems from your dismissal, but what I can't figure out is, you are constantly making up for your sorrow to everyone but me."

"I'm not sure I understand. I just feel that you don't like me," shared Dylan.

"And I feel you don't like me. It's as if I'm your only failure in life and you go out of your way to help others to run away from actually being a part of me. Am I making any sense?" asked Hunter.

"You're making perfect sense, but I want you to know that you're my heart, Hunter," stressed Dylan.

"I appreciate that, so what I want to say is, now that I'm a father, I know I can beat this drug dependence. I know it will be hard, but I can handle it. I'll have to for Maria. What I can't handle is being dismissed by you anymore," expressed Hunter.

"I promise you, son, that will never happen. I guess I was trying to be a role model to you by volunteering to work with special needs children and taking care of all my employees at the store," justified Dylan.

"I'm not sure I believe you, but I feel we're getting close to an abnormal reconciliation," said Hunter.

"Fair enough," replied Dylan.

Both father and son were tearing up. To prevent any more emotional feelings from rising, Hunter stood up and declared, "All this cleansing has made me hungry. Let's go for a ham sandwich."

Uncertain that Hunter was ready for a hug, Dylan stood up and patted his son on the back. The two then walked toward the facility.

After they feasted on the peace offering of ham on a bun, Hunter decided that he and Dylan should take a walk along Bayou Boeuf instead of participating in any of the Family Day games. During their father and son stroll, Dylan told Hunter about his class reunion. Dylan explained in detail all the highlights of the unforgettable three-day event. Hunter loved his dad's friends and was delighted to hear about all of their madcap misfortunes.

It was four o'clock, and Family Day was official over. While Hunter and Dylan stood on the side of Dylan's truck, they were both waiting for the other one to make a move. Finally, Hunter hugged his father and softly uttered, "I love you, Dad."

"I love you too," Dylan proudly replied.

As Hunter watched his father drive away, Dylan accidently peeled out on the gravel while turning onto the highway. Hunter grinned and said himself, "That is one crazy rebel."

For the next two weeks, Dylan, Sylvia, Maria, Kris, and Norma attended the remaining Family Days, and each of them had a one-on-one session with Hunter's counselor. On Hunter's last Family Day of his treatment, his younger uncle, Kris, was asked to leave by Janis Presley.

To fill the void from losing his girlfriend to an expensive bottle of Nicki Minaj cologne, Kris channeled his late father's talents and wrote a song titled "Tortured Love by Stolen Toilet Water." Kris decided he was going to perform the tune for the lonesome ladies in recovery. He hoped some of the females were in treatment for sex addiction. When Janis heard the lyric, "You gave up my tallywacker for your love of cheap-smellin' perfume," she stopped Kris from singing and ordered the vulgar folk singer to leave. Once again, Kris had to hand over his American Express card to Norma because of his immature behavior.

Hunter's after-treatment plan immediately went into effect when he was discharged from the recovery center. Dylan hired him for a manager-in-training position at Norma's Cajun Rage Quick Stop. Hunter going to work at the store would be a tremendous help to Dylan because of the loss of his deli manager to Dairy Queen and the loss of his weekend floor manager to paranoid schizophrenia. Hunter also attended Bayou Peace's outpatient program three nights a week.

While Hunter was in residential treatment, Norma bought the condominium right next to hers for her grandson and Sylvia. Therefore, the couple would have to live with Dylan for only a month until they could move into their own place. Norma's substantial gift couldn't have come at a better time because Sylvia was three weeks pregnant. Dylan and Norma could not figure out how or when Sylvia could have gotten pregnant until the couple came clean.

Hunter delivered the bun into Sylvia's oven during the drive from Destin to Cheneyville. The couple made love in the bathroom stall of a Jack in the Box in Baton Rouge when they stopped to eat dinner. Hunter told his counselor, Stan, that he and Sylvia had stomach problems due to eating Jack's Spicy Chicken Sandwich. Oblivious to what the lovebirds were actually doing, Stan walked around the parking lot, drank his milkshake, and smoked two cigarettes as Romeo and Juliet received a gift from God that was not listed on the drive-thru menu.

Dylan was overjoyed to become a grandfather for the second time. He felt a newborn would create new hope for his and Hunter's uncertain relationship. Norma was also excited to hear that Sylvia was expecting. The only thing that Norma wished would have happened differently was the location of the conception. She thought that Hunter and Sylvia could have at least made a baby in the restroom of a Raising Cane's Chicken Fingers instead of a Jack in the Box. Norma had always admired Todd Graves, the founder of Raising Canes, because he was a Louisiana man who attended LSU and became a hugely successful entrepreneur by following his dreams. The way Todd Graves put chicken fingers on the map nationwide was very similar to her departed husband, Frankie's, approach to make pork jerky the new white, dried-meat snack sensation of the South.

CHAPTER 20

Baptizing, Bankruptcy, and Blissful Beginnings

Over a short period, many life-changing moments occurred for the Jacobs and their extended family.

Just a few days before John John planned on seeing his lawyer to file for bankruptcy, he was approach by a national bank. Johnny Boy's Bistro was located on prime property. John John and Debbie owned the building and the land. The extremely generous offer from the bank was enough money for the rowdy Rachels to live comfortably for at least two years. Debbie was excited and ready to sign the papers. Although John John was happy to be relieved from a serious amount of debt, he was disappointed he had let his dream drown in a sea of bad business decisions and stupidity.

Steven Jacobs was also approached with an important business proposal. Dylan offered to buy out his brother's share of Norma's Cajun Rage Quick Stop. Steven didn't hesitate to sell his portion of the family business, especially since his mother and brother continuously disregarded any input he had to offer. Dylan was ecstatic to get Steven out of the way so that he could prove his faith in Hunter by offering him a promising career. Norma and Dylan were overjoyed that Hunter was enthusiastic to learn everything there was to know about the family's unique one-stop shop for gas, jerky, and over-the-counter therapy. Hunter's paid internship would allow him to earn a decent income to support his daughter, the baby on the way, and Sylvia, who had only one semester left to graduate from the Gorgeous Garments Online Fashion Design Academy. Debbie was actually the one who encouraged Sylvia to take the leap into the stimulating field of glitter and glamour.

In another life, Debbie must have been a gypsy princess because of her love for over-the-top flamboyant fashion.

The ostentatious, self-made clothing designer was the mastermind behind all her daughters' and nieces' pageant, prom, and baptism dresses. The only time Debbie felt defeated in the brutal world of pageant attire designing was when her oldest daughter, Amanda, lost the Little Miss Hollywood Cenla Pageant. Years later at a pokeno party, Debbie had a chat with Trisha Baker, who was one of the judges from the beauty contest. Trisha, a plump, gaudy-looking woman, had several margaritas and spilled the beans regarding Amanda's low scores. Trisha told Debbie that Amanda lost the chance of becoming Little Miss Hollywood Cenla because she did poorly in the sports attire category. The tipsy critic revealed to Debbie that her daughter looked like Andre Agassi in a tennis dress. Instead of punching the sloshed woman in the face, Debbie noticed that Trisha's margarita glass was empty and offered to get her a refill.

"That would be lovely," said Trisha.

"I'll be right back. I want to hear the dos and don'ts of the regional pageant circuit," expressed Debbie.

Debbie took the glass from Trisha and walked to the kitchen. She grabbed the pitcher and poured the glass half full of margarita. She wanted to leave room for an extra touch of something special to add to the frozen beverage. The mischievous mother sneaked into the bathroom next to kitchen, lifted her skirt, and released a small amount of urine into the brew. "Just a little golden sprinkle to enhance the lime and tequila," Debbie said to herself. She then strolled back into the living room with the pee cocktail in her hand and gave it to Trisha. Trisha thanked Debbie, and then the clueless alcoholic took a sip.

"Oh, it tastes a little bitter," Trisha complained.

"I'm sorry, it may need some altering, just like your lack of judgment," replied Debbie.

It was two days before Halloween when John John and Debbie decided to treat Dylan, Phoebe, and Stuart to an overnight trip to Shreveport to gamble at Sam's Town Casino, dine at the Superior Steakhouse, and attend a Halloween party. The costume party was for John John and Debbie's daughter Amanda and her wife, Cindy.

Cindy received her undergraduate degree from Centenary College, and her old college buds who were unable to attend her actual marriage ceremony in Vermont wanted to give the happy lesbian couple a party with a horror twist.

For the first time ever, Stuart couldn't believe that he wasn't the one who planned a group outing. He was happy, and at the same time, he was hesitant because he wasn't in charge.

The trip offer could not have come at a better time for Phoebe. She just happened to be in Alexandria meeting with her interior designer when John John called. At first, Phoebe declined the invitation because she didn't like to gamble, nor did she celebrate Halloween, but when John John told her that they were going to be eating at Superior Steakhouse, she reconsidered. The best prime rib Phoebe had ever eaten was at Superior Steakhouse, not to mention, the owner's wife, Karen Barbaree, had spent thousands of dollars on Cane River Angel Jewelry.

In such a short time, Hunter's work ethic and dedication to Norma's Cajun Rage Quick Stop proved to his father that he could be trusted. Therefore, Dylan was definitely ready to join his friends for an overnight excursion.

On the morning of the group's mini-vacation, Stuart, who relapsed from his micro-managing disorder, rented a van so that they could all ride together. He got a good rate on a five-passenger van thanks to Leigh Ann Kirsch. Leigh Ann, the owner of the local Avis Rent A Car, used to date Stuart back in the college days. They broke up because of Stuart's severe obsession with his past.

Debbie appointed herself the driver and decided to take the longer way to Shreveport, by way of Highway 165 North instead of the much shorter route of I-49. Her puzzled passengers did not understand why she took the Camp Hardtner Road exit while driving through Pollock, Louisiana. Debbie drove down several backwoods roads to get to her final destination. Stuart was having a nervous breakdown as Debbie managed to hit every bump and hole on the dirt roads.

"I'm leasing this van that you're tearing up, Debbie!" shouted Stuart.

"Your life desires have been nothin' but rental hallucinations! So shut up and enjoy the ride!" Debbie yelled back to Stuart.

After hitting one more gigantic pothole, Debbie finally arrived at the mystery stop. She ordered everyone to get their frightened asses out of the van. John John, Phoebe, Stuart, and Dylan complained about the hot October weather the entire time they were getting out of the rental van.

"All right, you bunch of whiners! Strip down to your underwear!" Debbie demanded.

John John and Dylan obeyed the fiery female drill sergeant and started stripping down to their undies while Phoebe and Stuart glared at Debbie as if she were crazy.

"What are you doing? Preparing for the leading lady's role in the remake of *Deliverance?*" Stuart asked Debbie.

"I'm gonna choose to ignore that remark, especially comin' from a paranoid jackass," replied Debbie.

Stuart looked over at Dylan (wearing LSU boxers) and John John (wearing tighty-whities). The predictable follower then decided to strip down to his Polo Ralph Lauren briefs. Phoebe remained clothed as Debbie, who was only wearing a bra and Spanx panties, waited for the timid jewelry designer to disrobe.

"What is this? A southern-style submission of a former African American virgin?" Phoebe asked her bizarre buddies.

Everyone laughed as Debbie grabbed five beach towels and a boom box out of the back of the van.

"Listen closely, my beautiful, buff cult. We are all standin' here to take part in a baptism of forgiving our inescapable imperfections! Now, are there any questions before we hike to the waterfall to cleanse our justifiable sins?" Debbie asked her baffled disciples.

As Phoebe took off her clothes, John John chuckled.

"What's so funny, John John? I'm sure you've seen me in my bra and panties at one time or another in our pitiful life," scolded Phoebe.

"No, that's not it, baby girl. You're a brick house. You're mighty, mighty—just lettin' it all hang out and all that other stuff. I was just laughing because I'm just happy that Debbie bleached my under drawers before we left for this secret adventure. Ya know, I'm the type of no-good bastard whose underwear is yellow in the front and brown in the back," John John explained.

Debbie led everyone to the waterfall that she swam in as a child, and they were all impressed with how beautiful and private it was. Immediately, the men began horse playing while the ladies slowly got in the freezing-cold water. There was no need for Phoebe and Debbie to pace themselves, because John John did a cannonball from the top of the ledge and landed in front of them. The women were soaked from the childish titan's splash. For hours, the middle-aged ragers had a blast swimming, dancing, chicken fighting, and washing off their worries.

Out of the blue, the friends separated into two groups. Phoebe, John John, and Dylan gathered in the cave below the waterfall, and Debbie saw that Stuart was sitting by himself on the sand, so she sat down beside the lonesome accountant. Stuart had a sad expression on his face as he watched the clear waterfall from the cliff. Debbie smiled at him as she ran her fingers through his wet, thick, gray hair.

"You have such great hair. John John would give up his shotgun collection and his LSU season tickets to have your full head of hair," said Debbie.

"That's about all I have going for me, my gray mop," Stuart replied.

"I'm not gonna throw you a pity party, Stuart. I suck at it. Hell, I can't even host a decent Tupperware party," joked Debbie.

"I don't know, Debbie. It's like no matter what I do, I can't be happy, and I work so hard at it. I mean, look at me … I'm in great shape, financially secure, and I'm free. I should feel like I'm the luckiest man in the world, but I can't love or allow myself to be loved. Last night, I walked around the overblown bar room that I paid close to nine hundred thousand dollars for and stood on the dance floor and looked at myself in the mirror. I know I must have stood there for an hour …" explained Stuart.

"What happened? Did ya have an Oprah aha moment?" asked Debbie.

"Actually, I came to the conclusion that I'm a miserable person with a fabricated memoir," answered Stuart.

"Oh shit. Stuart, I ain't buyin' that! So you love to live in the past, big bull balls! At least you're marinating in the good times. You'd really be an obnoxious buffoon if you chose to live back in Never, Never, Negative Land!" shouted Debbie.

"I honestly feel that my relationship with you all is more of a predictable ritual than meaningful camaraderie," stated Stuart.

"Spare me the relevancy crap! Stuart, we all love you more than sex and crawfish! Listen, it's not gonna be a difficult task for you to strive to be happy. You're just gonna have to stop depending on others and fond memories to pacify your low self-worth. Look at me. I just lost my restaurant … I'm fatter than the hard plastic pig on top of Dylan's store … menopause is around the corner … and I just fired my therapist for diagnosing me with intermittent explosive disorder! But I'm happy! Yes, I'm certainly happy!" yelled Debbie.

"Now, I did constantly warn you and your stubborn husband about losing Johnny Boy's Bistro, but no, you had to have your sister's incompetent husband do ya'll's bookkeeping," lectured Stuart.

"Um, Stuart, you're becoming a buzz kill for my baptizing plans," replied Debbie.

"What the hell does that mean?" asked Stuart.

"It means that I'm gonna take you into that water and wash out all your toxic insecurities. Yes, I'm gonna bathe you until you're sparkling clean of any doubts you may have had about being loved! Now, get up and let's start the Debbie Rachel baptism procedure!" ordered Debbie.

Debbie grabbed Stuart's hand and led him into the water. They walked across the pond until the cool water was up to Debbie's waist. She picked up Stuart as if she were a bride carrying her groom across the threshold. Debbie started speaking in tongues while she repeatedly dunked Stuart, the self-doubting sinner, into Mother Nature's christening pool.

Dylan, Phoebe, and John John were so engrossed in a discussion about Hunter's positive progress in recovery that they didn't even realize a strange baptism ceremony was taking place.

After Stuart's sentimental cleansing and Hunter's good report card, Debbie decided it was time for her and Phoebe to give the boys a bayou-style burlesque show. The fearless woman in the tummy-control undergarment ordered the men to sit down on the sandbank. She then told Phoebe to push the on button on the ghetto blaster.

"Did you just say ghetto blaster? Really, Debbie?" questioned Phoebe.

"Oh all right! Please turn the portable CD player on. Is that better, Miss Black Panther? Now get your skinny, socialist fanny up here so we can show these dirty, middle-aged men who the *real* Pussycat Dolls are!" yelled Debbie.

Phoebe turned the boom box on and ran to join Debbie, who was standing in the shallow water in front of the three confused southern studs. The song "I Know What Boys Like" by The Waitresses played during Phoebe and Debbie's erotic dance attempt. While Dylan and John John laughed hysterically at the struggling bump and grinders, Stuart couldn't believe that he was actually watching a reenactment of the group's wild history. Stuart was delighted because, for once, the neurotic cruise director wasn't in charge of his own déjà vu—thanks to Debbie's inventive planning.

After the terrible burlesque queens' act bombed, John John decided that he and his sexy sidekicks would show the ladies what a strip show should look like. He told the untalented women to sit down and ordered Stuart to select a song. Stuart looked at Debbie for a suggestion, and she told him to play song number eleven. He pressed the fast-forward button to eleven and ran over to join his arousing cohorts, who were facing the two harsh critics. The tune "It's Raining Men" sung by the Weather Girls came on, and a horrifying adaptation of the most intensive dance scene from the movie *Magic Mike* was performed. As John John was dancing, Phoebe looked over at Debbie and stated, "I didn't realize that Johnny boy had so much hair on his back,"

"Hey, its' a good thang. When I shave his back on the front porch, the birds fly down and pick up the fuzz, and it makes a good nest," Debbie replied.

John John realized that Phoebe and Debbie were less than impressed with his naughty presentation, so he took his underwear off and threw it at them. Dylan followed the big man's lead and tossed his boxers at the women. For some odd reason, Stuart refused to play follow the leader and walked back to shore. After Dylan and John John showed their bare derrieres to the bored females, the two men turned around and gave the women a peek show of their hidden jewels.

Phoebe and Stuart hooted at the nude dancing nuts, but Debbie wasn't as amused. She eyeballed her husband's package and said, "Your pee pee looks like a dying tulip. That little beef whistle hasn't been blown for years."

Debbie then inspected Dylan's ding dong and said, "And, Dylan, your boy Hunter has you beat by a long shot."

After they all shared a hearty laugh, Debbie snatched up Dylan and John John's underwear from the sand and told Phoebe that she had to come with her to pee in the woods. As the wicked women departed with the men's undies in their grubby hands, Stuart remained standing on land and watched his buck-naked buddies do handstands in the water.

Debbie and Phoebe reached the perfect spot in the woods to use as an outdoor Porta-Potty. Debbie instructed Phoebe to stand in front of her to keep guard while she tinkled. After Debbie peed, she struggled to pull up the Spanx over her knees and fell frontward on the ground. Phoebe turned around and was startled to see a strange man glaring at her and Debbie, who was lying on her stomach with her panty girdle up to her knees. The stranger watching the stunned ladies was Benny Maxwell, a young, cross-eyed, heavyset deputy with the Grant Parish Sheriff's Office.

"What kinda sick orgy is goin' on here?" Deputy Maxwell asked the ebony and ivory impersonators of Laverne and Shirley, who looked like they were in the process of a lewd act.

Back at the swimming hole, Dylan and John John swam as dolphins, showing their bare behinds to Stuart each time they dove in the water. Stuart noticed Phoebe, Debbie, and Deputy Maxwell walking up toward the waterfall. "Holy crap," he said to himself.

After the deputy saw the two nude, grown men frolicking in the pond, he turned to the ashamed ladies and said, "This is private land in Grant Parish, not some fruity bathhouse in some place like Californy!"

Deputy Maxwell ordered the five peace disturbers to wrap themselves in towels and follow him to his patrol car, which was parked behind their van.

He made them each hand over their driver's licenses and ordered the streakers to line up in front of his car while he called in each of their license numbers. Debbie and Dylan were the only ones with a criminal background that was reported by the dispatcher on the receiving end of the police radio. Debbie's arrest for road rage in 2006 came up, and Dylan's two DWI charges were also conveyed. Deputy Maxwell got out of his patrol car and moseyed up to the guilty party of five.

"Well, it looks like we got us an irate woman driver and a sloppy drunk in this here nekkid, tree-huggin' society," barked Deputy Maxwell.

Stuart and Phoebe stared ahead while Dylan, John John, and Debbie were biting their lips to keep from laughing at the cocky deputy's crossed eyes. To take his mind off the deputy's active, wandering eye, Dylan focused on the man of law's nametag.

"You wouldn't happen to be related to any of the Maxwells in LaSalle Parish, would you?" Dylan asked the sheriff's deputy.

"Yeah, what's it to ya?" responded Deputy Maxwell.

"My stepfather, Frankie Dubois, employed several Maxwells at his pork jerky factory in Olla," stated Dylan.

"Your stepdaddy was Frankie Dubois?" asked Deputy Maxwell.

"Oh yes, the late great country singer and dried pork king is my stepdad," Dylan proudly replied.

"Mr. Frankie paid for my daddy to go to trade school. It's also a tradition in my family to play his album, *Hillbilly Love*, every Christmas morning. 'I Found Christ in K-Mart' still brings tears to my eyes," expressed the sentimental deputy.

"Oh God, not this again," Phoebe mumbled to herself.

"Hell, let's just consider this little weird trespassin' incident as a warning. Now, ya'll go on," Deputy Maxwell told the five bare bandits.

They thanked the young man and got into the van. Just before Dylan entered the soccer mom vehicle, Deputy Maxwell called him over. Dylan walked over to the deputy and saw that the man had tears in his eyes.

"Are you okay, Deputy?" asked Dylan.

The emotional law enforcer then embraced Dylan and said, "God bless you and your family."

During the ride to Shreveport, the wild bunch reminisced about how a spontaneous side stop to a waterfall turned into a mortifying experience.

"The odd thing about this impulsive act that we've just completed is not one of us was inebriated," declared Stuart.

"I know. We don't need to be high to fly stark-naked into the woods," added John John.

"Okay, ya'll are starting to sound like bad teen actors in a drug prevention public service announcement," stated Phoebe.

"It is rather refreshing not to have to be plastered to do something out of the ordinary," expressed Dylan.

"I agree, Dylan," said Phoebe.

Everyone was silent, reflecting about the Stay Sober and Have Fun theory until all of sudden Debbie blurted, "All right, I must admit to ya'll, I took one of my little nephew's Adderalls before we left this morning,"

The drug-free crew (except for Debbie) arrived at the casino hotel just in time to take a shower and change into their costumes before their dinner reservation at eight. Phoebe and Dylan, both dressed in nursing scrubs, were the first ones waiting in the hotel lobby for the others. Five minutes passed before Stuart arrived. He was dressed up as an LSU football player. Stuart looked at Dylan and Phoebe and said, "Wow, two nurses, how original."

"They were all out of oversensitive accountant costumes at Party City, so we had to settle on being nurses," Dylan replied.

Just as Stuart sat on the couch beside the two evil nurses, the elevator door opened, and out walked John John and Debbie. John John had a stringy, longhaired wig on and was dressed in a tux shirt with ruffles, which was unbuttoned down to his navel, along with tight, black, leather paints. Debbie was wearing a long, white, heavy sequins gown, and she had a coal miner hard hat on top of her long, brown wig.

Phoebe, Stuart, and Dylan could not figure out who the couple was supposed to be.

"Who are ya'll supposed to be?" asked Dylan.

"I'm seventies rock icon Meatloaf," John John announced.

"I thought you were Mamma Cass during her heavy drug days," uttered Stuart.

"And I'm Loretta Lynn as the coal miner's daughter," proclaimed Debbie.

"Oh my God, Norma would love your costume," Phoebe said to Debbie.

"Who do ya think helped me designed this exquisite gown?" responded Debbie.

"Well, I'd like to stand here and have ya'll envy my sexy rock star persona, but we need to get out of here like a bat out of hell—no pun intended," said John John.

"I certainly don't want to be late for our dinner reservation at Superior Steakhouse," stated Phoebe.

"Shouldn't we all do a shot of tequila or something before we go out in public looking like the Village People?" asked Stuart.

"Hey, what happened to our no-drug pact? We don't need to get all liquored up to have a good ole time," Debbie answered.

"Such encouraging words coming from an Adderall addict. Besides, there was never an agreement to an alcohol-free weekend," Stuart scolded Debbie.

"All right, kids, let's save the arguing for the van. Now, let's go. Meatloaf is hungry," John John said to the uptight football player and country singer.

As Stuart, Phoebe, and Dylan followed behind John John and Debbie to the valet parking office, Debbie leaned over, grabbed John John's arm, and griped, "That will be the last time I baptize that ungrateful bastard."

"Settle down, Loretta," John John replied.

The oddballs had just finished eating char-grilled oysters and prime rib when the other diners finally stopped staring at them and accepted that they were having dinner across from five loud *Let's Make a Deal* contestants. Right after John John ordered Superior's hot buttered pecan pie, chocolate molten soufflé, and southern comfort bread pudding for everyone to share for dessert, Debbie's cell phone rang. It was her daughter

Amanda. Debbie took off her hard hat and straightened her teased-up wig before she answered her phone.

"Hey, baby girl … wait, wait, what's wrong?" Debbie asked her daughter.

Debbie remained on the phone with her distraught daughter for ten minutes while the others, who couldn't wait any longer, devoured the delectable desserts. As the worried mother listened to her daughter's complaints over the phone, she saw her husband getting ready to eat the only piece of bread pudding left. Debbie pushed the mute button on her phone and then snatched John John's right arm to prevent him from sticking his fork in the only bite of pudding.

"I'm warning you: you take the last bite, and you'll be one big chunk of meat without your loaf," Debbie advised John John.

John John granted his pudding-dependent wife's wishes and placed the small portion of dessert in front of her while the others laughed at his vulnerability. Debbie finally got off the phone with Amanda, gobbled the sliver of bread pudding, and announced, "The Halloween party is off."

"Why? What happened?" asked Phoebe.

"A horrible fight broke out between SpongeBob Square Pants and Marilyn Monroe. Apparently, Marilyn brought Mariah Carey to this drag queen shindig and SpongeBob had just ended a three-year relationship with Mariah. Therefore, Marilyn and SpongeBob got into a nasty brawl, and the police were called," reported Debbie.

"I'm tellin' ya, there ain't nothin' worse than a catfight between two gay dudes. Honey, do you remember the time we had that partners ceremony in the banquet room of the restaurant?" asked John John.

"Hell yes, I do. Those fuming grooms went after it before the ceremony even started. Hell, those divas tore down the rainbow backdrop I made out of chicken wire and colored tissue," said Debbie.

"Hey, hey, let's not make this a two-hour mystery movie of the week. The party is over, and we can all go back to the hotel. There, see how easy that was," said Dylan.

"We're not going anywhere until I get a piece of that pecan pie that ya'll gobbled down in front of me while I was tryin' to calm my baby girl down," Debbie warned.

It was 10:45 p.m. when the group arrived back at the hotel lobby. Debbie was holding her hard hat with her wig stuffed inside it, and John John's fake hair was tied in a ponytail (courtesy of Phoebe when they were at the steakhouse waiting on Debbie to finish eating her much deserved dessert). As the worn-out troop walked toward the lounge to get a nightcap, a group of college boys chanted, "LSU! LSU! LSU!" at Stuart. The old football player smiled at the young men and said, "Yeah, yeah, go Tigers. Now y'all go on and leave this ancient fan alone."

Debbie and Phoebe sat down on the sofa, and the men plopped down on the sofa across from them. A young, pretty barmaid approached the five and told them that the special for the night was a bucket of Budweiser beers for fourteen dollars. Surprisingly, the former party animals all ordered Irish coffees. After the waitress left, John John asked, "Is anyone up for a game of blackjack?"

"I'm gonna pass," replied Stuart.

"No, thank you," answered Phoebe.

"I'm too tired," added Dylan.

"Since we all have decided to have a calm night, now would be a good time for my dashing rock star of a husband to ask Dylan a very important question," announced Debbie.

"Honey, let's not do this tonight," John John told Debbie.

"What is it, John John?" asked Dylan.

"I'd rather not do this right now," requested John John.

"Oh come on, John John, we're all family. Spill the beans," encouraged Phoebe.

"I just don't want to put Dylan in an awkward position," uttered John John.

"It's okay, brother. Ask me anything," Dylan said to John John.

"Ask him," Debbie ordered her nervous husband.

"Do you think Dylan and Debbie may have had sex before ya'll got married? Is that what's troubling you?" Stuart asked John John.

Dylan gave Stuart a dirty look and said, "Stuart, why don't you go find a slot machine to play. I'm sure there's one with an eighties theme to make you feel relevant."

Debbie interrupted what could have been an ugly argument between Stuart and Dylan by saying, "All right, let's not go there, fellas. I spent too much time this afternoon on christening Stuart into a self-regulating thinker."

"Cut the bull crap. For God's sake, John John, ask Dylan whatever the hell you need to ask him!" demanded Phoebe.

"Go ahead, baby," encouraged Debbie.

"Just ask him," added Stuart.

John John cleared his throat and proceeded to ask Dylan what seemed to be the million-dollar question. "Okay, you know that I recently came into a decent amount of money by selling my building to the bank, right?"

"Yes, I'm aware of this," answered Dylan.

John John continued explaining, "Well, it's not enough money for me to retire on, and ya know how I am with my pride and all …"

"I know, man," interrupted Dylan.

Debbie felt that John John had taken too long with his request, so she jumped in. "Dylan, what my chicken-ass husband wants to know is would you consider him opening up a catfish takeout station inside Norma's Cajun Rage Quick Stop?"

Everyone anxiously waited for Dylan's response. Dylan had a flat expression on his face while he appeared to be thinking about John John's essential request. After many seconds of silence, Dylan said, "It would be my honor, brother." Phoebe, Debbie, and Stuart cheered as John John and Dylan raised their glass mugs of coffee and made a toast in honor of their new business venture.

Shortly after the mini celebration of John John's lip-smacking catfish merging with the celebrated red pig (the mascot of the everlasting Aunt Dewy's Pork Jerky), everyone decided to call it a night. They all hugged one another and went to their rooms for a good night's sleep.

The next morning while John John, Dylan, and Stuart slept in, Debbie and Phoebe met Debbie's daughter Amanda and her wife, Cindy, for breakfast. Phoebe had brought the newly married couple a gift since she was unable to attend their wedding in Vermont. The skillful jewelry designer made two beautiful gold pins that were two dog paws that appeared to be holding hands. Amanda and Cindy had met while walking their dogs and they both worked in animal healthcare. Amanda was an adorable, blonde-haired woman who could pass for Debbie's young twin sister, and Cindy was a tall, slim, boyish female who also had blonde hair. Both ladies were thrilled with Phoebe's present. They immediately pinned the golden paws on each other's blouses. During the entire breakfast, Cindy and Amanda told Debbie and Phoebe about the hideous lovers' battle that unfortunately ended the Halloween-slash-marriage party.

After the ladies ate breakfast, Debbie and Phoebe walked the newlyweds to the parking garage. They all hugged, kissed, and said their good-byes.

While Debbie and Phoebe were walking back to the lobby, Debbie stopped by the valet parking booth and instructed the attendant to have the van out front in an hour. She also asked the attendant to find a few cardboard boxes and place them in the vehicle. Phoebe thought that Debbie's request was an odd one but didn't bother asking her why she wanted the cardboard. When the ladies reached the elevator, Phoebe told Debbie that she would make sure that Dylan and Stuart were up and ready to go. The plan was everyone would meet in the lobby in forty-five minutes.

When Debbie arrived at her suite, she suddenly realized that she didn't have her room card, so she knocked on the door for John John to let her in. When John John opened the door, he had only his underwear on, and there was a melted chocolate mint, shaped as a lucky horseshoe, imprinted on his forehead.

"What the hell is on your forehead? Did a bedbug crap on your brows?" asked Debbie.

John John wiped off his forehead and discovered that he had forgotten to take the complimentary chocolate off his pillow before he slept and drooled on top of it. He walked over to the mirror and began to laugh at himself, along with Debbie.

No one took a shower, but John John did wash the melted chocolate horseshoe off of his face. They were all dressed in jeans and sweatshirts when they met in the lobby. Ironically, everyone was wearing Menard High School class of '83 baseball caps that Stuart had put in their welcome bags the first night of the reunion. The five friends looked at one another and started to cackle.

"Oh my God, everyone is wearing their caps! This couldn't have worked out better even if I had planned it!" cheered Stuart.

"We all look like campy grandparents waiting to see our grandkids play Little League ball," Dylan remarked.

Once again, Debbie decided that she would be the driver for their trip back to Alexandria, and this time she took the I-49 route. The weather was partly cloudy and looked as if it might rain.

Right when they entered Natchitoches Parish, Debbie noticed a steep hill of grass beside an overpass. She pulled over to the side, turned on the hazard lights, parked the van, and ordered her perplexed passengers to get out of the vehicle.

"What is it, honey? Do we have a flat?" John John asked.

"No, we don't have a flat, but I do need you to get your big, fat, flat ass out of this van," Debbie ordered John John.

The group got out of the van and watched Debbie take two large cardboard boxes from out of the trunk. As she flattened the boxes by jumping up and down on them, she pointed to the top of the hill.

"Our last activity before we end this weekend," Debbie, the new leader, announced to her flabbergasted followers. She gave John John one of the compressed boxes and handed the other one to Stuart.

John John looked at Phoebe and said, "Come on, let's take a free ride."

As Phoebe and John John hiked up the hill, Debbie instructed Dylan to turn the van radio up, which was already on the classic rock station. She then held her arm out for Stuart to escort her to the hilltop of brown grass. John John and Phoebe were the first ones to ride down the knoll on the cardboard sleigh, and before Stuart and Debbie took the plunge, Stuart gave Dylan thumbs up for selecting such a cool song to play, which was "The Battle of Evermore" by Led Zeppelin. The middle-aged chums had a wonderful time gliding on their magic (cardboard) carpets. They took turns sliding down two at a time. The only minor malfunctions that occurred were the light rain falling from the dark clouds plus and John John and Debbie's inability to slide down together. The couple's weight prevented the takeoff, so they had to separate and ride with a lighter partner to avoid a Wide Load sign from being placed on their backs.

After twenty minutes of participating in the redneck version of sledding, Phoebe and Dylan decided to take a break. Phoebe stood by the van and watched Stuart and the tubby twosome slither down the small mountain while Dylan was in the minibus, attempting to find an eighties radio station at Stuart's request. A flash of lightning appeared, followed by thunder when a state police car pulled up behind the party van. Debbie, standing on top of the hill, was the first one to see the flashing blue lights. John John and Stuart had already slid down the hill before Debbie could warn them about the police. Phoebe saw Debbie pointing to two state troopers, and then she yelled for Dylan to get out of the vehicle. Dylan stepped out and saw the two officers coming toward him and Phoebe.

"Call me crazy, but I don't think these two policemen are gonna be fans of Frankie Dubois's hit song, 'I Found Christ in K-Mart,'" Phoebe expressed to Dylan.

CHAPTER 21

Fried Turkey Stuffed with Holiday Secrets

On Thanksgiving Day morning, Norma and Sylvia were in Norma's spotless kitchen. The two talked about Hunter and Sylvia's wedding plans while the proud grandmother was dying her future granddaughter-in-law's hair sparkling burgundy. The expecting mother and the young man in recovery decided to be married on Christmas Day. Norma's first husband, Brent, agreed to have the ceremony and reception at the Jacobs family mansion. All family on both sides were extremely happy that Hunter and Sylvia decided to tie the knot, especially since Hunter was now sober and allowed everyone to see the truly incredible person who Sylvia had always known him to be.

Norma decided to have an evening Thanksgiving dinner. The only tasks Norma had to complete were to heat up the Spinach Madeleine, the cornbread dressing, and the sweet potato casserole and thaw out the cranberry salad. She had brought all the premade food from the Main Dish Casserole Shop.

John John agreed to come over early to fry the turkey. Debbie would not be attending Thanksgiving at Norma's because she and her younger daughter, Savannah, were going to spend the holiday at her sister Darlene's house, and John John was not invited. Darlene was upset with him for refusing to hire her to work at Johnny Boy's Catfish Takeout. John John never trusted Darlene, ever since he caught her stealing a huge jar of pickle chips from his restaurant a few years ago. Debbie didn't care that her husband didn't want to hire her sister because she was finished with the fried seafood business for good. Debbie had her own dream to achieve. In fact, she and Sylvia had been seriously thinking about opening up a toddler pageant gown store. She even asked Stuart if he would be interested in leasing his man cave to her. He told her that there wasn't a snowball's chance in hell that he would allow his Bayview Yacht Club to be turned into a boutique for Jean Bennett Ramsey fanatics.

Phoebe was another extended family member who would not be attending Norma's turkey day observance. The talented jewelry artist was going to take her son, Michael, and his fiancée, Carmon, for Creole cuisine at Mr. B's Bistro in the French Quarter to celebrate Thanksgiving. Michael had met Carmon two years ago at the Jazz Festival. Carmon, a petite, stunning, dark-skinned black woman, was just as beautiful as Michael was.

Phoebe fell in love with her future daughter-in-law the first day she met her, which was the day Carmon graduated from Loyola University Law School. Phoebe also invited a mystery guest to attend her holiday dinner—and that guest was Shane Miller, the manager of the Produce Department at Rouses Supermarket.

Shane, a medium-built African American man with gorgeous, copper-colored eyes, was ten years younger than Phoebe. Right away, the two hit it off when Shane showed Phoebe how to pick out good asparagus. Ever since meeting at the market, Phoebe and the vegetable connoisseur had spent every day together. Shane and Phoebe had a lot in common. He lost his wife of five years to breast cancer, and he was well read. Before he became the produce manager at Rouses, Shane worked as a newspaper reporter for the *Times-Picayune*. The low pay along with the pressure of working under a deadline led him to the stress-free career of maintaining pineapples and eggplants.

Minus the absences of Debbie and Phoebe, Norma had a condo full of family and friends, which included Dylan, Stuart, John John, Kris, Hunter and Sylvia, Steven and Lauren, Brent and his new girlfriend, and the new girlfriend's daughter.

Brent's new love was Liz Benowitz, a stylish, wealthy, sixty-four-year-old Jewish woman whose money came from her third husband, who owned Oriental rug stores in New Orleans, Baton Rouge, Lafayette, Lake Charles, Alexandria, and Shreveport.

Brent encouraged Liz to bring her daughter, Caroline, because he felt she would be a perfect match for Stuart. Out of all Dylan's friends,

Brent liked Stuart the most. Caroline was slightly overweight and had a big nose. She looked like a black-headed Bette Midler. She was raised by her father (Liz's first husband) and grew up in Beverly Hills, California. Brent knew that Stuart would be fascinated with Caroline because she was an executive producer for several reality and game shows that had made pop culture history.

Norma's dining room table (set for twelve) was exquisite. Her Lenox Eternal china and silver goblets were beautifully displayed. Even Lauren was mesmerized with how lovely her mother-in-law's table looked. Norma, dressed in a St. John apricot pant suit that Steven and Lauren gave her for her birthday, stood at the door and greeted each guest as they arrived.

Meanwhile, John John and Kris were in the kitchen, sampling the cranberry punch, which consisted of cranberry juice, vodka, and red wine. John John had on an apron that read: Piss Off! I'm Cooking! Kris was wearing khaki pants and his best Bob Marley T-shirt. John John had started drinking the potent punch earlier in the day while injecting the turkeys with his secret Cajun spices.

Dylan, dressed in jeans, a white dress shirt, and a tie, entered the kitchen. He saw the jolly turkey fryer trying to persuade Kris to try a deli spiral treat. Debbie had John John bring over a box of the unpopular appetizers to make up for her absence.

"What's going on here?" asked Dylan.

"Chef Paul Prudhomme here is getting plastered, and he's insisting that I try one of these thawed-out pinwheel pieces of crap," answered Kris.

Dylan walked over to Kris and grabbed the paper cup of punch from his hand and poured it into the sink. Dylan turned around from the sink, glared at John John, and asked, "Do you think it might be possible not to add one more addict into the family this holiday season?"

"He's seventeen! My God, you and I started drinkin' at twelve!" responded John John.

The tipsy, big man took a bite into a spiral treat, and half of it fell down on the kitchen floor. Kris watched John John accidently step on the piece of food while he was swaying back and forth.

"You've been drinking since you were twelve, you say? And how's that working for you?" Kris asked.

Before John John could reply to Kris's condescending question, Stuart, Hunter, and Sylvia entered the kitchen. Stuart had on a coat and tie. Hunter was dressed almost identical to Dylan, but he had a black tie on, and his father was wearing dark-blue tie. Sylvia looked lovely in her simple, black dress. Hunter looked at John John guzzling his punch, and then he saw Kris's T-shirt with the famous Reggae singer smoking marijuana on the front.

"I have so much to be thankful for this holiday season. I especially give thanks to my strong support system," Hunter expressed to John John and Kris.

"Damn it, you two!" Dylan shouted at Kris and John John.

"Dad, it's really okay. I was only joking with them," explained Hunter.

John John placed his hand on Dylan's shoulder and said, "Calm down. What's wrong with you?"

"He's upset because Marie is with my parents today instead of spending Thanksgiving with us," Sylvia answered for Dylan.

"Dad also hasn't had a drink in twenty days, so he's a little agitated," added Hunter.

"Well, today should be one hell of a test for both of y'all," uttered Kris.

Norma called out for everyone in the kitchen to come to the living room. When Dylan, John John, Kris, Hunter, and Sylvia entered the room, Norma was waiting to introduce Liz Benowitz and her daughter, Caroline, who had just arrived along with Brent, Steven, and Lauren. The new arrivals all looked dashing in their holiday attire.

After the introductions were made, Liz complimented Norma for having such a charming and spacious condominium.

"Thank you," said Norma.

"Brent told me you had a Dottie West museum. I just gotta see this," requested Liz.

As Norma took Liz and Caroline to the legendary room dedicated to Dottie and her late husband, Frankie, Brent strolled over to Stuart and asked, "How about that Caroline?"

"She seems very nice," answered Stuart.

"If she's anything like her mother between the sheets, you're in for a real treat," Brent added.

Stuart didn't know how to respond to Dr. Jacobs's inappropriate comment. Dylan, who was standing in front of the bar where Steven was preparing a cocktail, looked at his brother after hearing the crude remark from their father and uttered, "Will you at least show me a bottle of vodka?"

Steven smiled at his alcohol-craving brother and replied, "This is only a minor challenge in your duties of becoming a role model."

Meanwhile, in the chamber devoted to two long-ago country artists, Liz and Caroline were amazed with all the photos, costumes, albums, and memorabilia on display. As Norma was explaining the old black-and-white photograph of Aunt Dewy's Jerky Factory with the notorious pig statue placed on the roof, Liz interrupted the unconventional tour guide.

"Hey, that's the pig on top of your little shop-and-stop store!" declared Liz.

"Yes, it is," Norma replied.

Liz nudged her daughter, and she shouted, "How adorable! We adore that bright, red porker, and this is coming from two Jewish broads!"

Norma and Caroline grinned as Liz chuckled at her own statement. After Liz finished laughing, she suggested to Caroline that Norma's peculiar exhibit would be perfect for one of those bizarre documentaries that she produced.

While Norma was in the process of showing the ladies a Dottie West gown that was displayed on a mannequin, Liz once again interrupted her.

"You have the most beautiful skin. Geez, even under this track lighting, you're complexion is gorgeous. I would kill for your skin ... I was gonna try that Lifestyle Lift, you know that procedure that Pat Boone's daughter talks about on television," explained Liz.

"Are you talking about Debbie Boone?" asked Norma.

"Yeah, yeah, the chick that sang that sappy 'You Light Up My Life' garbage. As I was saying, this Lifestyle Lift is supposed to be a safer alternative to the traditional facelift, and I'm like oy vey, I'll just continue to use Doctor Leibowitz ... he's my tune-up specialist in Miami," Liz clarified.

"I always say that beauty is skin deep, but under a well-done procedure, one's soul shines even brighter," added Norma.

Liz looked at Caroline and said, "I love this woman."

After cocktail hour had passed, Norma called everyone to the dining room. There was no seating chart, so the guests sat wherever they wanted to. Brent made sure that Stuart and Caroline sat next to each other. Norma was seated at the head of the table, and Kris sat at the other end. Norma insisted that Hunter say the blessing, and he was honored.

"God, I wish to thank you for this joyful day … my very supportive fiancée … my daughter as well as my child on the way … my loyal family, especially my father … the new friends we've made today, and most importantly, giving me a second chance … Amen," Hunter expressed.

Everyone said amen, and then Kris looked over at Stuart and mumbled, "What is this, the *Hunter Jacobs Show*? I mean, come on, is narcissism step thirteen in his road to recovery?"

Instead of answering Kris, Stuart kicked the obnoxious teen under the table.

While everyone was eating frozen cranberry salad, John John's portion slid into his lap after he attempted to cut it.

"Damn it, this is like eating freezer-burned Jell-O," joked John John.

Kris and Liz were the only ones who laughed at John John's frozen salad mishap. Dylan got up and told John John to follow him into the kitchen so that he could get the cranberry stain off his unfitting apron.

When the two men entered the kitchen, Dylan immediately reprimanded John John for his childish behavior.

"Not today, John John. I can't deal with your outlandish temperament! And take that damn foolish apron off!" demanded Dylan.

As John John took off his apron, he looked at his livid buddy and said, "Okay, man, I'm sorry. Things could be a lot worse, ya know. Debbie could have been here to intensify your humiliation toward your friends. Ya know, I don't need this. I'm out of here. Let me know how the fried turkey is."

"Wait, wait, please don't leave. I don't know what's wrong with me. It's like I'm going through this menacing detox from my standard selfish ways," pleaded Dylan.

"Holy turd balls, the mysterious rebel just might have found happiness. Everything is at a content standstill in your life, and you can't stand it," John John confirmed.

"Touché, the fried catfish king has made a substantial point," admitted Dylan.

John John looked at the fried turkey and all the trimmings displayed on the kitchen island and replied, "Well, this royal pain in your ass is fixin' to pour another glass of this forbidden fruit punch and then go into that there dining room to watch your daddy be a matchmaker for Stuart and that hot Hollywood executive in there … and I'm gonna put my apron back on."

The two old friends hugged and then walked back into the dining room.

When John John and Dylan entered the room, Kris was picking up everyone's salad plates. He had promised Norma that he would be the butler for the day to make up for lying to her about pretending to be sick to get out of taking his algebra final. Just as John John and Dylan sat down, Norma instructed Kris to go to the kitchen and prepare to serve.

"All right, boss lady, I'm going," Kris replied.

"Liars must repent," uttered Norma.

"Yeah, yeah … don't be surprised if there's a lethal substance added to your store-bought Spinach Madeleine," shouted Kris as he entered the kitchen.

Norma looked over to Liz and Caroline and explained, "I promise our dinner wasn't purchased at Walmart. I bought everything from the Main Dish, which is a wonderful take-out casserole shop."

"I love the Main Dish! Their lasagna is fabulous. It's better than sex. I appreciate the fact that they don't use cottage cheese. I hate that stuff. It's bumpy, lumpy, and just appears to be old," stated Liz.

John John looked over at Liz and asked, "Wait, are you talkin' about an ingredient you don't like in lasagna or the trials and tribulations of having sex with old Doctor Brent Jacobs here?"

Norma, shocked by John John's inappropriate question, spit out her wine as Liz, Caroline, Brent, and Stuart burst out into laughter. Dylan stood up and ordered John John to come with him into the kitchen again. Before John John could respond to Dylan's demand, Liz intervened.

"Dylan, honey, don't fuss at your hilarious friend. It's all in good fun. Oy vey, the whole family is comedians—comedians, I tell ya. Caroline, you should grab a camera and film these people for your reality shtick," said Liz.

Suddenly, they all heard Kris's voice coming from the kitchen. "Bon appétit … get your butts in here!" shouted Kris.

They all grabbed their dinner plates and headed toward the kitchen. When everyone entered the kitchen, there was Kris wearing a hairnet (in honor of all cafeteria ladies in the United States), and he had a large serving spoon in each hand.

"Serve you! Ya'll don't be shy. Come and get it!" Kris yelled at the family and guests.

As everybody lined up to be served fried turkey and pre-prepared side dishes, Norma, who was standing in front of her eldest son, Steven, muttered to him, "I should have taken your advice, son, and enrolled Kris when he was five into a boarding school for bad boys who have old mothers." Dylan watched Steven snicker at his mother's wisecrack, and for the first time in many years, he felt there could be a potential bonding in the making, and then he saw Steven tell Lauren to hang in there and that they should be finished with this dreadful dinner soon. Dylan quickly came back to reality.

Kris saw that Liz and Caroline were the first two in the serving line and said, "Sorry, ladies, the Main Dish was fresh out of kosher cuisine."

"Kris, stop it. I mean it. Put those spoons down and get to the back of the line," Norma demanded.

Once everyone fixed their plate and took their seat at the dining room table, Norma made a touching toast, and then everybody began to eat. Brent, Dylan, Caroline, and Norma complimented John John on the turkey. Kris took his first bite of the spicy bird and said to John John, "Damn, this is good." John John gave Kris a fake smile.

"What? You don't think I'm sincere?" asked Kris.

"Nah, it's just hard to take praise from a punk wearing a hairnet," answered John John.

"All I can say is it's sure nice to have a home-cooked meal for once—even if it was prepared by casserole clerks from the Main Dish. At least it's a local business," Steven stated.

"You'd have a home-cooked diner if you were ever home," Lauren responded. She then began eating at a rapid rate. To avoid an argument between the couple in trouble, Brent changed the subject by giving an exciting announcement about his dear ex-wife, Norma.

"Norma, tell our guests your exciting news," requested Brent.

Before Norma could say a word, Kris corrected Brent by saying, "What do you mean—*our guests?* This isn't your home."

"That's enough, cafeteria man. Shut up and let Momma share her good news," Dylan ordered his belligerent younger brother.

"Thanks, Dylan, for the warm, fuzzy introduction … umm, it's really no big deal. I was asked to be the grand marshal of the Alexandria Christmas parade," Norma announced.

"It is a big deal!" shouted Sylvia.

"Wonderful! I love parades!" added Liz.

"What an enormous honor," chimed in Caroline.

"You've turned down the grand marshal invitation from the Mardi Gras Association for years. Why now?" Stuart asked Norma.

"Because this is a Christmas parade—not a Mardi Gras one," Hunter answered for his grandmother.

"Why would you turn down the offer to be grand marshal for Mardi Gras?" Caroline questioned the modest hostess.

"It's because of a tragedy that happened to her friend's daughter-in-law many years ago in New Orleans," Hunter answered for Norma.

"I gotta hear this. What the hell happened?" probed Liz.

"I'd rather not say. It was such a horrible incident," Norma replied.

"Oh, come on! Tell us!" demanded Liz.

"I really don't feel it's appropriate to talk about, especially during Thanksgiving dinner," Norma said.

Liz looked at Brent and demanded, "All right, Brent, spill the beans. I know you must know what your lovely ex-wife won't share with us."

Brent cleared his voice and began to tell the Mardi Gras misfortune story. "Norma's friend Gert Waters—"

"Oh, I love Gert Waters. She bought many rugs from third ex-husband ... oh I'm sorry. Please continue, Brent," interrupted Liz.

"After consuming several Hurricanes at Pat O' Brian's, Gert's daughter-in-law, Elizabeth, ran in front of the *Wizard of Oz* float to try and catch one of the red slipper necklaces that the little people dressed as munchkins were throwing ... well, Elizabeth stepped out too far in front of the float and was crushed instantly," explained Brent.

"Yeah, and when the speeding float came to a sudden halt from running over the drunk woman, munchkins were flying into the crowds as if these poor little people were being shot out of a cannon," added Kris.

Liz and John John were the only two to laugh at Kris's commentary. While trying to stop laughing, Liz said, "I'm so sorry to laugh, but, Caroline, I'm tellin' ya, if you had a camera or at least a damn tape recorder, you'd make millions off these outrageous people."

"Really, Mother? Please stop," pleaded Caroline.

"I'm sorry, I'm sorry," Liz uttered.

Caroline looked at Norma and said, "I can definitely understand why you'd be hesitant to ride on any float."

"Is this why you refuse to watch midget wrestling?" John John jokingly asked Norma.

Liz laughed even harder. Sylvia saw that Norma had tears in eyes. She held her second mother's hand and said, "This is very difficult for Norma. Her friend's daughter-in-law's freak accident brings back the painful memory of her only true love, Frankie's awful death."

"Was he also run over by float?" asked Caroline.

"No, he was in the parking lot of Norma's Cajun Rage Quick Stop during Hurricane Rita, and the very strong winds blew the pig off of the roof, and it tumbled down on Frankie and killed him," Sylvia explained.

"Wait, you're tellin' me a woman is trampled by a float and Norma's husband was murdered by a pig statue—and it's the same pig that's on the top of the store today?" asked Liz.

"Yes," answered Sylvia.

Liz excused herself from the table and dashed to the bathroom where she laughed until she could barely breathe. Caroline, once again, apologized to everyone for her mother's behavior. Norma told her that it was okay.

Lauren, who had eaten every morsel of food on her plate, asked everyone if they were ready for dessert. John John was the only one who was even close to finishing the second course. Kris looked at Lauren's clean dish and said, "Wow, somebody made a happy plate." Steven, Dylan, and Norma also found it odd that Lauren, who usually ate like a bird, devoured her meal in a matter of minutes. Lauren stood up and announced that she was going to start preparing the dessert. She had brought two Louisiana yam cakes from the French Market Express in Natchitoches and a gallon of Kroger Private Selection Cherry Cordial ice cream.

As Lauren walked into the kitchen, Norma looked over at Kris and said, "You need to go help Lauren."

"I haven't finished eating," replied Kris.

"That's not my problem. I'm not the one who tried to get out of taking my math test by faking to be sick. Now, get up and go help with dessert," Norma demanded.

Brent looked at Kris and added, "Back in my day, the help always ate in the kitchen,"

"Back in my day—that phrase is so overused today," muttered Kris as he headed toward the kitchen.

When he entered the kitchen, Kris saw Lauren shoving rolls in her mouth as if she were a squirrel storing acorns for the winter. He asked the bread gorger if she needed any help, and she politely refused. Kris turned around, went back into the dining room, and sat down.

"Ah, wait a minute, garcon, aren't you supposed to be helping with dessert?" Hunter asked his younger uncle.

"After taking a breather from scarfing down the rest of the Sister Schubert yeast rolls like a vampire going in for a fresh neck, Lauren told me she had it under control," Kris replied.

"I understand. Us ladies save all of our calories for this glorious day," uttered Norma.

Liz entered the dining room after regaining her composure in the restroom and asked, "Okay, what outlandish story did I miss while I was in the bathroom?"

"You didn't miss anything. In fact, you've arrived just in time for my big announcement," replied Brent. The doctor waited for his new girlfriend to sit down, and then he continued, "I've just purchased a remarkable piece of art, and after dessert, I want you all to come see it."

"Where is it?" asked Norma.

"I have it stored in the storage space behind the convenience store," Brent answered.

"We can't stay long. Remember, we're invited over to the Newburgers' tonight," reminded Liz.

"Oh, Brent, I'd love to see whatever it is you're so excited about, but Kris and I, well actually just Kris, needs to clean up," stated Norma.

"Nonsense, this won't take long. I promise," Brent replied.

After everyone agreed to make a short trip to the storage unit, John John said, "Well, while ya'll eat that fattening dessert, I'll just finish up the rest of this healthy cranberry punch. Ya know, I gotta keep my fierce physique in check."

Later that evening, all who were present at the Thanksgiving dinner were waiting outside of the storage unit for Steven to arrive. While they waited, Norma, who was looking at the famous pig statue on top of the store with her namesake, pointed out to Dylan that the light inside the pig was still out. Dylan promised her that he would call an electrician to take a look at it. Steven finally pulled up to the unit, got out of his Mercedes Benz, and waved the key to the padlock in front of everyone.

"Where's Lauren?" Norma asked her oldest son.

"I dropped her off at the house. She wasn't feeling well," Steven answered.

"I hope it wasn't something she ate," uttered Norma.

"She'll be fine," Steven replied.

Steven gave the key to his father, and before Brent opened the padlock, he announced, "Norma, my dear first wife, we all pitched in and felt this would perfect for you,"

"Wait, this is a gift for me, not a piece of art you purchased?" inquired Norma.

Brent did not answer her. He opened the lock, rolled up the door, and there stood a magnificent eighteen-foot-long pig float made of fiberglass, papier-mâché, and Styrofoam. Norma couldn't believe her eyes. She was touched beyond belief.

"This is what you'll be riding on for the Christmas parade!" cheered Brent.

Norma immediately began to cry and said, "I can't believe what you all have done! Oh my God, this must have been very expensive."

"Don't get too attached to it, Momma, because we're selling it to the Avoyelles Tourism after the holidays. They're gonna use it for their Cochon De Lait Festival in Mansura," Steven explained.

As Norma hugged and kissed Brent as well as each one of her sons, Liz climbed up onto the incredible float and shouted, "Caroline! Use your cell phone and get a video of me on top of this! Oy vey! Who'd believe a Jewish American princess on top of a damn pork float!"

After Norma had thanked everyone for the beyond generous gift, they all went their separate ways. Dylan, Hunter, and Sylvia headed to Forest Hill to pick up Maria. Brent and Liz had another gathering to attend. Kris and Norma were going to clean up and then watch the movie *Sister Act*. Ever since Kris was five years-old, it had been a tradition for him and his mother to watch the comedy on Thanksgiving night, and Stuart invited Caroline to see his extraordinary bar (the replica of the Bayview Yacht Club), and she accepted his invitation. Stuart had promised John John that he would tape all the football games that were played on television earlier in the day, so John John tagged along with the couple, who was set up by Brent the matchmaker.

It was 11:45 p.m., and Norma was sleeping when Kris sneaked out of the condo and drove to Walgreens. Right when he entered the drugstore, he was shocked to see Lauren at the checkout. She was loading laxatives on the counter when she saw Kris. Kris smiled at her and said, "Hi,

Lauren. Bye, Lauren." He then turned around and started walking out the electronic doors.

"Wait, Kris, please wait," said Lauren.

"I'll be out in the parking lot," Kris replied.

Lauren paid the cashier, grabbed her bag of secret purges, and met Kris in the parking lot.

"What are you doing out so late?" asked Lauren.

"It's personal, just like those little cleansing friends you just purchased," answered Kris.

"You're too bright for me to lie to you. I admit I do have a body image problem, but it's not as bad as it used to be," clarified Lauren.

"Hey, we all have our drawbacks," replied Kris.

"Is Steven still at your house?" asked Lauren.

"No," answered Kris.

"He told me that he was going to watch a movie with you and Norma and that he'd probably be late getting in," stated Lauren.

Kris grinned and said, "Steven? Your husband, Steven? Watching a feel-good comedy with his mother—not to mention me, his half-brother, who he wishes would have been sold to the gypsies before he ever laid eyes on me. Are we talking about the same dreadful person here?"

Lauren didn't respond. She looked as if she was trying her hardest not to cry. Kris saw that she was getting upset and said, "Hey, look, maybe there was an emergency at the hospital and he had to go see about a patient or something like that."

"We both know that's not it. At any rate, why are you here?" probed Lauren.

"I guess since we're on the subject of personal drawbacks, I'll be honest with you … umm, my friend Todd Sesser's sister is in town for the holidays. She's a freshman at LSU, and along with gaining the famous freshman fifteen pounds, she also gained an appreciation for having sex. So, being the cautious and courteous man that I am, I wanted to get some condoms before I tap on her bedroom window."

"You're too young to buy condoms. Do you want me to buy them for you?" asked Lauren.

"Nah, that's not necessary. Hunter let me borrow his driving license, but thanks anyway," replied Kris.

"All the men in your family must carry the same promiscuous gene," said Lauren.

"Yeah, that's about the only genetic factor we all have in common … ya know, I'm starting to have second thoughts about pursuing this whole naughty college girl fantasy, I think I'm just gonna go back home," Kris explained.

"Do you want me to take you to that porno shop on Bolton Avenue?" asked Lauren.

"Geez, Lauren, I'm not a teenage nymphomaniac. I'm just a seventeen-year-old horny male who apparently is looking for love in all the wrong places. Believe me, I'll get over it, but thank you," joked Kris.

"I know we're not very close—I don't even think you like me—but can this accidental meeting be our secret?" pleaded Lauren.

"My lips are sealed," Kris replied.

Lauren gave Kris a weak smile and then turned around and began walking toward her vehicle. Kris remained standing in the same position as he watched the sad woman walking away. Suddenly, he yelled, "Hey, Lauren!" She turned around, and Kris shouted, "I do like you! I mean, just a little, but I do like you!"

"A small amount of acceptance is better than nothing!" Lauren yelled back.

"Wait, I didn't say I accepted you. We're just one level above tolerating one another!" hollered Kris.

"Bye, Kris! Behave!" Lauren shouted back as she was getting into her car.

Meanwhile, at Stuart's ultimate man cave, he and Caroline were sitting at a table in the middle of his bar. Debbie had picked up John John a few hours ago. John John had one too many cranberry cocktails, and he was also furious with Stuart. Stuart accidently recorded the Macy's Thanksgiving Parade instead of the NFL games that he was supposed to tape for the devoted football fan.

Caroline and Stuart sipped red wine and talked for hours about significant events that occurred in the entertainment industry back in the eighties and nineties. Caroline was ten years younger than Stuart, and their age difference made for stimulating debates. At first, she felt the bar was a bit too much, but after getting to know Stuart, Caroline thought that it was fascinating that he lived in the past and she was paid to bring the past back to the future. Stuart couldn't believe all the television shows, music documentaries, and reality series that Caroline had produced for the Sign of the Times network. Stuart actually liked VH-1 better, but he was still extremely awestricken with Caroline's work. Right after they had finished their conversation about the true meaning of the song "Release" by Pearl Jam, Caroline looked at her watch and saw that it was 4:30 a.m.

"Oh, Stuart, I'm gonna have to go. I have to catch a flight back to Los Angeles in two hours," Caroline stated.

"I'd love to take you to the airport," suggested Stuart.

"I'd like that," responded Caroline.

CHAPTER 22

The Dangers from Free Fried Chicken and the Pleasures of Riding a Pig

It was four days after Thanksgiving when Phoebe's cousin, LaToya, experienced an awful crash triggered by her craving for Church's Chicken. While she was driving an elderly man to his physical therapy appointment, LaToya saw the attorney Monty K. Earl standing in front of the chain restaurant, weaving a drumstick. Monty was the lawyer known for signing up clients by luring them with a free two-piece dark meat snack box. It was for only a few seconds that LaToya took her attention off of Monty and focused on the Free Chicken sign on the side of his van. The distraction of the free fast food caused LaToya to smash into the back of a city bus. She wasn't hurt, but her passenger endured a mild concussion from hitting his head on the glass.

Because of LaToya's disastrous attempt for fried bird, the unfortunate traffic accident resulted into a lawsuit, and her insurance was dropped. The former medical transporter was desperate to find another job. She called Phoebe for help, and Phoebe told her that she should call Dylan. The only job opening Dylan had at Norma's Cajun Rage Quick Stop was for a fry cook at John John's catfish take-out station. Dylan hired LaToya over the phone. After he hung up, Dylan laughed while thinking about how John John was going to react to central Louisiana's toughest food critic joining their team.

The next day at the convenience store, John John was at his station in the corner of the deli, cutting up Vidalia onions to add to his hushpuppy mix, when Dylan informed him that he would be getting a new employee.

"Thank you, Jesus. As long as it's not one of Debbie's family members, I'm ready to teach him or her all my tricks on how to fix the finest fried fish this side of the parish," John John bragged.

"Good deal. I know you'll like her. She has a good eye for fried food," said Dylan.

Ten minutes later, as John John was fileting catfish with an electric knife, LaToya and Dylan walked up behind him. Dylan tapped John John on his shoulder, and then John John turned around and saw him and LaToya, who was wearing a polo shirt with the store's logo (the red pig) embroidered on the left side.

"John John, I'd like to introduce you to the newest member of our family under the roof of which the awesome pig stands," said Dylan.

John gazed at LaToya and smiled at her.

"Well, well, looky here," teased John John.

Before John John could say anything else, LaToya interrupted him, saying, "I'm here to work. I don't want any trouble from you. I'm just here to do my job."

John John put out his hand for LaToya to shake, and she apprehensively did. While the two were shaking hands, John John smiled at the uptight, new crew member and said, "Well, I'm really glad you're here … now, let's sell some fish!"

LaToya felt John John was honestly being sincere, and he was. She smiled back at the gentle giant with the electric knife in his left hand and began telling him how to cut the fish.

As Dylan walked away from happy work couple, he started laughing from hearing the two bicker at about the correct way to filet a catfish.

The offbeat working relationship between the prior restaurant owner and the former medical transportation driver definitely paid off. Fried catfish dinner sales tripled during the following two weeks.

The night before the Christmas parade, Dylan was over at his mother's condo. He and Norma were waiting for Phoebe to come over. She was coming in from Houston, where she gave a lecture and showed her new line of eye rings at a women's exposition. When the doorbell rang, Kris flew down the stairs to answer it. He was eager to see if Phoebe had any gifts (New Orleans Saints memorabilia) for him. Kris opened the door, and there stood Phoebe.

"I'm sorry, Kris, no Saints stuff on this trip," said Phoebe.

"Ah, Phoebe, that's okay. You can make it up to me on Christmas," replied Kris.

Kris ran back up the stairs as Phoebe walked into the den. Norma and Dylan were excited to see her. They each gave her a hug and a kiss. Norma asked her if she was hungry and told her that there was some leftover Spam from hers and Kris's dinner. Phoebe graciously declined.

"Are you sure? I could make you a sandwich," Norma offered.

"Oh, as tempting as a fried Spam sandwich sounds, I think Dylan and I are gonna grab a bite at the Pitt Grill," Phoebe said.

"Come sit down," said Norma.

"I really can't stay long. I just wanted to come by and give you a little something that I think you could use for tomorrow," Phoebe explained. She then took a small box from out of her purse and gave it to Norma.

Norma saw the initials C.R.A. printed on top of the box and announced, "Oh my, this is from Cane River Angel. I know it must be extraordinary." She opened the box and pulled out a fourteen-karat gold pig broach paved in natural red diamonds. "Oh, Phoebe, it's beautiful," sobbed Norma.

"Dylan told me about your surprise float a few months ago, so it gave me time to design a special piece to go along with the ah, I guess one would say, pork theme."

For several minutes, Norma told Phoebe how much she appreciated the astonishing gift, and then Dylan informed the thoughtful jewelry designer that it was time to go eat.

Later, at the Pitt Grill, as Phoebe was reading the menu, Dylan was thinking to himself that perhaps the reason Phoebe called this meeting was a chance for her to express her true feelings about their relationship. In such a short time, Dylan had evolved into a solid individual who finally grasped the true value of life. The onetime rebel gained the trust back from his son, stopped smoking and drinking, spent more quality time with family and friends, and continued to work on being a better person. The only thing missing in Dylan's new and approved existence was a soul mate—and what better person than Phoebe to fill in the last gap of Dylan's wish list.

After they ordered, Phoebe looked at Dylan and said, "I guess you need to know why I asked you to meet with me,"

"Okay," responded Dylan.

"Where do I start? Oh God, Dylan, this is the most difficult thing I've ever had to tell you," cried Phoebe.

"You're in love with me," replied Dylan, followed by a smile.

"Come on, don't patronize me. What I have to tell you is extremely serious," said Phoebe.

"I wasn't being facetious," Dylan replied.

For the next two hours, Phoebe justified to Dylan in detail about her hidden secret. Dylan was in shock when Phoebe shared the news about her past life-changing mistake. At one time during the intense conversation, Dylan had to excuse himself and went into the men's room and vomited. Phoebe's unanticipated newsflash would profoundly affect Dylan's entire family.

The weather was sunny and cool on the day of the Alexandria Christmas parade. Phoebe had planned for everyone to come to her condominium in the Hotel Bentley to watch the parade from her balcony since the parade would be coming down the street in front of the hotel. She arranged to have a bartender serve champagne, and she ordered several appetizer platters from the Diamond Grill, which was located across the street from her condo.

Only Debbie, John John, Stuart, Brent, and Liz were at Phoebe's party during the parade. The rest of the crew wanted to stand on the side of the street to get a closer look at the very special grand marshal. Everyone, including Norma, planned on attending Phoebe's get-together after the parade.

Phoebe was thankful when Stuart yelled for everybody to come on the balcony because the parade had started. Liz was a huge fan of Cane River Angel Jewelry and would not stop asking Phoebe question after question. Stuart's announcement couldn't have come at a better time. Phoebe dashed away from her obsessed fan and made it to the balcony in record time. It did not take long for the folks standing on the balcony to recognize Dylan, Hunter, Sylvia, Maria, and Kris, who were all standing across the street. After the Shriners had passed by on their four-wheelers, Kris saw everybody on the balcony and shouted, "Hey, Debbie and Phoebe! Show us your boobs!"

Dylan popped Kris on the back of his head and lectured, "There are kids here! For once, don't be an idiot!"

After consuming more than a few glasses of champagne, Debbie followed Kris's demand and lifted her tacky Christmas sweater up and showed her bright pink brassiere off to Kris and the many other parade watchers. As Kris gave her a thumbs-up, Dylan hit him on the back of the head again. John John and Liz were the only two who laughed at Debbie's peek show. Phoebe was humiliated. She grabbed Debbie's arm and escorted her back into the condo. Liz nudged Brent and said, "I'm tellin' you, honey, your freakin' family is nuts … and I love it!"

As always, Phoebe's stern speech about manners to Debbie resulted in the two of them having a laugh fest in the kitchen. After Debbie promised Phoebe that she would behave, the two joined the others back on the balcony and watched the parade.

Once all the high school bands marched and Santa rode by on his sleigh, rounding out the parade was the fabulous pig float. Norma made a lovely grand marshal. She was dressed in a Mrs. Clause outfit and had her diamond pig broach pinned above her heart. Frankie Dubois's music played loudly through the speakers as Norma tossed Aunt Dewy's Pork Jerky sticks to the cheering crowd. At first she was apprehensive about throwing anything out to the people because she had read in the parade guidelines that hurling hard candy had caused many minor injuries to the delayed parade goers in the past.

Norma had tears of joy when she saw her family and friends on each side of the float. She looked up, waved to her loved ones on the balcony, and blew kisses to her family standing on the street. Norma would cherish the glorious moment forever.

Two hours later, Phoebe's post-parade party was at its peak. In honor of Norma, John John and Liz were dancing to the *Dottie West Greatest Hits* CD. Stuart was giving Debbie and Brent a full report on Caroline, the newest love of his life, while Debbie and Phoebe munched down on the hors d'oeuvres. Suddenly, Hunter, Sylvia, and Maria arrived, followed by Dylan, Kris, and Norma. They all applauded when Norma walked in the room. Phoebe had the bartender pour the grand marshal a glass of champagne as Liz and Debbie admired Norma's shimmering pig broach. Everyone had a great time eating, dancing, and drinking. Phoebe made sure she had sparkling grape juice on hand for the nondrinkers.

Norma was in the middle of telling everyone about her exciting venture when the doorbell rang. Kris opened the door, and it was Lauren.

"Hey, Lauren, where in the hell is Steven?" asked Kris.

"He's in Hawaii, deep-sea fishing with a few of his colleagues," answered Lauren.

"That sucks," uttered Kris.

"Doesn't though," agreed Lauren.

As Lauren walked over to Norma and gave her flowers, Hunter, who was standing by Kris, said, "I can't believe that prick would actually miss his own mother's parade to go fishing."

"Who's gone fishing?'" asked Phoebe.

"My jackass of an uncle, Steven," answered Hunter.

"Ya know what's so sad? No one even realizes that he and Lauren weren't present for Norma's big day," Debbie added.

"I bet Norma did," said Sylvia.

"Let's drop it for now. All of you know it's inevitable for Steven to pull such a heartless stunt," expressed Dylan.

The small group of protesters then looked over at Norma, who was holding little Maria with her right arm and holding the flowers that Lauren gave her with her left hand. The grand marshal was thanking Lauren for the roses when Liz interrupted, "Oy vey, you look like the rodeo queen of a country Christmas."

After Lauren complimented Norma on her broach, she then darted toward the bar for a glass of much-needed champagne. Unexpectedly, the doorbell rang again. Hunter opened the door, and it was Debbie and John John's youngest daughter, Savannah, and five other young ladies. The girls were dressed in cheerleader uniforms because they had marched in the parade. Hunter let the cheering squad in, and they walked to the center of the den. "May I have everyone's attention! The Menard High School cheerleaders wish to give our grand marshal an appreciation cheer!" announced Savannah.

Debbie looked at Phoebe and remarked, "That's my baby girl."

Liz looked over at Brent and uttered, "This is a psychotic circus ... I love it!"

Once the cheerleaders had everybody's attention, they performed a cheer by spelling out Norma's name. Norma was moved by the spirited performance. After the brief show, Savannah and her cheer mates ran up to Norma and gave her a hug. Hunter, who was holding Maria, and Kris were standing by Norma and the cheerleaders.

"Wow, I wonder how long it took the superficial sisterhood to come up with such a dynamic and difficult cheer," Kris said to Hunter.

"They heard you," Hunter said to Kris.

Savannah strolled up to Kris and spoke loudly enough for all to hear. "Kris, I can't believe you're here. I thought for sure your mother would have locked you in your room for days after you were caught leaving campus during lunch and attempting to buy a daiquiri at the Top Shelf drive thru by using your fifty-year-old brother's ID."

Kris turned to Hunter and said, "Cheerleaders are evil people."

"Why haven't I heard about this?" Norma asked Kris.

Surprisingly, Sylvia spoke up. "I was at the house when the dean of students called, and I pretended to be you, Miss Norma. By the way, you and Kris have an appointment with the principal the Monday after the holiday break."

"I don't understand. How did you pull it off?" Norma asked Sylvia.

Sylvia did a spot-on impersonation of Norma. Her impression was so good that everyone applauded except for Norma and Kris. After a few seconds, Norma did eventually giggle at the Hispanic impersonator. Everyone continued to chat, eat, and drink as Norma approached her youngest, devious son. Kris reached in his back pocket, pulled out his wallet, and handed his American Express card to Norma. "Happy Holidays, Momma. I take it it's gonna be a lonely Christmas for me."

"If I didn't love you so much, I'd kill you," replied Norma.

During all the fun commotion, Lauren nonchalantly snuck out after she had six glasses of champagne and a dozen pecan tassies. Once again, no one was aware of her absence.

After many cocktails were consumed and tours of Phoebe's condo slash art studio were conducted, the party started winding down at eight o'clock. Norma, Kris, Brent, Liz, the cheerleaders, Hunter, Sylvia, and Maria all left at the same time.

Phoebe, Dylan, Stuart, Debbie, and John John stayed at the art deco condo. The five old friends sat in Phoebe's living room and caught up with one another. Stuart was sprawled out on the sofa between John John and Debbie. His feet were in John John's lap, and he was laying his head on a pillow in Debbie's lap. Dylan and Phoebe were sitting in Queen Anne armchairs across from the relaxed three on the refurbished sofa (that was once in the bridal suite when the Hotel Bentley first opened 1908).

Stuart shared the good news about his long-distance relationship with Caroline. Ever since Thanksgiving Day, the two stayed connected every day through Skype. He focused on Debbie when he admitted that he actually knew what being in love felt like. Debbie and the rest were extremely happy for him.

Phoebe also revealed to the group that she was in a relationship. As she gave the minimal details of hers and Shane Miller's connection, John John, Stuart, and Debbie kept looking at Dylan to see what his response was. In the back of their minds, they always felt that the rebel and the artist would eventually be together. Dylan kept a poker face the whole time that Phoebe was talking.

Dylan didn't have much to say when it was his turn to share. He gave two positive reports. The first one was about Hunter, and the second one was about the good work John John had done with the catfish station inside of Norma's Cajun Rage Quick Stop.

John John took over where Dylan left off. He boasted about the customers' raving reviews over his food, the high sales profits, and his newborn bromance with LaToya. He and LaToya had gone to Buffalo Wild Wings after work for two Sundays in a row, to eat Caribbean jerk wings and watch the UFC fights on the huge flat screen.

"What the hell, I can't even get you to come watch sports at my bar ... why LaToya?" Stuart asked John John.

"A fella can have more than one BFF, Stuart," John John replied.

Stuart threw a couch pillow, and it hit John John directly in the face.

Last but not least, Debbie rehashed her aspiration of working with Sylvia to open a toddlers' pageant dress shop. Since Stuart rejected the offer to rent out his man cave to the new Diane von Furstenbergs of glamorous fashion designed for the preschooler who wants it all, Debbie and Sylvia decided to search for a building to open their new business, which they named Sassy Baby's Collections. The gang was somewhat leery of Debbie and Sylvia's wish to provide a much-needed service for the overaggressive stage mothers and fathers from all over the south.

It was midnight, and after everyone had discussed their present progressions and future goals, Phoebe announced that it was time for everyone to leave. She hugged each one of her friends and told them that she would see them at Hunter and Sylvia's wedding. Dylan was the last one to leave, and before he walked out the door, he hugged Phoebe again.

"I'm here for you, and everything is gonna be fine," Dylan whispered in Phoebe's ear.

CHAPTER 23

Let the Light Shine

It was Christmas and the morning of Hunter and Sylvia's wedding. In Norma's kitchen, Hunter, Brent, Dylan, and Kris sat around the island and ate chicken fried steak and scrambled eggs. Dylan and Hunter had spent the night, and it was a tradition in the Jacobs/Dubois household to eat steak and eggs on Christmas morning. Sylvia and the baby spent the night with her family on Christmas Eve, and she also felt that it was bad luck to spend the night with her groom the night before they would be married.

As Norma served breakfast to the men, Kris informed everyone what he got for Christmas, which was a two-hundred-dollar gift certificate to Game Stop the *True Blood* DVD set, and an Aero-Tray, which was invented by Norman Korpi. Norman was a cast member of MTV's very first *Real World*.

Norman invented the portable, ergonomic area for labtops. Oddly enough, both Norma and Frankie watched *The Real World* back in 1993. They were fascinated with the first reality show and they were big fans of Norm, the artist. Norma saw the Aero-Tray in a travel magazine and felt it would be the perfect gift for her son, the songwriter.

Kris was anxiously anticipating what type of New Orleans Saints memento Phoebe would be giving him.

Due to the night before being Christmas Eve, there was no rehearsal dinner. As an alternative, Norma asked the out-of-town guests to come over to her condominium for a light lunch and cocktails. Except for Caroline (Stuart's new girlfriend), all of the out-of-town guests were from

Phoebe's family unit. Her in-laws, the Surys, and her son, Michael, and his fiancée, Carmon, were coming.

Michael and Carmon were the first ones to arrive at the brunch.

"Where's your mother?" Kris asked Michael.

Michael gave Kris a small gift wrapped box and replied, "Mom is on her way back from Lake Charles. She spent Christmas Eve with Grandmother Evelyn."

"Poor woman," uttered Dylan.

"I know, right? You couldn't pay me enough to spend Christmas with that Grinch—and she's my grandmother," Michael agreed.

"We can't choose our family, but I can choose to open this gift right now," suggested Kris.

"Phoebe told us that you would be waiting for this. I hope you like it," Carmon said to Kris.

As Kris unwrapped his present from Phoebe, he stated, "I don't think this gift will have anything to do with the Saints, but if it's from Phoebe, I know that it will be good!" He opened the box, and it was a silver men's ring with the word *Purity* engraved on it. "What the hell is this?" Kris asked.

"It's a Christian purity ring," Carmon answered.

Dylan, Hunter, and Michael laughed at Kris's facial expression as the disappointed teen held up his ring for everyone to see. Norma grabbed her son's hand to get a closer look at the ring.

"Oh, what a beautiful purity promise ring," expressed Norma.

"Now why in the hell would the woman who has always given me a gift pertaining to the New Orleans Saints give me a freakin' abstinence ring … and I'm sure you had nothing to do with this, my dear mother," pointed out Kris.

"Actually, the gift does have something to do with being a saint," Norma replied, then burst into laughter along with the others.

"Y'all suck!" shouted Kris.

Suddenly there was a knock at the door. Norma told Kris to answer it. Still upset about his gift, Kris stomped to the front door. As he left the kitchen, Hunter yelled, "Hey, Kris! Don't lose your precious virginity on the way to the door!" Kris responded by shooting his middle finger at Hunter and the other jolly Christians.

Kris opened the door, and it was the Surys and Lauren. Lauren was carrying a big pot of grillades and grits, and Dr. Sury was holding a large glass bowl of salad. Lauren had volunteered to cater the out-of-towners' brunch for Norma.

Kris welcomed them in and offered to carry the pot of food, but Lauren told him that it wasn't necessary. Everyone greeted the Surys and Lauren when they walked in the kitchen. Lauren and Dr. Sury placed the food on the kitchen island, and then Lauren asked Norma, "Have you set that beautiful table in the dining room yet?"

"I thought we'd do casual and eat off of paper plates today," answered Norma.

"Oh, of course we are," Lauren sarcastically said.

"Hey, where's your worst half?" Dylan asked Lauren.

"He's over at the Thompson's for their annual milk punch and Bloody Mary's Christmas Day open house," replied Lauren.

"We just left the Thompsons', and I didn't see Steven anywhere," reported Christy Sury.

To change the direction of the conversation, Norma said, "My goodness, I went to the Thompsons' open house every Christmas morning that I was married to Brent."

Lauren didn't say anything. She turned around and saw that there was plenty of chicken fried steak left on the counter next to the oven. Kris observed the uptight housewife's facial expression and said to himself, "In three, two, one, she's going in for the kill." Kris was correct. Lauren began chowing down on the leftover steak as if she were a toy poodle attacking a doggy treat.

Norma directed everyone to the living room so that they wouldn't be so cluttered in the kitchen. Once they got to Norma's spacious sitting room, the Surys immediately went over to their grandson, Michael, and his fiancée, Carmon. Michael explained to his grandparents that Phoebe had been somewhat sad during the holidays because she had broken up with her boyfriend and she really didn't want to go to Lake Charles to see her mother for Christmas Eve. While preparing everyone's drink, Dylan eavesdropped and heard every word that Michael told his grandparents.

Meanwhile, back in the kitchen, Hunter and Kris sat on the counter and watched Lauren scoff down the last piece of steak while she converted the top of the kitchen island into a serve-yourself buffet. Lauren looked over at Hunter and asked him a question, but he couldn't understand what she was saying because her mouth was full of fried meat.

"You might want to swallow that last piece of fat so that I can understand your question," replied Hunter.

Lauren swallowed her last bite of deep-fried beef and re-asked the questions, "How is Sylvia? Is she ready for her big day?"

"Dad and I went by the condo this morning, and she appeared to be fine. Actually, she didn't want to see me with today being our wedding and all that stuff. All the women in her family are there helping her get ready. My house looks like a packed stadium at an Enrique Iglesias concert," stated Hunter.

Both Kris and Lauren giggled at Hunter's analogy.

"Lauren, I can't express how nice it was for you and Uncle Steven to let me and Sylvia stay at your beautiful camp on False River for our honeymoon," Hunter expressed.

"You're very welcome," replied Lauren.

Suddenly the doorbell rang, and Kris hopped off the counter. "I hope this is Phoebe with my real Christmas present!" Kris shouted as he ran out of the kitchen.

Right before Dylan could answer the door, Kris shoved his big brother to the side and opened the door. It was Debbie, her daughter, Savannah, and John John, who was wearing a Santa Claus costume. "Well, if it isn't Santa, Mother Teresa, and their daughter, Savannah the snitch," Kris announced as he opened the door for the Rachels to enter.

Minutes later, the doorbell rang again, and once again, Kris pushed Dylan out of his way to open the door. This time it was John John and Debbie's eldest daughter, Amanda, and her wife, Cindy. Kris was very disappointed when he saw the spiked, blonde-haired Bobbsey twins.

"It's Mrs. and Mrs. Whoever," announced Kris as he let the couple in. As the ladies walked in, Amanda gave Kris a fruitcake and wished him a merry Christmas. Kris looked at the cake and then said to himself, "Oh, a fruitcake. How appropriate for the occasion."

Just before Kris closed the door, Stuart and Caroline arrived. Kris opened the door wider to let them in and announced, "It's the intolerable accountant and some woman who apparently is glutton for punishment."

"Very funny, Kris," Stuart replied as he and Caroline walked in.

Finally, an hour into the brunch, Phoebe rang the doorbell. To avoid being trampled by Kris, Dylan didn't even attempt to answer it. When Kris opened the door and saw that is was Phoebe, who was holding a New Orleans Saints watch in her hand, he screamed, "At last! You came bringing my gift in celebration of Baby Jesus's birthday! Amen! Now, give it to me!"

"I thought this silver Saints watch would go well with your purity ring," Phoebe said to the overly anxious teen.

"Very funny, Wanda Sykes—you're not. I love it," responded Kris. He then gave Phoebe a hug followed by a kiss on her cheek.

"I take it everyone is here?" asked Phoebe.

"Everybody who's relevant is—and then some," answered Kris.

It was as if Phoebe was a movie star making her way down the red carpet when she entered Norma's living room. Everyone, except Lauren, ran toward the latecomer to hug her and wish her a merry Christmas.

Lauren, who had several holiday toddies and half of the fruitcake that nobody wanted, told everyone to enjoy the grillades and grits and that she would see them all at the wedding. Kris walked her out to her vehicle.

"Are you all right?" Kris asked the suffering woman, who had cake crumbs and bits of green candied cherries all over her lips.

"I'm fine. Merry Christmas, Kris," replied Lauren.

Back inside Norma's condo, Brent waited patiently for everyone to finish greeting Phoebe before he made an important announcement. "As you all know, I've been seeing a wonderful woman by the name of Liz Benowitz ... who by the way, is over at my house overseeing the caterers and wedding planner for my grandson's wedding. Well, tonight before the wedding, I'm gonna ask Liz to be my wife ..." announced the proud doctor. Everyone cheered, and then Brent continued, "Phoebe here was nice enough to design a beautiful ring for me, and I should have had her design another one for my lovely first wife, Norma here, for doing such an incredible job raising our sons as well as putting up with me through all my other marriages."

"Oh, Brent, that's really not necessary—the giant pig float was thanks enough," said Norma.

Before Brent could finish his announcement, Michael raised his glass of champagne and announced, "While everyone is here, I also wish to make an announcement ... Carmon and I recently found out that the newest member of the Sury family will be arriving in six months!"

Phoebe asked, "I'm gonna be a grandmother?"

"And I'm gonna be a great-grandmother?" added Christy Sury.

"Yes!" answered Carmon.

"I'll toast to that!" hollered John John. Santa then guzzled his spiked cranberry juice.

During the rest of the brunch, Michael and Carmon had a good visit and caught up with his grandparents (the Surys).

Kris and Hunter stayed in Kris's room and played the newest and the most violent video games. Before the young men started to play, Hunter laughed when Kris threw his purity ring on his never-been-used condoms in the top drawer of his dresser.

Norma took Caroline to her closet to choose an outfit for the wedding. Delta Airlines lost Caroline's luggage, and Norma insisted that she wear one of her loud ensembles.

Stuart, John John, Debbie, and Dylan were in the kitchen listening to Phoebe explain her recent breakup with Shane. Their age difference was the main reason for the split. Shane was too liberal and wanted to change the world, and Phoebe had become more conservative with age. She appreciated Shane's world peace viewpoint, and she was all for positive activists and their causes (as long as they wore Cane River Angel Jewelry). When it boiled down to it, the two were complete opposites with very different passions for life. Phoebe felt that Shane would have been a great boyfriend if they were living in the sixties. She informed the crew that she and Shane ended the relationship on good terms.

"Never trust a man who works in the vegetable and fruit department in a supermarket," Debbie said to Phoebe.

"Hey, I started out in the produce at Winn Dixie!" shouted John John.

"Need I say more?" replied Debbie.

"We still love ya, Stella, even though you lost your grove," Stuart said to Phoebe.

The backyard looked magical at the Jacobs' family home. There were lit-up lanterns placed in the oak trees and white roses were on each of the tables under the humongous white tent. Floating white roses with lights covered the pool, and the gazebo was also wrapped in white lights and roses. It was obvious that Hunter and Sylvia chose white to be the color theme for their wedding.

Liz Benowitz did a praiseworthy job overseeing the staff to make sure that Hunter and Sylvia's special night would take place in a heavenly winter wonderland atmosphere. Although the wedding took place on Christmas night, the date did not prevent anyone from attending. All the employees from Norma's Cajun Rage Quick Stop, Hunter's friends from high school, and sixty members of Sylvia's family were in attendance.

It was a clear and comfortably cool night. The temperature was in the lower sixties. Hunter, Dylan, and Marla Rodrigues stood under the beautifully lit gazebo and waited for the bride. Marla taught Spanish at Louisiana College, and she was also an ordained minister. Hunter and Sylvia wanted the ceremony done in both English and Spanish. Hunter and his father looked dashing in their black tuxedoes and dark-blue bowties. On the left side of the gazebo, a lovely woman began to play Pachelbel's *Canon in D Major* (the popular wedding song) on the harp.

Maria was the flower girl and the first one to walk down the aisle. The three-year-old looked like the number-one princess of all pretentious child pageants. Debbie and Sylvia had made Maria's royal-blue tutu dress that was covered in diamond rhinestones. The flower girl looked like a tiny blueberry that had rolled in a pile of cheap cubic zirconia stones. Maria held a basket of white rose petals as she slowly walked toward the gazebo. She did not toss any of the petals. Instead, she waited until she got to the third row on the groom's side and poured out the entire basket of rose petals into LaToya's lap.

"Oh no you didn't, little gurrrl," said LaToya.

As the guests laughed at LaToya's reaction, Maria ran directly to Dylan. The proud grandfather held his little petal pusher while they waited on the rest of the bridal party to walk down.

The second female to walk down the aisle was Amy Purser. Amy, a pale, freckled, natural redhead, was Sylvia's matron of honor. The two had worked together at the Pitt Grill. Amy had on a simple turquoise, sleeveless dress and had a white rose in her hair. She held the bouquet of roses in her left hand because she only had two fingers on her right hand.

Amy's middle, ring, and pinky fingers were chopped off a few years ago when she was cutting a head of lettuce while preparing a side dinner salad for a customer at the diner. Amy thought it was funny that every time she held up her right hand in front of Maria, Maria would say, "Stickem up," because with Amy only having her grooming finger and thumb on the right hand, it resembled a gun.

As the seven-fingered bridesmaid strolled down the aisle, Debbie noticed her bright red hair, her bouquet of white flowers, and her gaudy blue dress, and then she leaned over to John John and joked, "Look at her, she looks like a patriotic Howdy Doody in gown. Sylvia should have asked me to be her matron of honor ... hell, we're gonna be business partners." John John snickered at his opinionated wife's comment.

In fact, John John did rent the doublewide trailer two lots down from his and Debbie's mobile home for a six-month trial basis. If Debbie and Sylvia's new business adventure actually took off, he would eventually buy the vacant store space next to the Tobacco Plus and make it a permanent home for Sassy Baby's Collections.

The harp player began to play "Here Comes the Bride," and everyone stood up. Sylvia looked beautiful in her bright-blue Mexican wedding dress with white roses crocheted along the neckline. Her flamboyant dress hid her pregnancy well. Sylvia's tiara was made of fabric silver roses and she decided to dye her hair from red back to black. The pretty bride was escorted by her father, Santiago Carrillo, a short, bald, fairly dark-skinned man with a thick, black mustache. Mr. Carrillo was wearing the same tuxedo as Hunter and Dylan. Tears of joy rolled down the bride's cheeks as she saw Hunter waiting for her. Hunter and Dylan were also shedding tears of happiness. It did not take long for the tears of bliss to spread throughout the crowd (especially the female guests). Phoebe, Debbie, Norma, Liz, Christy Sury, and even Kris cried.

After the minster performed the brief ceremony in both English and Spanish, Sylvia and Hunter said their I-dos, and then it was time for the reception. Sylvia's family had prepared masses of Mexican food, and Norma had hired the Spirits Catering Bus for those guests who had a taste for central Louisiana's finest seafood dishes.

The wedding cake was blue with white roses, and Sylvia had Betty Wenkel, the best wedding cake specialist of the South, make Hunter's groom's cake. Because of Hunter's as well as his father's, uncle's, and Norma's obsession with clean-smelling products, Betty made an edible Glade PlugIn.

A mariachi band played as the wedding party entered the tent. While Hunter and Sylvia's families posed for pictures, the rest of the guests helped themselves to food and drinks.

After the photos were taken, the bride, groom, and their families walked into the tent and the reception was in full force. Guests were dancing, eating, and waiting in line at the frozen margarita and sangria machines.

Liz Benowitz ran up to Norma and showed her the engagement ring that Brent gave to her an hour before the wedding. Norma congratulated Liz and thanked her for helping make her grandson's ceremony such a special event. Norma was sincere when she told Liz, "Welcome to the jungle."

Meanwhile, at one of the open bars, Phoebe's son, Michael, who had never been a big drinker, was ordering his fifth shot of tequila. Steven and Lauren were standing behind the amateur drunk. Steven noticed that Michael was swaying from side to side, and he said, "Hey, you better slow down, son. The party's just getting started."

"Thanks, Dad, I appreciate your fatherly advice!" Michael loudly slurred.

Phoebe, who was standing a few feet from the bar talking with Dylan, Carmon, and Kris, heard every word that Michael shouted to Steven. When she saw her son giving Steven an unexpected hug, she rushed over to them.

"I told that man to stay away from tequila," said Carmon as she, Dylan, and Kris followed behind Phoebe.

When they arrived at the uncomfortable situation, Michael's arms were still locked around Steven. Steven and Lauren were stunned by the big man's actions. "Let him go, Michael," ordered Phoebe.

"Tell him, Ma. Now's the time ... tell him," demanded Michael.

"Oh lord," Dylan said to himself as Michael finally detached from Steven.

Phoebe told Carmon to take care of her sloshed fiancé, and then she asked Steven and Lauren to come sit at a table where they could talk privately. As the worried couple followed Phoebe to find an empty table, Kris looked at Dylan and asked, "What the hell is going on?"

Dylan told his younger brother that he would explain everything as they watched Phoebe, Steven, and Lauren from afar.

Phoebe asked Steven if he remembered the night that she and Dylan visited him at Tulane when they were seniors in high school. Steven told Phoebe that he barely remembered them coming to see him. His memory started coming back when Phoebe explained in detail what happened that night. Steven took Dylan and Phoebe to his fraternity house where they were having a Jimmy Buffett beer bash. The fraternity turned the basement into a beach, and everyone funneled Dixie beer for hours to the tune of "Brown-Eyed Girl." Phoebe specifically remembered the song that kept playing that night because she had brown eyes and she was the only brown girl at the social. Dylan had left with a promiscuous Phi Mu pledge, so at the end of the night, Steven took Phoebe back to his dorm room. Phoebe had always had a crush on Steven, and she didn't fight him when he wanted to seduce her. Although Phoebe was very much in love with Garrett, Steven was her dream pass, and unfortunately, the man who took her virginity was also the man who got her pregnant. The only people who knew about Phoebe's secret were Garrett, Michael, Garrett's parents, and eventually Dylan. Phoebe did not tell Steven and Lauren why it took her so long to tell the truth about Michael's biological father. In fact, she didn't know why herself. She was just glad to finally come out with the hidden secret that she'd held in for thirty-one years.

Steven's mouth dropped and Lauren excused herself from the table. As Lauren stood up, Phoebe apologized to her.

"No worries, Phoebe. Nothing takes me by surprise anymore," replied Lauren.

When Kris and Dylan saw Lauren dashing off, Kris said, "And there she goes, off to the table of sopapillas and beignets."

Steven, who was still in shock, told Phoebe that he would get in touch with a family therapist and they could all meet to discuss his future involvement with Michael. Phoebe grinned and replied, "Honestly, Steven, I know you must be overwhelmed with this sudden news, but really, neither I nor Michael need or want anything from you."

"No, no, Phoebe, as ironic as this must sound, I'd really like to work something out … now please excuse me while I go get inebriated … and I'm serious, I want to make this right," responded the new father-to-be.

As Steven darted toward the bar, Dylan walked up to Phoebe and said, "I can definitely see us pulling an all-nighter at the Pitt Grill tonight." Phoebe replied by giving Dylan a smile.

An hour into the reception, guests were still having a blast. Hunter danced the night away. It was extremely odd for Hunter to dance without being intoxicated, but he enjoyed attempting to twerk sober with LaToya, Carmon, Christy Sury, and several of his female coworkers from Norma's Cajun Rage Quick Stop.

Debbie was inside helping Michael sober up. She fixed him a pot of coffee and made him eat an orange. She had always heard that oranges could cure hangovers. Eventually, Michael began to feel better. He even laughed a few times during Debbie's story about the time she had too much tequila at the El Chico Café in West Monroe and passed out face first in a platter of macho nachos.

197

Sylvia spent most of the night visiting with her relatives. She would sneak away every once in a while to join Hunter on the dance floor. The only glitch that occurred during Sylvia's fairytale wedding was when she caught Kris trying to persuade her thirty-seven-year-old, non-English-speaking aunt, Naiara, (whose name meant *of the Virgin Mary*) to go out to his vehicle and make out while they listened to Shakira on his Sirius radio.

Unlike Kris, Stuart had no problem achieving love during the celebrated affair. He and Caroline spent the majority of the night on the front porch, sitting on a swing. Caroline was wearing Norma's midnight-blue sequin blazer that she ordered from the Joan River's collection on the infamous night she caught Kris with the limping escort. Sadly, Miss Rivers passed away a day after Norma purchased the blazer.

The sparkling jacket was the only clothing item of Norma's that Caroline could wear. Truthfully, the blazer was rather tight on her, but she wore it because Norma insisted and the airline was still searching for her luggage. The two new lovebirds had an in-depth discussion about Stuart going to Los Angeles for three months to assist Caroline with producing a reality pilot about hit pop artists from the eighties and early nineties who live together for a month and work together on new material for a one-night-only concert. Stuart was beyond excited for the once-in-a-lifetime opportunity to share his pop-culture knowledge about trivial matters that occurred back when he was young and innocent. After he gladly accepted Caroline's offer, the two shared a passionate kiss. After their intimate smooch, Stuart told Caroline that they had better head back to the reception because he heard John John yelling out his name.

When Caroline and Stuart arrived back at the tent, John John, who was standing next to the disc jockey, waved for Stuart to come over. The disc jockey and the mariachi band took turns playing sets throughout the night. John John's daughter, Savannah, had found the song "I Feel for You" by Chaka Khan on her iPhone and gave it to the DJ to play. John John, Dylan, and Stuart sang this song to Green Wave fans when LSU beat Tulane thirty-three to fifteen on November 24, 1984. Right as the song started, John John grabbed Stuart's hand, and they both shouted for Dylan to join them on the dance floor. Dylan, who was standing next to Hunter, said to his son, "Oh God, I'm not in the mood for this."

"I know, Dad. Dancing sober is new to us, but go ahead and try it. I promise it's not that bad," Hunter suggested. Dylan winked at his son and then strolled over to the dance floor.

John John and Stuart were dancing as if they were being touched by Jesus at the Brother Love's Traveling Salvation Show. Dylan was not as animated as his buddies. He swayed from side to side and snapped his fingers, and that was about as wild as he got.

The guests enjoyed watching the men perform although they were confused about what the three men were trying to validate.

Liz spotted her daughter witnessing the middle-aged boy band make fools of themselves and ran over to Caroline.

"I've been at this fiesta, hoedown, reception, or whatever the hell you want to call this for hours! And I'm just now seeing you!" scolded Liz.

Liz immediately showed her daughter the gorgeous engagement ring from Brent Jacobs that Phoebe designed. As Caroline gushed over the stunning ring, Liz noticed the blazer her normally conservative daughter was wearing.

"What the hell are you wearing? Oy vey, you look like the opening Vegas act for Wayne Newton." Before Caroline could respond, Liz called Phoebe, Norma, and Debbie over. When the ladies arrived, Liz said, "You ladies know a lot about fashion. Look at what my daughter's wearing. She looks like a lounge lizard!"

"Ma, Delta lost my luggage, and Norma here was nice enough to lend me this blazer from the Joan River's collection," Caroline replied.

"Oh, I adore Joan Rivers! I love it! I'm still in shock that she died!" yelled Liz. She then went to touch the sparkling jacket and accidently knocked Caroline's drink out of her hand. Caroline bent down to pick up the plastic champagne glass from the ground, and the back of the blazer tore in half.

"Oh God, Norma, I'm so sorry," pleaded Caroline.

"No worries, honey. The shopping network is on twenty-four hours a day. I can always buy another one," Norma said.

Debbie reached behind Caroline and ripped a large strip of the glittery material off of the blazer and then announced, "I could use these scraps for my new business."

Once again, Phoebe, Debbie, and Norma congratulated Liz, and then Liz grabbed Caroline's arm and told her to come with her to spread the news to others about the engagement. While Norma was complimenting Phoebe on Liz's ring, she noticed that Phoebe looked distracted. "Is everything all right, honey?" asked Norma.

"I'm fine, just a little tired," Phoebe replied.

"I know it's been a long day. Look, I want you two to come over tomorrow afternoon for tonight's leftovers," Norma told Debbie and Phoebe.

"I'm in. The only thing I've got to do tomorrow is take John John's mother to Walgreens' after-Christmas sale," announced Debbie.

"What time?" Phoebe asked Norma.

"For some odd reason, Steven wants to have a family meeting at noon. I'm sure it's about all the things Dylan and I are doing wrong at the store or it could be that he's having marriage troubles. Who knows—with these three boys I've raised, it could be anything. Heavens, Phoebe, just come over at noon. You're family. I'm sure it's nothing you haven't already heard or seen," Norma replied.

"Yeah, Phoebe, you're like the redheaded stepchild of the Jacobs," joked Debbie.

"You mean more like the black sheep of the family," added Phoebe.

The wedding reception started winding down at eleven o'clock. After LaToya lectured Sylvia's mother about putting too much cilantro in the enchiladas, she volunteered to drive Michael, who had sobered up, and Carmon back to the Hotel Bentley.

Sylvia and Hunter stood at the front of the tent and said thank you and good-bye to all of their guests and family members.

Steven sat alone and nursed a scotch as he thought about his actions while watching his father, Brent, and soon-to-be-stepmother slow dance to the last song of the night.

After Norma instructed the caterers to pack all the leftover food in her vehicle, she looked over at Kris and asked, "Well, what movie is it gonna be tonight?"

"You choose," responded Kris.

"How about *Problem Child?*" Norma suggested.

"Okay, only if we can watch *Serial Mom* afterward," Kris joked.

The mother and son grinned and then hugged.

Dylan, Phoebe, John John, and Debbie were standing in front of the Jacobs' home talking when Caroline approached them. "Have you guys seen Stuart?" she asked.

"No," answered Debbie.

When you find him, I'm sure he's gonna want us all to come over to his bar for a nightcap," John John told Caroline.

"Oh no, that won't be happening tonight. It's gonna be just the two of us," Caroline stressed.

"Well all righty then," replied John John.

All of a sudden, they heard Stuart yelling down from the balcony of the two-story home. "Hey!" shouted Stuart.

They looked up and saw him on the balcony, holding up his bottled beer to make a toast.

"He's acting out the scene from *Fandango* where Kevin Costner makes a toast from off of the cliff. This is all wrong! I'm supposed to be Kevin Costner's character!" Dylan shouted to John John.

"Shut up, Dylan. Let him have at it," John John replied.

John John, Dylan, Phoebe, and Debbie lifted up their glasses and waited for Stuart's tribute.

"Here's to us ... and what we were," Stuart shouted to his lifelong friends.

"And what we'll be," shouted John John.

Stuart smiled as he looked down at his four comrades and repeated, "And what we'll be."

Meanwhile, on top of Norma's Cajun Rage Quick Stop stood the gloomy pig statue. All of a sudden, out of the blue, the interior light came on and lit up the bright-red pig.

About the Author

David Luck is a Louisiana native who is a true believer in intensive laugh psychotherapy. He has a thirty-year career span in finding humor as a television news reporter, mental health technician, and a marketing specialist. David's first novel, *Too Fat To Dance*, landed him the honor of being the 2012 grand marshal of the Alexandria Mardi Gras parade as well as representation from a powerhouse entertainment attorney who happens to be the most beautiful Housewife of Atlanta.

About the Book

Southern Fried Life is a comedy that validates the special bond between five middle-aged friends who actually relive their youth for one long weekend. For three fun-filled days, these unique individuals leave behind their worries of unplanned pregnancies, divorce, bankruptcy, substance abuse, bizarre baptisms, unfair kiddy glamour pageants, poorly fried catfish, and a freak accident caused by a fake pig. This amusing story is a reminder to all that one should always take time to smell the bacon.

"It's mid-life crisis fried over easy and seasoned to hilarious perfection. This hysterical story proves that when life throws you a side of nasty pork – make jerky!"

> Phaedra Parks
> Attorney, TV Personality,
> Producer, Mortician and
> Author of the best-seller,
> *Secrets of the Southern Belle*

"*Southern Fried Life* is a gumbo full of tragedies, love, laughter, bad behavior, honest mistakes and friendships that will last forever."

> Norman Korpi
> Artist, Filmmaker, Star of
> MTV's *The Real World*
> and Inventor of Aero-Tray